How to Succeed at Love

Michael Zwell, Ph.D., is a teacher of peer counseling and a consultant for the College for Human Services in California. A Woodrow Wilson Fellow, he received his graduate education from Yale University and taught sociology and anthropology at Rutgers University. He does ongoing marriage and family counseling and consults at preschools, community organizations, and colleges.

How to Succeed at Love

Michael Zwell

A SPECTRUM BOOK

Prentice-Hall, Inc., *Englewood Cliffs, New Jersey 07632*

Library of Congress Cataloging in Publication Data

Zwell, Michael.
    How to succeed at love.

    (A Spectrum Book)
    Includes index.
    1. Interpersonal relations. 2. Interpersonal
relations—Problems, exercises, etc. 3. Intimacy
(Psychology) I. Title.
HM132.Z9   301.11   78-3408
ISBN 0-13-435024-3
ISBN 0-13-435016-2 pbk.

$$301.11$$
$$Z97h$$

© 1978 by Prentice-Hall, Inc.
Englewood Cliffs, New Jersey 07632

A SPECTRUM BOOK

Printed in the United States of America

10   9   8   7   6   5   4   3   2   1

PRENTICE-HALL INTERNATIONAL, INC., *London*
PRENTICE-HALL OF AUSTRALIA PTY. LIMITED, *Sydney*
PRENTICE-HALL OF CANADA, LTD., *Toronto*
PRENTICE-HALL OF INDIA PRIVATE LIMITED, *New Delhi*
PRENTICE-HALL OF JAPAN, INC., *Tokyo*
PRENTICE-HALL OF SOUTHEAST ASIA PTE. LTD., *Singapore*
WHITEHALL BOOKS LIMITED, *Wellington, New Zealand*

To those whose love has reached me:
Patricia O'Bryan
Leo Zwell
Etta Zwell
Penny Jeannechild
Harvey Jackins
Felice Pace
Judy Kay
and many more

Contents

ix

List of Exercises

xv

Preface

All people have relationships. We are social animals and have been so for millions of years. We generally work, play, eat, and often sleep with other people. We watch television with some friends, play cards with others, and drive to work with still others.

Most of us have many important relationships, with our parents, our brothers and sisters, our lovers/spouses, our children, our close friends, our work associates, and so on. These relationships are sometimes satisfying, sometimes frustrating, and frequently infused with many feelings. Whether they go well or poorly, however, we usually do not feel in control of them. If things go well, we feel lucky. If they go badly, we feel as though there is nothing we can do about it, that "This is just the way it is." When things feel good with another person, we sometimes cannot remember why we ever felt bad or fought with him or her; and when we are fighting or not speaking to one another, we wonder what we ever liked about each other in the first place. Or we wonder, "How did we ever get into such a miserable place with each other?" We do not want to snap at our partners and friends, but it seems as though we cannot help it.

My goal in this book is to help people take charge of their intimate, or primary, relationships, to help us prolong the highs and reduce the lows in our ongoing interactions. To do this I present a theory of how human beings operate, illustrate it with many examples from different relationships, and provide thirty-six exercises and techniques so that it can be applied to the reader's own relationships. This theory is based on an understanding of the role thinking and feelings play in human behavior.

The functioning of human intelligence is undoubtedly the most advanced and adaptable process we know of, the highpoint of an evolutionary development that has been going on for millions of years. We of all creatures have the unique capability, not to act on the basis of rigid patterns of behavior, but to respond freshly and creatively to each immediate situation. Although the ability to think and act outside of patterns is rudimentarily developed in our closest relatives, the apes, their functioning is in no way equal to our own. Our ability to think is the basis upon which human society and culture exist.

We alone of all animals can analyze every situation, compare it to everything we have known and learned in the past, and create new responses to deal with the circumstances at hand. This is not only the means by which every great scientific advance has been achieved, but it is also the process every one of us uses every day. First we receive information from the environment: what is happening, what the place and/or the people look like, and so on. Second, we instantaneously compare and contrast these data with all the information we have stored in our memory: what similar things have happened to us, what we have read or been told, what we have done before, and so on. Third, we formulate our behavior based on what will bring the best results. For example, maybe we fix the toaster ourselves, or take it to be repaired, but in either case our behavior is based on what we think is most appropriate, given all the circumstances, for getting the toaster fixed.

Part of the information we have with which to evaluate the present is speculation about the future. We often cannot know what is going to happen the next minute, month, or year, but we do have a tremendous amount of information upon which to base predictions. For example, we have every reason to believe that if we stop eating right now we will eventually feel hungry and need nourishment. This knowledge is based entirely on past experience and things we have been told. It is rational to use this information to help choose what behavior is most sensible in the present. We may not feel like going out to tend the garden today, but if we want to eat three months from now we had better do it anyway.

So, based on our knowledge of the past and the present and our best inferences about the future, we can choose what we do right now. This process is not something we have to consciously set in motion; it is the natural way the human mind operates. It is the means by which human beings have adapted to more kinds of environments than any other species. And by using our intelligence we have the power to control our lives and our relationships and shape our destinies. We are no longer fated to react blindly out of rigid inherited or learned patterns. We can *think*, and act flexibly on our thinking.

Of course we do not act on the basis on our best thinking all the time; the state of the world and many of our relationships are ample evidence of that. We sometimes eat things we know are not good for us, we say mean things to people we love, and some of us set fires and start wars. These actions are not based on our intelligence. What seems to happen is that the process by which we select new and flexible responses to situations is hindered by painful emotion or tension. We do not think so well or clearly when we are upset or anxious, for example. At the height of anger we do many things we later regret. When grieving we sometimes do not feel like eating, let alone looking for a job or meeting new friends.

It is not the distressful emotion itself that interferes with our thinking and constructively acting, but rather the inhibition of its release. The natural response when we feel bad is to cry; the natural response when we feel scared is to tremble, perspire, and laugh; the natural response to embarrassment is to laugh or giggle. The crying, laughing, trembling and perspiring are the body's physiological release of the painful feeling.

When we feel bad and do not cry, or feel embarrassed and hold in our laughter, and so on, we store the distress instead of releasing it. We record the negative feelings in our memory along with the incidents with which they are associated. Then, when we are in some way reminded (usually unconsciously) of the distressful event, we again feel the unreleased painful feelings. More importantly, we tend to respond to present situations in the same way we responded to similar ones in the past, in which painful emotion was held in. Rather than taking all the information into account and acting flexibly and creatively, we do exactly the same thing we did before in a similar situation. Our behavior falls into a predictable pattern: "Oh, Allen is *always* shy in groups"; or, "Whenever Majorie loses at cards, she gets furious and walks out." When we act in these patterned ways, our behavior is controlled by our past hurts, not our functioning intelligence.

In reality, *we can take charge of our lives in the present.* The feelings from the past are simply feelings, meant to be released and gotten rid of. By releasing our painful feelings by crying, laughing, trembling, raging, and yawning, and doing our best to think clearly, we can take control of all aspects of our lives, particularly our love relationships. Does this sound farfetched? Unrealistic? Silly? It would not be surprising, because our problems often feel too complicated and difficult to solve. Read this book and try some of the exercises. See if you *can* decide how you would like things to be and what steps must be followed to bring it about. Of course, as circumstances change your wants and needs may change, for which your flexible intelligence is well suited. You can use your creative thinking process to make your relationships as good as you deserve.

In this book I have tried to convey the idea that working on relationships can be fun, and does not have to be nearly as serious or scary as it sounds and sometimes feels. Getting to know our friends and partners better is an exciting learning experience, which usually will help us feel better about ourselves in the process. The exercises I have included are designed to be enjoyable as well as helpful and should leave the reader with valuable insights and personal satisfaction.

Many examples of relationships are presented to demonstrate how particular aspects of them are affected by past hurts, and how we can work through these feelings. The names of the individuals involved and some of the details of the relationships have been altered to preserve privacy. In some cases the example is a composite of several persons I have counseled. I have tried to include people from a variety of ethnic, racial, and class backgrounds, as well as both homosexuals and heterosexuals. Some of the relationships examined are between husbands and wives, lovers, parents and children, close friends, and co-workers. Such a diverse sample was included because the theory is applicable to *all* relationships, and the tools and techniques contained in the thirty-six exercises will produce a noticeable improvement wherever they are used.

In the text I have avoided using "he," "his," and "him" as impersonal pronouns describing both men and women. I think the use of these terms contributes to our unconsciously emphasizing men and devaluing women. I have instead used the term "s/he," to be read as "she or he" (or "he or she"), and used "his or her" or "him or her" where appropriate. It is a little more awkward, but it brings the language of the text more in line with the reality of two sexes.

I enjoyed writing this book. I want it to make a real difference in the quality of readers' relationships. And I have no doubt that it *can* make a difference—so go to it!

I wish to thank Penny Jeannechild, who provided detailed and substantive feedback on the whole text as well as contributing original thinking in the chapter on sex; Patricia O'Bryan, who gave me emotional support and encouragement throughout the endeavor and provided valuable input at several crucial points; Robin Fragner and my parents, Etta and Leo Zwell, who read and commented on the manuscript; and Judy Kay, Don Flory, and Ann Young, who loved me and listened to me think, laugh, and cry over the book.

How to Succeed at Love

one
Love Is Natural

Frankie and Johnny were lovers,
Oh Lordy, how they could love. . . .

How does the rest of the song go? Well, as you may remember, she shoots him dead because he "loved" another woman. Turn on the radio, and what do you hear? Men and women heartbroken, ready to kill themselves, murdering, maiming, and emotionally crippling each other, all in the name of love. I can't live without you! You are the only one for me! You are my special angel!

What is love? What is this feeling that men and women supposedly kill and die for? Is it the transitory, once-in-a-lifetime feeling you read about in romantic novels, the moment you have been waiting for, your dreams come true? It seems as if every moment of your life has led up to this one, everything you have hoped and prayed for culminating right now this very minute—you have *fallen in love.*

Oh, Mary, I can't tell you what it was like. When I saw him standing there, it was love at first sight. Oh, I can't think about

1

anything else! He has big green eyes and dark brown hair, and a beautiful smile. . . . Oh, I can't tell you how much I love him!

Or is it the way you felt toward that one and only person for whom you waited your whole life, with whom you were fated to spend the rest of your days in enchanted bliss and ecstasy?

My own Beloved, who hast lifted me
From this drear flat of earth where I was thrown. . . .

Elizabeth Barrett Browning,
"Sonnets from the Portuguese"

When I was younger I remember asking myself, "Well, what if I don't find 'my own Beloved'? Or what if I find her and she doesn't want me? Will my whole life be wasted then? Will I have to settle for someone else and live forever in the sorrow of having missed 'My Own True Love'?" And, I'm embarrassed to admit, I still have these feelings sometimes.

Is this love? Is love something to be seldom found and easily lost, to be jealously guarded from all the evil forces threatening to take it away? This is the message that is drummed into us every day, through books, television shows, commercials, popular songs, billboards, and many other forms in our culture. The myth that love is something to be read about daily but experienced rarely is at times amusing and occasionally hilarious, but its daily unfailing repetition leaves its mark on all of us. We, the very perpetrators of and actors in the myth, are also its victims; for the tragedy is that we are not prepared for actual human relationships with real people, who are not gods or goddesses but human beings like ourselves. People do not always say and do the right thing at exactly the right time. They are not always there whenever they are needed or wanted. They do not always completely understand—in fact, sometimes they do not seem to understand at all! The problem of how to cope with human beings in our daily lives seems far removed from anything we learned in romantic novels and movies. We have almost no cultural models that bridge the gap between our ideals of love and the reality of our ongoing struggles. Although Americans watch television an average of five hours per day, we see very little to help us deal with the problems of maintaining real relationships.

The myths of love are just that, myths. Love is not a once-in-a-lifetime feeling or something dangerously scarce or something that you can experience with only one person at a time. We have believed these fantasies mainly because we have been bombarded with them from infancy on. Unfortunately, as we hear them over and over again without contradiction, these myths become recorded in our brains as misinformation—that is, we "learn" to accept false ideas as being true. All the misinformation we have received makes it very difficult for us to think clearly about love and our own lives. What is love? Who loves you? Whom do you love? Why? Is jealousy a natural part of love? Can you love two people at once? Can men love only women, and women men? These are questions which are hard to think through, made more confusing by our internalized myths about love and our own conflicting feelings and fantasies.

In this book I shall present a theory about love and demonstrate through discussion, case studies, and exercises how this theory can be applied to your own relationships. Some of what you will read may directly contradict current myths in our culture and what we have all been taught to believe. When this happens, I urge you to do your own best thinking, using all the knowledge and information you have at hand.

WHAT IS LOVE?

Love is a sickness full of woes,
All remedies refusing;
A plant that with most cutting grows,
Most barren with best using.
Samuel Daniel (1562–1619)

In the absence of meaningful definitions of love in the wider culture, I will propose one here: *Love is the way people naturally feel toward each other in the absence of painful emotion.* When people are not feeling hurt, angry, scared, or embarrassed in any way, they will feel love toward other people to the extent that they know them. Hard to believe? Bear with me.

How would we feel toward other people if we were feeling good all the time? Do you remember a time on a beautiful spring day when you were walking in a park and started a conversation with a complete stranger? Remember how much you enjoyed it? Or the time that person started talking with you in the supermarket while you were both waiting to be checked out? When we are feeling good about ourselves and the things we are doing, it is usually a joy to make contact with another person. Our attitude toward strangers is one of openness and curiosity, and we are delighted with the other person. Unless, of course, we are on an unlit city street late at night, in which case we are scared; or we are coming home from a bad day at work and do not feel like being friendly to anybody; or we just do not feel safe with the way another person is looking at us. These are all times when our own negative feelings prevent us from being open to appreciating other people.

I begin each college course I teach by individually introducing each member of the class to the whole group. I ask them who they are, what they do, why they are there, and what they like about themselves. Often this turns out to be the highlight of the course, because people in the class are totally fascinated with each other. They (and I) are excited to find out who someone else is and what his or her life is like. This has happened often enough for me to learn that the main barrier to people making overtures to strangers is their own fear and embarrassment. In the absence of these feelings we would all feel good about human beings we meet.

"But," you protest, "what about when a stranger pulls a gun on me and demands my money? Am I supposed to love him or her, or be curious about who s/he [read this word as "he or she"] is?" No, you are not "supposed" to feel love for or be curious about anyone. When painful emotion is being experienced—that is, when we are feeling grief, anger, fear, or embarrassment—positive feelings are usually covered over. In this example, the feelings of fear and anger, however justified, certainly block the appearance of any good feelings on your part. And, of course, the fear and hurt the robber is experiencing are blocking his or her good feelings toward you. This example does not contradict the premise that we feel good about people in the absence of painful feelings. Rather, it shows that in the presence of anger and fear we do not feel good about and are not open to others. (I will be the first to admit that it is difficult to feel good about someone who is robbing you!)

When there is no painful emotion present, how do we feel toward people as we get to know them better? Doesn't it seem reasonable that we would like them better and better and appreciate them more and more? We would have the joy of doing things and spending time together, sharing our thoughts and feelings with each other, touching one another, seeing each other's creativity and intelligence in action, and so on. All these things involve seeing and experiencing each other's human qualities more and more, which would naturally result in our feeling better and better about each other. This is what love is, the way people naturally feel toward one another. It is not something rare or forbidden, or for that matter something deeply mysterious. Rather, it is the feeling we have when we are in touch with the human qualities of other human beings—their loving, caring, thinking, creativity, and zest. These are some of the ways human beings are when their behavior is not based on the effects of painful emotion.

This natural feeling seems far removed from what really happens in relationships. People do not feel good all the time, and they do not always feel good about each other. There are millions of divorces in this country every year, and many more unhappy marriages and relationships. If people love each other more as they know each other better, why all the trouble staying together? Why do we have so much difficulty remaining friends with one another? Quite simply, painful emotion and behavior associated with it get in the way. Let me illustrate this premise with an example.

Jonathan and Barbara have been married for almost eleven years. Jonathan is an assistant manager in a small variety store, and Barbara works as a teacher's aide in an elementary school. They have two boys—Robert, aged eight, and David, aged six—and own a small house in a residential neighborhood. Barbara describes their marriage as follows:

It's okay, I guess, we get along. We don't talk to each other very much, but I suppose that's what happens after you've been married for eleven years. We like each other fine, I suppose. We don't fight very much. . . . Mostly Jonathan has his life and I have mine. That's okay, but I wish that we shared more with each other. It seems that Jonathan isn't interested in my life very much, and doesn't want to share his with me either. So we live in the same house and do a few things together and love each other and everything, but it feels like something is missing. [Anything else?] Well, Jonathan has a pretty short temper, both with me and with Robert and David. He is quick to get angry, and then he is very difficult to talk to or be around. We pretty much have to leave him alone until he settles down. I wish he wasn't like that. . . . Also, I wish he would do more around the house. . .[she laughs].

For Jonathan, also, the marriage is less than perfect.

It has changed a lot over the years. I don't know, maybe I'm bored or something. I still care about Barbara; it's not that. I don't know what it is. We each go our own separate ways mostly. Maybe we don't interest each other very much any more. I work hard and feel under a lot of pressure, and just don't feel good most of the time. I guess I tend to get troubled with how things have been going lately—I guess over the last couple of years. It seems like Barbara doesn't care about me anymore. When I try to talk to her about the things that interest me, she doesn't listen. Sometimes she gets angry, but mostly she ignores me. Most of the time I don't feel too good, and being with Barbara doesn't help. I guess this is just the way it is in marriages, but it's too bad.

After eleven years, the love seems to have gone from Jonathan and Barbara's relationship. But did it really disappear? Are boredom, minor irritation, and disappointment all that are left in the marriage? Perhaps on the surface it appears so, but there is actually much more happening. This segment from a counseling session with both of them brought out some deeper feelings.

COUNSELOR: Jonathan, what do you like about Barbara? Say it directly to her.

JONATHAN: Well, um . . . you are good looking (*laughs*). . . . You cook well. . . . You take good care of the kids. . . . You manage the money pretty well. . . . (*Anything else you like about her?*) You get along well with people. . . . You're pretty smart (*laughs*).

COUNSELOR: And you, Barbara, what do you like about Jonathan?

BARBARA: I like how hard you work. . . . I like the way you play with Robert and David. . . . You do your job very well. . . . You're handsome (*laughs*). . . . You're friendly to your in-laws (*laughs*). . . . We've had some good times together.

COUNSELOR: Do you remember one?

BARBARA (*pause*): Well, the camping trip last year to the mountains was lots of fun. David and Robert loved it, and so did I.

JONATHAN: I did, too.

COUNSELOR: All right, let's move on to what's not going well in your relationship. How about you first, Barbara.

BARBARA: Well . . . I guess the thing that bothers me the most is that it seems like we never talk to each other any more. Whenever I try to talk with him about something, Jonathan cuts me off somehow and goes back to his paper or television or something else.

COUNSELOR: How do you feel and what do you do when that happens?

BARBARA: What usually happens is that Jonathan will snap at me or something, and I'll leave him alone after that. I suppose I feel hurt and a little angry.

COUNSELOR: Okay, let's hold it here and give Jonathan some time. What are the problem areas you see in your marriage?

JONATHAN: Let's see. Well, one of them is when I get home from work. I'm usually pretty tired and just want to relax and read the paper. This is one of those times when Barbara wants to talk to me. I want to be alone for awhile, but she doesn't seem to understand that. After awhile I get angry and say something I shouldn't. That usually stops it.

COUNSELOR: Anything else?

JONATHAN: Well, I guess I feel guilty about it, and end up staying away from her for quite awhile. This kind of thing seems to happen quite a bit with us.

This is of course merely a portion of the total process of working through what is going on in the relationship. It does provide a clue, however, as to what often goes wrong. Jonathan and Barbara still care for each other, but they each have other strong feelings that get in the way of feeling and expressing their love. It is not that they do not love each other any more; rather, their feelings of love are covered over by other painful feelings. This has been demonstrated in hundreds of cases in which people have released their negative feelings by talking, laughing, crying, and so on. After the painful emotion is gone, the feelings of love which were always there are uncovered and again experienced. In the case of Jonathan and Barbara, it took several sessions of much talking and copious release of feelings before they were both strongly in touch with the love they have for each other.

HOW PAINFUL EMOTION BLOCKS
OUR FEELINGS OF LOVE

Why is it so difficult for us to feel good about those we love? Four main things seem to happen: (1) Our painful emotions are triggered by things our partners do (and vice versa); (2) when we feel bad we tend to take out our feelings on our partners; (3) we have chronic feelings of not being worthwhile and not being loved, which are based on old hurts and are constantly making it difficult for us to feel good about ourselves and our partners; and (4) we develop expectations of our partners based not on who they are but rather on how close they come to filling old needs that were not filled in childhood. Let us take a look at each of these factors.

Factor 1: *Our negative feelings are triggered by our partner's behavior.* In most relationships, the things our partners do that bother us are behaviors that they repeat over and over again. With Jonathan and Barbara, for example, Barbara continually wants Jonathan's attention when he gets home from work. Her behavior fits into a pattern which plays almost every day when he comes home. Barbara's behavior itself is not bad or wrong; it is merely inappropriate. Jonathan is usually tired when returning home and is not ready to listen to what Barbara's day was like. It is in response to Barbara's demanding his attention at this time that Jonathan feels angry and annoyed. His feelings are triggered by her patterned behavior.

Jonathan's behavioral response of getting angry and shouting at Barbara to shut up also forms a pattern. His response does not vary much and occurs almost every time Barbara wants his attention and he does not feel like giving it to her. This behavior pattern of Jonathan's is also inappropriate: Barbara does not deserve to be yelled at merely because she wants to talk to Jonathan when he is not ready to be talked to. In response to Jonathan's anger and yelling, Barbara's own feelings of anger and hurt are ignited.

This example is typical. The things that trigger our negative feelings are our partner's behavior patterns that are inappropriate to the actual situation. It would make much more sense for Barbara to wait until Jonathan relaxed awhile before telling him about her day. It would also make more sense for Jonathan to say to Barbara, "I'd like to relax now; let's talk after dinner," rather than getting furious at her. Their behavior is rigid and unproductive; in other words, each new interaction with one another is not approached flexibly and creatively, but instead involves the same old responses. Compare the following two interactions, each occurring just after Jonathan returns home from work:

I. Both Jonathan and Barbara respond out of rigid behavior patterns:

BARBARA *(busy in the kitchen)*: Hi, Jonathan! How was your day?

JONATHAN *(takes off his coat, sits down in a chair, and starts reading the paper)*: Okay.

BARBARA *(coming out of the kitchen)*: Anything interesting happen at work today?

JONATHAN *(head in the paper)*: Nope.

BARBARA: I had a good day today. This afternoon Robert and David and I went to the swimming pool, and we had lots of fun.

JONATHAN *(head remains buried in the paper)*: Humm.

BARBARA: Aren't you interested?

JONATHAN *(in a heated tone)*: Goddammit, can't you leave me alone for awhile? I haven't been home for two minutes and yak yak yak, it's the kids this and the kids that. Can't you just keep quiet for awhile? *(Barbara feels hurt, remains silent, and goes back into the kitchen.)*

II. Jonathan and Barbara respond freshly and creatively to the situation:

BARBARA*(busy in the kitchen)*: Hi, Jonathan! How was your day? *(Comes out of the kitchen and gives Jonathan a kiss.)*

JONATHAN: Hi, Barbara *(hugs her)*. . . . My day was all right . . . pretty tiring . . . *(sits down and picks up the paper)*.

BARBARA: I'd like to tell you some of the things that happened today. Want to listen?

JONATHAN: Yes, but not right now. I'm awfully tired, and I'd just like to relax and read for awhile. How about during dinner?

BARBARA: Fine . . . *(returns to the kitchen)*.

Barbara and Jonathan had the same conflicting needs in both interactions, Barbara to talk about her day and Jonathan to have some quiet space. In the first interaction they were responding out of rigid behavior patterns, setting off each other's hurt and angry emotions. In the second interaction, by letting each other know directly what they wanted and were feeling, they established good communication despite their differing concerns. Their painful emotions were not triggered, largely because their partners were not behaving rigidly but were rather responding to what the particular situation warranted.

Why are our painful emotions triggered by our partner's behavior patterns? Why can we not just think all the time and always respond appropriately to every circumstance? What seems to happen is that we are reminded, either consciously or not, of distressful situations in our past that have some similarity to the present. Thus reminded, we "play back" the feelings and behaviors recorded at that time. These recordings constitute our rigid behavior patterns. To illustrate, here is a later portion of Barbara and Jonathan's counseling session:

COUNSELOR: Barbara, what are you reminded of when Jonathan shouts at you to leave him alone? *(pauses a moment)* What is your first thought?

BARBARA: My father used to yell at me a lot.

COUNSELOR: Can you remember a specific time?

BARBARA: Well, one time, I guess I was about six, and I think I was playing in the kitchen, pretending I was baking something. I must have made a mess, because when he came in he was furious. . . . He screamed something at me, I don't remember what. . . .

COUNSELOR: Make a guess. What might have he said?

BARBARA: Something like, "What are you doing?" *(said in a loud, angry voice)* And then he hit me *(she starts crying, and cries for several minutes).*

COUNSELOR *(after she has stopped crying of her own accord)*: What happened next?

BARBARA:: I guess I was sent to my room. It wasn't fair . . . *(starts crying again).*

Here we see that Barbara's response to Jonathan's angry behavior is rooted in distressful experiences from her past. Her fear and hurt from such incidents with her father get called up in the present and prevent her from thinking clearly about how to respond to Jonathan's anger. Similarly, Jonathan's angry response to Barbara's desire for his attention is rooted in his own particular hurtful experiences from his past. This is true of all rigid patterns of behavior—they are all based on the ways each of us has been hurt. Rigid behavior patterns do not develop in response to all distressful events, however. They seem to develop particularly when the natural healing process of emotional release—laughing, crying, trembling, raging, sweating, and yawning—is inhibited. Thus, when we are hurt and do not completely release or discharge the feelings, we record in our memory everything that happens in the situation—the feelings, the circumstances, the physical appearance of the people involved —without evaluating any of the information. This mixed-up recording of feelings and circumstances is the basis of the behavior pattern that later is replayed when we are in some way reminded of the painful experience.

An event occurred a few years ago that well illustrates the different consequences of discharging or not discharging painful emotion at the time of a distressful experience. Ginny and her four-year-old son Eddy were at a gas station, waiting in the office while their car was being serviced. Eddy was approaching the chained German shepherd watchdog with curiosity when it suddenly leaped on him and grabbed his head in its jaws. For almost fifteen seconds the dog had its teeth on the boy's head while the mother stood watching, frozen in terror. Finally Eddy was freed by the station attendant, luckily suffering only minor head lacerations. He, of course, was terrified, and was crying and shaking a great deal. Ginny put aside her own feelings and spent the next hour and a half encouraging Eddy to continue crying and shaking, having him look at the dog (before they left), asking him to tell her what happened, and reminding him how scared he was. With her encouragement, he cried almost continuously for an hour before moving on to laughter and finally to feeling okay.

The result of this event demonstrates the tremendous healing ability of the discharge process. The physical wounds healed relatively quickly, and there was no apparent emotional scar from the incident. When Eddy sees a dog, he approaches it cautiously, closely observing it to see whether or not it is friendly. If it is, he goes ahead and plays with it. Otherwise, he leaves it alone. What Eddy has done is to integrate into his thinking and behavior the information that some dogs are dangerous. He does not automatically respond with fear whenever he sees large dogs; rather, his experience gave him more information with which to choose how to relate to any particular dog. Because he discharged his feelings of terror concerning the incident, they in no way exert any control over his behavior around dogs.

Ginny, on the other hand, did not take the opportunity at the time or soon thereafter to release her own feelings of terror over watching her son being mauled by a big dog. Her terror was every bit as real as Eddy's and not releasing her feelings had the effect we might have expected. Although Eddy did not develop a fear of dogs, Ginny did. When she sees a large dog, she has an involuntary, momentary response of fear: Her face slightly whitens, she sweats, and she backs away a little. She has internally recorded a mixed-up message, attaching her feelings of fear and terror to the incident. When she sees a large dog she is reminded (usually not consciously) of that incident, and the fear and associated behavior are stimulated again, or "restimulated."

This then is the mechanism by which we develop negative feelings in response to our partners' behavior. Usually the behavior to which we are responding is part of a rigid pattern and not the product of our partners' best, flexible thinking. In other words, what bothers us is that part of our partners' behavior is based on how they were hurt in the past. Whether our partners are yelling at us or consistently burning dinner, their behavior can be traced to earlier painful incidents in which their distressful emotion was not discharged.

The reason we are bothered, however, is based on the ways *we* were hurt in the past. Their behavior reminds us, as Barbara was reminded by Jonathan's angry outbursts, of distressful situations in the past that were in some way similar to the present one. The feelings that were internally recorded during those past events are then re-experienced. We do not have to respond to our partners' yelling at us by yelling back or by pouting. We act out these behaviors only because our painful feelings are triggered by our partners' patterns. This interactive dynamic between both people's patterns is one of the major factors preventing us from feeling and expressing love for each other.

Factor 2: *When we are feeling bad we tend to take out our feelings on our partners.* Many times when we are angry at our partners or do not feel love for them, it has little or nothing to do with them. Witness the following short interactions:

A: Good morning!

B: Good morning? What's so good about it? Who do you think you are, Mister Cheerful?

Or

A: Jack, let's spend the evening at home tonight relaxing. I'm feeling pretty tired.

B: Oh, you're always feeling tired. Living with you is like living with a bag of bones. I'm sick of it.

Or

A *(very cheerfully)*: How's it going?

B *(leaning over the engine of her car, hands and clothes covered with grease)*: Oh, shut up.

Or

B *(when A comes over to give B a hug and a kiss)*: Leave me alone.

In these exchanges the first person is doing very little to provoke the second, yet the venomous replies of the latter indicate that some strong feelings are involved. What seems to be happening is that the interaction is serving as a vehicle for the person to release some of his or her feelings and tensions by yelling at or in some other way taking out frustration on the other person. Have you ever had a conversation such as the following?

YOU *(seeing your friend looking rather depressed)*: Is anything wrong, dear? You look a little sad.

S/HE *(grumbling in a low voice)*: No.

YOU: Are you sure? You hardly ate any dinner, and you don't seem like yourself.

S/HE *(shouting)*: Listen, bug off. I'm okay, and nothing's wrong. I don't want to talk about it. Now *lay off*.

What did you do to deserve such treatment? You were just trying to help when you were hit with all these feelings. No doubt you felt hurt and angry in response, and perhaps you even struck back with your own verbal artillery. Nevertheless, your partner's unprovoked attack on you was in no way your fault. What happened? Why do we pick on the people we love most, even when they are not at fault? It is not just that they happen to be there at the right time; do you know anybody who would respond to a stranger's "Good morning" by saying "Who do you think you are, Mister Cheerful or something?" This kind of behavior is generally reserved for our loved ones, as crazy as this may seem. The explanation lies in the nature of the circumstances surrounding such interactions.

Whenever people take out their feelings on another person, either physically or verbally, you will find that they are in some way feeling hurt themselves. This is clear in all the above short encounters. We have all had experiences similar to the woman fixing her car. We are working on something and it is not going well. We get more and more frustrated, but have no outlet for these feelings. Then our partners come along and we dump all our frustration right on them; often we feel much better, but they feel awful. In this example it is clear that we use interactions with our friends to unload feelings we accumulated in contexts unrelated to them.

Another situation to which I am sure many can relate is what often happens when a person first arrives home from work. The dialogue between Barbara and Jonathan presented one such case. Barbara's simple attempt to discuss her day was sufficient to provoke an explosion on Jonathan's part. To understand why he responded in this way, here is another segment of a counseling session.

COUNSELOR: What do you normally feel like when you come home from work?

JONATHAN: I'm pretty tired . . . I have a pretty long day, and when I get home I want to sack out.

COUNSELOR: What is it like at work for you?

JONATHAN: Good . . . I make enough to live on. . . . Sure would like to make more, though . . . *(laughs)*. . . . I like the responsibility I have. I'm hoping I'll move up soon.

COUNSELOR: Anything else good about it?

JONATHAN: Well, I don't have to drive too far to get there *(laughs)*.

COUNSELOR: What's hard for you about working?

JONATHAN *(laughs)*: That's an easy one . . . *(yawns)* . . . I spend most of the day dealing with people's problems. . . . Everybody is always complaining about everything. I get really sick of it.

COUNSELOR: Can you remember a particular time?

JONATHAN *(pauses)*: . . . Well, last week this guy came in and wanted to return a shirt he had bought. It had a tear in it all right, but it looked like it had been worn quite awhile. I told him he needed a sales slip to return it, and he got pretty heated. I kept being nice to him, but he was screaming away, going on and on. I hated him! *(laughs)*.

COUNSELOR: What would you have liked to have said to him?

JONATHAN *(laughs)*: I'd have told him to shut up.

COUNSELOR: Pretend that I am he, and tell him now.

JONATHAN: Shut up.

COUNSELOR: Shout it at him, and shake my shoulders while you're at it.

JONATHAN: You've got to be kidding.

COUNSELOR: Try it. Sometimes it helps loosen up the feelings. If you start hurting me I'll let you know.

JONATHAN: Shut up! *(shaking the counselor's shoulders)* . . . *(continues yelling and shaking for awhile, laughing as he does so).* . . .

The session continued with Jonathan alternately laughing and getting angry for several minutes, and then bringing his attention back to the present with the help of the counselor. One of the things this session demonstrates is the extent to which Jonathan has feelings at work which he does not normally express. Although the session involved a simulation of the experience at work and was not the real thing, the feelings that surfaced were as real as those in the actual situation. In fact, these feelings surfaced precisely because he was reminded of the real situation, and because the counseling session provided enough safety to allow him to get the feelings out.

Jonathan does not usually discharge his frustrations around work (as most of us do not). Instead, he arrives home tired and irritable, and when Barbara tries to converse with him, he explodes at her with all his pent-up feelings. Why does he take them out on her? The main reason is that he has no other place to get rid of the feelings. His job, like most, is not set up so that he has the opportunity to release his painful emotions. Could you imagine Jonathan crying after a distressful exchange with a customer or his boss? Of course not, because it is simply not socially acceptable to do so.

Having no other outlet for his feelings, Jonathan comes home and lets go at Barbara and his children, the only people in his life with whom he feels safe enough to get angry. The intimacy found in the primary relationships in his family is usually sufficient to allow him to express his feelings and frustrations. In addition, the patterned dynamic in Jonathan and Barbara's relationship insures that Barbara will not get angry back; she instead feels hurt and withdraws. The family thus serves as a "safety valve" by which he (and we) can let off steam that has built up from other distressful experiences.

This is not a particularly rational system for several reasons. First, it places undue pressures on intimate relationships. In this example, the cause of Jonathan's accumulation of feelings was his job, but the family bore the consequences. It is as if all the daily distresses felt by both partners are funneled into their relationships with each other and with other loved ones.

Second, the act of taking out our feelings on other people at best restimulates their own painful feelings from the past and at worst physically and emotionally hurts them. This result is most obvious when people act out their feelings by beating someone, but any form of physical or verbal abuse has a harmful effect on other human beings. Unless the recipients of the abuse release their own painful feelings over the event, it will add another groove to the distress recording which blocks them from behaving and thinking at their full potential. None of us wants this to happen to those we love.

Third, when we take out our anger and pain on our partners, they react with their own pain and hurt. Often they in turn take their feelings out on some undeserving person, such as a son or daughter, in a kind of chain reaction. The behavior conforms to a pecking order, analogous to that seen in chickens or baboons: The boss picks on the employee, the employee goes home and picks on his or her spouse, and the spouse picks on the children. Although this example is oversimplified and not entirely accurate, it does point out how distress is passed on by people taking out their feelings on each other. Jonathan might seem to feel better after dumping his feelings on his wife, but his behavior has hurt her and their relationship.

I would like to draw a distinction here between real discharge, which is the process of physically releasing distress, and *dramatization*, which involves acting out feelings and directing them at other people. Discharge includes the physical mechanisms of laughing, crying, trembling, yawning, sweating, and raging. These are all natural processes and do not have to be learned by any human being—in fact, we have to be consistently punished to keep us from discharging when we need to. This physical release is the natural response to painful experiences (discussed in greater detail in Chapter 7).

Dramatization, on the other hand, includes behavior such as whining, yelling, physically beating someone, angry door slamming, moping, and so on. These acts all indicate that the person is in some way "hurting" (i.e., feeling hurt, angry, embarrassed, or scared) but is unable to release the painful feelings or ask for help directly. The feelings are instead "acted out," or dramatized. Dramatizations are patterned responses to hurt, developed at an early age at those times when painful incidents occurred but our discharge was inhibited. Let me give an example of a dramatization that I am very familiar with, one of my own.

When I was in grade school and living at home, there was a characteristic behavior I enacted when frustrated or feeling bad. (It did not particularly matter what the immediate cause of the feeling was.) I would pick up on the slightest reason, get quite angry, and then go into my bedroom, slamming the door as hard as I could and locking it. Of course, this only happened when my parents were around. This behavior was clearly in response to my feeling bad, but it did not alleviate the feeling. My mother often came to the door and asked me what was wrong and if she could come in, but I always told her to "Go away and leave me alone." This behavior was all dramatization on my part. Looking back on it, I remember lying on my bed and secretly wishing my mother would somehow break open the door, come over and hold me while I cried and cried, ridding myself of those horrible feelings. Rather than discharging my painful feelings, however, I was acting out or rehearsing a behavior or distress pattern which I reenacted whenever I was feeling bad.

When Jonathan yells at Barbara and when she responds by withdrawing and feeling bad, both are dramatizing their feelings rather than discharging them. The result is that neither of them is actually getting rid of the feelings, so they carry them around for hours or days. No wonder the love seems to be gone from their relationship! With so many other feelings present and distressed behavior being acted out, there is little space left for appreciating one another.

Dramatizing and discharging our feelings around our partners have quite different consequences. When we act out our feelings and take them out on our partners, it tends to restimulate their past painful feelings, from similar incidents, resulting in the kind of encounters Jonathan and Barbara have. When we discharge in front of our partners, however, it has a different effect. They may feel embarrassed or uncomfortable, but the discharge usually will not encourage them to take out their feelings on us. On the contrary, often our crying or trembling reminds our partners that we are human beings who have feelings and can feel hurt by things that happen to us.

Unfortunately, at the present time we do not usually release our feelings around our partners but instead take out our feelings *on* them. Why we do this will be discussed later, but now it suffices to say that this dramatizing is a major factor preventing us from feeling and expressing love for our partners.

Factor 3: *We have chronic feelings that we are not worthwhile and are not loved. These feelings, based on old hurts, make it difficult for us to feel good about ourselves, and hence, feel good about our partners.*

Do you remember a time when you saw a toddler, full of curiosity, about to pick up some delicate object when an adult voice suddenly shouted out, *"Don't touch that!"*? If you remember, the adult was quite angry, rushed over to the toddler, and roughly moved him or her to a different spot. At this point the toddler probably started to cry.

Or do you remember a time when you were at school and someone made fun of your looks, your clothes, or some aspect of your behavior? It was embarrassing to have your classmates ridicule you, even if it was supposedly done "in good fun." It probably bothered you for a long while afterward.

Or try recalling your earliest memories. What is your first memory? Your second? Ask a friend the same question. Probably the things you each remember are early incidents that were either physically painful or emotionally scary, embarrassing, or in some other way hurtful.

We have all experienced literally thousands of events in our lives that were upsetting. When we were hit, made fun of, forced to overeat or to go hungry, pushed around, told we were stupid or lazy, made to sit still, or threatened with physical violence—these all constituted new hurts. If the feelings about these experiences were not discharged, they became mixed in with the brain's recording of the associated event. The other thing conveyed during the incident and recorded along with the feelings and the actual circumstances is the misinformation about us. Do you know a woman (or a man) who you think is very smart but who thinks of herself as stupid? Or a man you think is handsome who sees himself as ugly? In both these cases, the person's self-image is based on past unreleased distressful experiences in which they were directly or indirectly told they were stupid or ugly. Events in which such expressions are directly stated are easy to understand. In an incident I observed recently, for example, a group of ten-year-old boys were riding a school bus. One of them, Billy, was the target of ridicule from several of the others. Some of the things said were "Phew, are you *ugly*" and "You're so ugly you should keep your head in a paper bag!" and so on. There was much laughter and snickering by all the boys except Billy, who remained silent. Whatever their intentions, the effect of their ridicule was to pass on to Billy the message that "You are ugly." This message was internally recorded along with the embarrassment and any other bad feelings he was experiencing at the time.

We can use the term *invalidation* to describe this kind of

experience, in which a person is told in some way that s/he is not okay. Even when the invalidating message is not stated directly, its consequences are nevertheless the same. If a student speaks out in class and everyone laughs at what s/he says, the message that "You are stupid" is communicated and recorded as clearly as if it were stated in so many words. For more examples, think of your own early experiences and the kinds of messages that were communicated to you.

One component of all invalidating messages is the implication that we are not good or not okay, that we are bad for looking the way we do, for saying the wrong thing, for wanting to examine and play with that pretty glass vase, and so on. (Why else would they laugh at us or scold us unless we were bad?) Thus the message that we are not okay has been recorded over and over again, associated with most of the innumerable distressful events we have experienced. With enough repetition and attached to so much undischarged painful emotion, the distress pattern is now how we see ourselves.

Of course we are all okay. We may have done things that did not make sense, but we only did them because we were hurting—which does not make us any less worthwhile human beings. We were all born with tremendous potential to develop into capable, intelligent adults. The only reason any of us has not achieved this potential is that we were hurt and made to feel worthless. We must draw a distinction between the human being and the distress recordings which were laid in through no fault of our own. If an intelligent, energetic infant is systematically told that s/he is no good, does that make him or her any less worthwhile a human being? Even if s/he is hurt so much that s/he starts believing it, this does not affect the inherent worth of the person. Logically we have no reason to assume that we are anything but lovable and worthy people. Unfortunately, how we feel about ourselves is based not on logic but rather on how we have been hurt.

Another message that seems to be recorded along with

most undischarged distressful experiences is "I am not loved." For if they loved us would they hurt us? Would they hit us or make fun of us? As adults, many of us have come to the *intellectual* realization that our parents, for instance, did those things as a result of their own hurts; but at least in part because we were not able to release our feelings about what happened, we still, at a *feeling* level, do not understand why they did it. It *feels* like we must have done something to deserve it. After all, they are our parents. Why would they treat us that way if they loved us? So we internalized the message that nobody loves us. Like the message saying that we are not okay, this has become chronic through repetition.

Having these feelings of not being loved and not being okay affects both our ability to feel the love others have for us and our capacity to feel and express love toward other people. For how can we accept other people's love when we "know" that we are unlovable? What usually happens is that we tend to deflect other people's expressions of love away from us; we either laugh it off, ignore it, or quickly say "I love you" right back. Often we just do not believe it. Have you ever had a thought similar to those following after someone has told you that s/he loves you?

Hmmm . . . She doesn't *really* know me at all.

Or

She just has a blind spot when it comes to me.

Or

I guess she's not as smart as I thought she was.

The implication is that something must be wrong with our friend for him or her to love and appreciate us. Why do we not believe them? Our feelings about ourselves are not based on logic or common sense, but rather are rooted in past, hurtful experiences. These feelings continually make it difficult for us to accept and feel love from our partners.

They also make it hard for us to feel and express love toward our partners. For how can we be expected to care for and appreciate another person when we feel that nobody appreciates us? What seems to happen is that when people are themselves hurting it is difficult for them to pay attention to other people. This is a natural result of the phenomenon of restimulation, through which we are reminded of past hurtful experiences by present situations. Many things having to do with love remind us of past experiences associated with embarrassment, fear, grief, or anger. When these feelings are restimulated, it is very difficult for us to think clearly about what to do. (We know how strong feelings can block rational, caring behavior—witness the number of murders committed by people who know and love their victims.) As the whole area of love is one in which we all have had many hurtful experiences, often perpetrated by those whom we loved the most, it is no wonder that our feelings of not being loved inhibit our expressing love well to others.

Factor 4 is concerned with why we choose the partners we do in the first place: the kinds of needs and wants for which we seek partners.

WHY WE CHOOSE OUR PARTNERS

Olivia: How does he love me?
Viola: With adorations, with fertile tears,
With groans that thunder love, with sighs of fire.

William Shakespeare,
Twelfth Night

Have you ever thought about why you and your partner are close friends, lovers, or spouses? Why did you choose each other rather than other people? Was it mere chance that you happened to end up together? Your meeting one another might have been the result of chance, but your liking each other and wanting to develop the relationship was not entirely the result of circumstance. True, you may each have been looking for someone to get involved with, but there are millions of available people in this country in the same situation. Some of your getting together was chance, some was common interests, and some was your mutual appreciation of each other's special human qualities—his sense of humor, her intelligence, his kindness, her sense of humor, and so on. The other element greatly affecting whom we choose as our partners is the extent to which they help us meet our needs and wants. For someone who loves to sing, having a partner who can sing on key may be a highly desired attribute.

It is entirely rational and sensible to try to fill some needs through a relationship. There are other things that we think of as "needs," however, which in the long run are harmful to relationships if we try to fill them. We need to distinguish between these different motivations before we can accurately describe the effect they have on relationships. For our purposes we can divide what we normally call "needs" into three groups: real human needs, what can be called "frozen needs," and false needs.

Real human needs are those things without which we would suffer some real physical or emotional damage. I think we can all agree that human beings need food, water, and sleep. Without these things people undergo noticeable damage. Similarly, we have needs which if not filled result in mental, emotional, or psychological damage. The damage is in this case less visible, but it is no less devastating. In fact, we only know these are real needs by having seen what happens to people when they are not met—namely, they develop rigid behavior patterns. A case study exemplifying this result will be presented shortly. Let us here list some of the real human needs involving other people.

Touching. We need to have physical contact with other human beings. This is not learned behavior, nor is it restricted to a few cultures. Rather it is universal among humans, that from the womb onward we need to touch and be touched. Without enough physical contact we will experience deprivation and hurt as a direct result, and without discharge will develop rigid patterns out of which we will operate when the hurt is restimulated.

Being loved. We need to have other people express their love to us. This is most important in our early years, but the need continues throughout our entire lives. Of all the human needs involving other people, this is the one that is most acknowledged. A person who does not feel loved is a hurt 'human being.

Loving. What is not usually mentioned is that the need to love other people is at least as important as the need to be loved. It is tremendously hurtful to be denied the right to express our love for other people. What is often the most painful about having loved ones die is not losing their love but rather losing them as human beings whom we love and care about. Indeed, when we do not have people to love we often redirect our love to pets, plants, and even inanimate objects such as automobiles.

Receiving validation. We need to be told over and over again that we are good, that we are doing good things, that we are appreciated. This might be considered one aspect of being loved, but like touching, is important enough to be listed separately. The absence of validation usually is a large contributing factor in our developing patterns that contain the message "I am not okay." This is an area in which almost all of us are hurting, having received little validation when we were growing up.

Being seen and treated as a unique person. We have a need to be respected as individuals, and not related to just on the basis of what racial, sexual, religious, or ethnic group we belong to. We are unique human beings *first*, and are only secondarily men or women; Protestants, Catholics, or Jews; white or black or Puerto Rican; and so on. Being treated primarily as a member of a stereotyped group effectively denies our full humanness and limits our potential.

Sharing thinking. Having people to share ideas with, to listen to us and respond from their own thinking, is a real human need. Without this interchange our ability to think clearly becomes impaired (not irrevocably so, fortunately). Just imagine what it would be like to talk about, but never receive feedback on, what you were thinking. It would be difficult to tell whether or not what you were saying was making sense. Interacting with other intelligences is a necessary aspect of healthy human activity.

Playing. We need to have people to have fun with, to be silly with, to try out new behaviors with—in short, to play with. It is well known that monkeys and apes do not grow up to be healthy adults if they are deprived of play at an early age. We are not about to try the same experiment with humans, but I am sure the results would be the same. We do have the examples of hundreds or thousands of people who grew up without peers or someone to play with. The particular way each person is affected is of course unique, but having no one to play with seems to be a hurt associated with much painful emotion. In addition, it seems to limit our ability to be creative and flexible, as play is one area in which it is relatively easy to step out of role-related behavior and try different things.

Knowing other human beings. This need is related to all of the above, but differs in that it focuses on being in touch with the whole person—experiencing another person's humanness in its entirety. This concept means not just appreciating what someone does or how s/he looks, but making contact with and enjoying the human being who does all those things or looks that way. The absence of knowing other people in this way seems to result in feelings of isolation, loneliness, and hurt. If not discharged, these result in the formation of patterns of behavior that affect almost all aspects of human interaction.

What distinguishes the preceding needs from other kinds of motivation is that these are not learned or taught in any way. They are not specific to any one culture, but are common to all human beings. Meeting these needs helps people to grow and develop, and their not being met is hurtful. Starving these needs is harmful in the same way that any other undischarged distressful experience is harmful: The painful feelings, the particular circumstances, and the invalidating messages all get glued together in the memory, forming a behavior pattern that operates whenever we are reminded in some way of the hurt. We can illustrate this with an example.

Frank is forty-five years old and works as a bricklayer. He has been divorced once and is about to get remarried. Frank functions very well in most of the things he does; he is a skilled worker, a good father, and a very nice person. One thing that did hurt his first marriage was his jealousy and possessiveness; whenever his wife wanted to spend time with her family or her friends, Frank felt hurt and angry, occasionally going so far as to strike her. Feeling trapped by his jealousy was in fact one of the main reasons she left the marriage. To help us understand the nature and cause of his jealousy, here is a condensation of part of a counseling session:

COUNSELOR: Hi, Frank. What are some good things that have happened to you recently?

FRANK: Not much. . . . I had a good weekend . . . went fishing with Greg *(his son)* on Saturday, and we each caught several bass. . . . Gloria and I went to a movie last night, and it was good.

COUNSELOR: Anything else?

FRANK: I finished a good job last week . . . felt good to finish it.

COUNSELOR: What do you want to work on today?

FRANK: I think I need to work on what happened last night. On the way home from the movies I asked Gloria if she wanted to get together tomorrow, and she said she was busy. She's going out with some girlfriends from work. I got pretty upset . . . I sort of got cold and turned off to her. I just dropped her off at her apartment and went on home. I know I shouldn't, but I still feel angry about it.

COUNSELOR: Talk more about how you feel.

FRANK: I just feel like she doesn't really care about me . . . if she did she would want to be with me instead of her other friends.

COUNSELOR: Can you remember a time while growing up when you felt like people didn't care about you?

FRANK *(laughs)*: Sure, all the time.

COUNSELOR: Who didn't care about you? What's your first thought?

FRANK: My mother . . . she was always too busy to be with me . . . *(yawns)*. She didn't really love me. At least that's what it felt like. She was never there when I needed her.

COUNSELOR: Is there a specific time you remember when you needed her but she wasn't there?

FRANK *(pauses)*: I remember one time . . . I must have been about four or five, and a couple older kids stole my ball. It was the only one I had, and I really loved it. . . . Anyway, I ran home crying, looking for mom, but she wasn't there . . . she was never there. . . .

(With gentle encouragement Frank continued to talk about the incident and his feelings about it. After several minutes he began releasing his feelings by crying.)

Here we see a good example of what happens when a real human need, the need to be loved, is not adequately met in childhood. If Frank's situation is at all typical, the incident he is describing was just one of hundreds in which his mother or someone else was not there for him when he was hurting. As the same kind of thing happened over and over again, the amount of distress he has in this area has grown larger.

Frank still has a real need to be loved. What happened, however, is that his early, unfilled need became frozen into a rigid behavior pattern which continues to operate. His present behavior and jealous feelings are based on the love he needed as a young person but did not get. A *frozen need* is a real human need that became locked into a distress pattern because it was not met in the past and continues to function in the present. His "need" to have someone there whenever he "needs" her is not related to his adult reality. Nevertheless, his feelings and the associated behavior pattern demanding more and more attention still take over despite their inappropriateness.

By their very nature, frozen needs can never be filled in the present. We can get rid of them by releasing the painful feelings associated with their not having been met in the past, but we cannot satisfy them as we can satisfy current human needs. Frozen needs are parts of recordings which play again and again; occasionally we can temporarily feel like the "need" is satisfied, but as soon as the pattern is restimulated the frozen need will be as strong as ever. Frank's need for constant attention from women he loves cannot be realistically met. He would perhaps feel better if Gloria were with him all the time, continuously giving him her full attention and love, but would this be good for either of them? Who, unless acting out of the effects of past, very painful experiences, would choose to be with one other person all the time? Even if Gloria did choose to spend all her time with Frank, he would not feel satisfied. Past unfilled needs simply cannot be filled by present behavior.

One of the costs of trying to fill frozen needs is that we tend to see other people and situations merely as elements we can use. While in the grip of his rigid pattern Frank cannot appreciate Gloria as a separate, unique human being, with real needs and interests and qualities of her own. Instead, he sees her as someone who either will or will not be with him, who will or will not meet his need. This very much hurts the chances of their developing and maintaining a good relationship. Fortunately, Frank is trying to free himself of the frozen need by discharging the feelings associated with the early experiences that caused it. Already his awareness of the pattern is making a difference in his love relationship.

Frozen needs function much in the same manner as drug addictions. When the need is not met, most of our energy and attention goes into getting it met. Frozen needs have no scruples; people acting in pattern will often do things hurtful to others. The most extreme examples are the murders that are committed for "love." Frank wanting his women friends to be chained to him is also a good example: While being controlled by his "need," Frank has no concern for what is good or bad for Gloria. The frozen need cries out "Me, me, me," disregarding the realities of the actual situation.

Almost all of us have frozen needs; because our nurturers often were hurting themselves and may not have had the resources, few of us had all our needs met. Because most of our frozen needs developed in relation to those we loved while growing up, they are restimulated by, and interfere with, our present love relationships. The feelings and behaviors called up are remnants of the past; their only proper place in the present is to be discharged so that we can be completely free to act appropriately now and in the future.

In addition to frozen needs, there are other perceived needs that are the products of past hurts. Unlike frozen needs, however, they never were real needs. An example of such a false need is someone who "needs" to eat sweets whenever s/he feels bad. This supposed need will not be found in an undistressed human being. Usually we can go back to a person's early experiences and locate exactly when eating sugary foods became attached to feelings of anxiety and discomfort. Although the person may feel the "need" very strongly, it will disappear when the feelings around those hurtful incidents are totally released.

We can see in the previous instance how something felt as

a need is really the product of past hurts and not a basic human need at all. There are some false needs, however, so common to our culture that most people accept them as being basic. We know that they are not for several reasons: (1) they are not found in all human beings in all cultures and are therefore not universal; (2) when people discharge their painful feelings around these so-called needs, they tend to disappear; and (3) when people meet their real needs and consciously avoid meeting these false needs, they appear to suffer no harmful consequences—in fact, they seem to be better off.

Let us list some false needs that are widely mistaken as real needs throughout our culture:

The false need to be taken care of. Because of things that happen to us in childhood, many of us have feelings of inadequacy about taking care of ourselves and taking charge of our own lives. We have been socialized to believe that everything will be okay once we find someone to take care of us. This is particularly true for women, but is not rare for men either. When the feelings of inadequacy and helplessness are eliminated and people receive support for taking care of themselves, the "need" to be protected and "looked after" goes away.

The false need to take care of. This need, reciprocal to the previous one, is also based upon hurt that was inflicted in childhood. The myths that men need to take care of women and vice versa remain myths, no matter how often they are repeated. There is no such thing as a real need to shelter and protect another adult human being.

The false need for sex. We do not have an uncontrollable "need" for sex. The idea that sex is a drive is a product of the overemphasis and misinformation around sex in our society. The supposed need for sex is in most cases directly linked to frozen needs for touching and loving which were not met in childhood. (This concept will be discussed in depth in Chapter 11, which focuses entirely on the role of sex in relationships.)

The question may be raised, why not use relationships to try to fill false or frozen needs? If one person wants to take care of the other, and the other wants to be taken care of, what is wrong with that? Let us take a hypothetical example of a couple, Tom and Martha. Suppose Martha wants to be taken care of: She wants to be supported, to have Tom handle the money, to have him decide where they live and how many children they have, and generally to be protected from having to deal with the realities of survival in the larger society. Let us further suppose that Tom feels the "need" to be in the protector role; for him to feel good about himself he needs to have someone at home waiting for him, someone who is dependent upon him for almost all her needs. They are both seemingly meeting their "needs."

There is nothing wrong with this arrangement in the sense that the people should feel guilty about what they are doing. There is a considerable cost, however, to maintaining such a relationship. Their "need" to be in these roles is the result of behavior patterns based on past hurts. Operating within these patterns has the effect of limiting the ways they can relate to each other, because they are not treating one another as full human beings. In fact, while acting within the patterns, they work to keep each other from taking charge of their own lives. Is Tom going to support and encourage Martha to go back to school if she wants to? Not if his feeling okay is dependent on her staying at home. Their "needs" for one another can only limit their potential as human beings.

This example is hypothetical because I do not know any couple who are happy trying to fill each other's frozen and false needs. What usually happens instead is that people feel frustrated and disappointed because no matter how hard they try, their partners cannot successfully meet their old needs for love, sex, attention, or whatever. Rather than accepting their partners for who they are, they want them to be superheroes and heroines who will bring joy and happiness where before there were pain and loneliness. Unfortunately, human beings do not work this way, despite our lovely myths.

To this picture of a couple trying to fill their old needs with each other, let us contrast the possibility of a rational love relationship. Here the two people feel good about themselves and each other, and continue to appreciate each other more and more as they share their lives together. They enjoy each other's company, but do not feel tied to each other out of fear; it is also okay for them to spend time away from one another. They encourage each other to set personal goals and to follow through on them, so that their lives can be as meaningful for themselves as possible. Not responding out of rigid patterns of behavior around each other, they each try to act freshly and creatively all the time, which enormously enhances the quality of the time they spend together. And when one of them is experiencing painful emotion, the other patiently encourages him or her to discharge the feelings.

This relationship is not a pipe dream. It is within the reach of every person, including you and your partner. Our behavior does not have to be controlled by patterns based on past, painful experiences. These patterns are not basic to us; they are not intrinsic parts of our being. Fortunately for us all, acquired, rigid patterns of behavior do not have to be kept forever. If that were so, I probably would not be writing this book, because my own old patterns of skepticism and self-doubt would have stopped me.

Two things seem to be necessary to completely free ourselves from the effects of past hurts, so that we can act creatively, flexibly, and zestfully in the present. The first involves going over our own life experiences and using the natural process of physical discharge—crying, sweating, trembling, raging, laughing, yawning, and talking—to release the painful feelings. We have discovered that even though the hurt occurred in the past, the act of discharging the related feelings in the present helps to separate feelings from past circumstances and undo the distress recording, which would otherwise continue to operate when it is restimulated. As the pattern disappears, it has less and less control over our behavior, leaving us free to think and act appropriately in every unique situation.

Second, we need to consciously act in ways that are human and not patterned. At any given moment we are capable of using our intelligence to evaluate all the available information and choose what behavior is appropriate in the particular situation. Even if our partner is screaming hysterically at us, we can still think about what response makes the most sense, and act on this thinking.

In this book we will focus on techniques to help us step out of patterns and act most sensibly in our relationships. These techniques will not provide ready-made solutions to our problems. By using them, however, we will be better able to be effective partners and to get what we deserve in our relationships. There are no rigid rules by which we can decide how to best behave, for every situation and every human being is different. The techniques and exercises in this book are designed to enable us to think more clearly about our own particular relationships and to encourage us to act appropriately.

If you read this book and try the exercises presented, I promise you that your relationships will improve in the following areas:

1. How you communicate with your partner
2. How you deal with your own hurts
3. How you respond to your partner when s/he is distressed
4. How you relate to young people and how you support their emotional, physical, and mental growth
5. How you take charge of your own life to get what you want and deserve

6. How much love you and your partner are expressing toward one another, and

7. How good you feel about yourself

We all are capable of improving our relationships and all aspects of our lives. The main things in our way are rigid patterns of behavior and associated painful feelings. One of them common to many of us is the feeling that "I can't do it." Well, of course we cannot if we let ourselves be controlled by the pattern that tells us we are powerless. This is the feeling, but it is *not* the reality. We are all intelligent, strong human beings, capable of making changes in our lives and our loves. We do not have to wait until our partners agree with us that things need to improve. Everyone can move independently to make things better. We shall see that one person taking charge of his or her behavior is sufficient to greatly improve a relationship; of course, two people taking charge is even better. In either case, the best time to start is right now.

two
Is What You Think You Want What You Really Want?

And only say that you'll be mine,
And in no other arms entwined. . . .

"Banks of the Ohio," traditional

Several years ago my wife and I separated. For weeks after our separation I walked around in a kind of daze. I volunteered few opinions and hardly participated in conversations, and mostly listened to others. I did not know what I wanted to do, where I wanted to go, with whom I wanted to be; in short, I felt completely lost. I managed from day to day by following the routines in my life: getting up in the morning, going to work, coming home, eating, and so on. Fortunately, I had some very good friends who paid attention to me and helped bring me out of my "identity crisis."

During this time I was not a complete hermit, of course. I did talk to people, and after a month or so I began to develop a new circle of friends who had not known me as a married or coupled man. Still, it was a long time before I learned to say "I" instead of "we." Before the separation I had not been aware of how much I had been defining myself as half a couple rather than as an individual. This was brought home to me by conversations such as the following:

PERSON I'VE JUST MET: Hi, my name is Frank. What's yours?

ME: Michael.

FRANK: How did you happen to come to this gathering?

ME: Well, *we* have been in this town for two years, and hardly know anyone here. So I decided it's time to start making some new friends.

FRANK: Where did you move here from?

ME: *We* came from Chicago. What do you do?

FRANK: I'm a painter, among other things. I also drive a cab, go to school, you know. . . .

ME: Last year *we* went down to the National Gallery. Have you been there?

This conversation might not have been unusual except that it occurred a few months after I had been separated. Frank had just met me and did not know my ex-wife; there was no good reason to include her in the conversation. For quite awhile I felt strange every time I used "I" instead of "we" in discussing my past experiences.

This is a common occurrence in love relationships. Our identities become defined in terms of our relationships, and we lose the sense of ourselves as individuals. This loss happens in the early stages of the dating process as well as in long-term relationships. Consider the conversation of a young couple just coming out of a movie theatre on their first date:

HE *(thinking this is a good way to start a conversation)*: What did you think of the movie?

SHE: I liked it. *(Actually I was bored stiff by it, but since he wanted to see it, he must like it.)* Did you?

HE: Yeah, it was pretty good. *(I was disappointed with it, but as long as she liked it I'm glad we came. I sure wouldn't want to go to a movie she didn't like on our first date.)* Would you like to go some place to get something to eat? *(I'm not really hungry, but she might be.)*

SHE: Okay, that would be fun. *(I'm not hungry, but if he wants to go he'll be disappointed if I say no.)*

From the very beginning of a relationship we tend to be afraid to assert ourselves as individuals. What is happening in this conversation is that both people are trying to please each other so much they are hiding their real selves, which of course lays a weak foundation for any ongoing relationship. As the relationship develops they will have to overcome not only their own fears about being assertive but also their partner's misconceptions about who they really are.

A third example of how self-identities are lost in relationships is the case of Betty, a woman who has been married for over twenty-five years. Married immediately after finishing high school, she had three children by the time she was twenty-three. She has spent her entire adult life taking care of other people's needs, and doing a good job of it at that. Now, however, her children are grown and no longer need to be looked after. In her early forties, she must find somewhere else to place her energy and attention. The issue came up in a counseling session as follows:

BETTY: I just don't know what I want to do. It feels like I can't do anything. I have no skills, no degrees, nothing. And even if I did have a college degree I don't know what I would want to do I've been at home my whole life; my children have been my life. Now that they don't need me any more, I'm not good for anything. I feel like some useless baggage.

COUNSELOR: Could you take a few minutes to appreciate how good and worthwhile you are, to counter some of those feelings?

BETTY: *No! (starts crying)* I'm not good . . . I can't do anything. . . .

This woman has devoted the major portion of her adult life to helping three human beings grow and develop into healthy, productive adults, and she feels as if she hasn't done and cannot do anything. Her self-image is almost entirely defined by her role in the family, that of wife/mother and nurturer. Because much of that role is no longer relevant to her life, she has gotten more and more in touch with feelings of inadequacy and worthlessness. These are of course just feelings; she deserves to feel proud and competent about the work she has done, and she is as worthwhile as any other human being. Her sense of herself as a whole person has unfortunately been submerged under the burden of living out a role that was unpaid, unappreciated, and temporary.

Why do we tend to lose the sense of ourselves as individuals when we become involved in love relationships? This is not an inevitable consequence of loving other people. It is quite possible to love and to retain the sense of ourselves as whole persons. What happens in many relationships is that our sense of identity gets lost in our attempts to cover up what we imagine to be the "bad" or unacceptable parts of ourselves, as we play roles we hope the other person will find appealing or pleasing. These roles hinder us from discovering our own desires and from maintaining our own sense of who we are and what *we* want.

This process starts early. We discover that love and acceptance come our way only when we conform to the norms our parents, school, and society prescribe for us. Our potential for being independently whole, competent, and intelligent humans is limited by the lack of support and attention. Instead of being encouraged to be whatever we want to be, we have been forced to take limited roles. Instead of being encouraged to think for ourselves, we have been *told* what is right and what is wrong. Instead of being encouraged to explore new and different horizons, we have been punished for stepping out of line. When we excitedly present new ideas that do not fit an accepted notion, we are told our thinking is wrong or silly. As we accept these limitations, we are rewarded with "love" and "approval," but it has a severe effect on our self-image and capabilities. Our self-image is of crucial importance with respect to how well our relationships work. As we said in the first chapter, if we perceive ourselves as basically undeserving of love, we find it difficult to accept when it does come our way.

As infants we were not allowed to explore and fully take charge of our environment to the extent we were capable. Most of us were literally caged in cribs. "Don't touch that, you'll break it" accompanies the containment of children by well-meaning adults. Of course, some control of children's environments is essential, but it is usually overdone for the sake of the parents' convenience. The effect is to thwart children's developing sense of themselves as powerful, independent human beings. Many times when a young person is told in a harsh tone not to pick up a plate or to stay out of the living room, it constitutes a new hurt. Unless the feelings connected to this hurt are discharged, s/he will internalize a recording connecting the desire to explore with the related painful feelings and the message that s/he was bad for trying to master the environment. This message is recorded thousands of times in all our early experiences, resulting in the development of chronic behavior patterns based on the sense of ourselves as being bad, incapable, and powerless.

Another place where we were constantly contained was the classroom. Fortunately, there are now many people working successfully to improve our educational system. The way our schools have operated is that from the age of five or six to seventeen, we were told what to do, how to think, where to sit, and when to go to the bathroom, for from five to eight hours per day, five days a week. Curiosity, creativity, and a desire for knowledge are natural human attributes, which were generally stifled by the educational environment in this country. Instead we were rewarded for adhering to rigid standards, for telling teachers what they wanted to hear, and for not fidgeting too much in our seats. And here, even more than in the home, discharging the painful emotion associated with the experience was strictly prohibited. Our training and education often consisted of learning the roles and rules of our society which contribute to making us feel powerless and inadequate. Not only were we rarely given the opportunity to think for ourselves, but we were actively punished for attempting to do so. Over and over we recorded the message that we are not in charge of our lives, that we must follow orders, that other people know better than we do. This is all false, and we had to be systematically punished over many years in order to be made to believe it.

Thus, from both the home and the school our self-images have been shaped by the ways in which control over our lives was taken from us. Our identities also have been affected more subtly by culture-wide phenomena. We have all been inculcated with the myth that a human being is only okay if s/he is coupled with another person, preferably one of the opposite sex. This myth is closely tied to our real needs and our frozen needs to be loved, but it is nevertheless still a myth. Despite the fact that in every happily ending movie the woman gets her man or vice versa, having an intimate relationship does not make a human being more worthwhile or in any way a better person. Cinderella may have felt better being a prince's wife than her sisters' maid, but it did not increase her value as a human being. Furthermore, in many intimate relationships people do *not* feel better than they did when they were single.

This myth that having a boyfriend or girlfriend brings joy and fulfillment haunts everyone in our culture. The harmful effect it has on relationships is that it supplies an external motivation for becoming intimate, whether or not it is appropriate under the particular circumstances. It makes us feel that we are not okay if we are single, that something must be wrong with us if we do not have a partner. If we are in a relationship, we feel we must maintain it at all costs or risk not being accepted. Consider the number of divorced people who suddenly are not invited to parties because they are now "single," an embarrassment. It *is* easier to function in our society if we are coupled. In most social and professional circles it is much more acceptable to be married or attached than to be single. As "unattached" persons we are stereotyped as being "on the make." Of course, people who are not in intimate relationships often are looking for partners. The on-the-make syndrome is another manifestation of the supposed need to have a relationship. We thus have developed patterns saying that we are not whole people by ourselves. Being human is not enough; we also must be part of a larger unit. No wonder, then, that we feel a driving "need" to pair up.

Any message that says "You are only okay if you are X" is hurtful to human beings. It is not true that we are only okay if we are married, or okay if we are beautiful, or okay if we are male, or okay if we are heterosexual. To believe these myths is to believe that our inherent worth as human beings is dependent on how we look or what we do, which is simply not true. In China today people do not marry until their late twenties. In the United States if we are not married by our late twenties we are considered slightly strange or abnormal. Is a single twenty-seven-year-old man or woman more worthwhile in China than in America? By cultural standards, perhaps yes, but intrinsically, no. Human worth is not dependent on how others see and treat us. We are okay whether single or coupled, no matter what we have been mistaught. It seems that we need to discharge the feelings attached to learning this myth, however, before this can be fully believed.

Another effect of this myth is that it interferes with our feeling and expressing love for people other than our partners. Part of the myth is that only one person must be the object of our affections. In fact we do love other people: our parents, our brothers and sisters, our good friends, and so on. Can we completely accept these feelings when they contradict what we have been taught to believe regarding the nature of "true love"? It is difficult to do so.

It is not our fault that we feel the need for partners. None of us has ever chosen to have distress recordings control our behavior and feelings. We accepted false information only because not discharging interfered with our mental processes of evaluation. We do need to love and be loved. The oppressive aspect of the recordings about being coupled is not that they say we need love, but that they limit love to one relationship. They imply that we can be committed to only one person, and s/he must be a member of the opposite sex. Not only does this deny us the right to love other human beings, but it also places a heavy burden on the love relationships themselves. How good can we feel about our partners (and ourselves) when we are required to shut off our feelings of love toward every other member of the human species?

Moreover, the patterned "need" to be paired becomes paramount and tends to overshadow our rational human needs and wants. Like frozen needs, the false need for one partner cannot be satisfactorily filled. Many people are happily married, but marriage itself does not bring happiness. If it did, there would not be nearly so many divorces. Trying to fill this false need only obscures what we *really* want and need to help us grow as human beings.

Another factor making it hard for us to have strong adult identities while involved in love relationships is that many of us never had the opportunity to develop identities as single, independent adults in the first place because of the patterns and feelings about being single that we acquired by the time we were in our midteens. We have either had boy- or girlfriends or been looking for them. In either case, we were not able to appreciate ourselves in the state of being "unattached" adults. Take the case of Ralph, an ex-student of mine at Rutgers University. Ralph is twenty-two and is about to graduate college. He is living at home with his parents, because he cannot afford to both support himself and pay tuition. Ralph and his girlfriend June are engaged and planning to get married as soon as he graduates. He talks about his relationship as follows:

We've been going together for a couple of years. I had another girlfriend before that, but that just didn't work out. We used to fight a lot. Anyway, June and I get along pretty good, and she wants to get married. I personally don't care, but if she wants to, I guess it's okay with me. I mean, I don't like being alone, being on the make all the time. It's a drag. I expect it will work out all right.

Ralph has no experience being a single adult taking full responsibility for his own life. His parents have been supporting him, and he has spent most of his life in the sheltered environments of home and school. The kinds of interactions he has had with people are limited, and for the whole of his relatively short adult life he has had a girlfriend who has been the major focus of his social life. What opportunity has he had to establish an identity for himself as a competent, grown man, capable of controlling his life? Instead of entering into a relationship from a position of strength and self-confidence, Ralph is acting primarily on his fear of being alone. There is no way that this will be conducive to developing a healthy and productive marriage. Hanging over his head will be a sense of inadequacy, based not on the reality of how good he is but on those fears related to his past experiences. This fact does not necessarily doom their relationship to failure; if it did, it would also doom millions of other relationships. It will, however, make it difficult for Ralph and June to determine what kind of relationship would be best for them, given their particular wants and needs. For if we do not know who we are, then how can we know what we want?

Another factor affecting relationships is what we may call *approval patterns.* These are rigid patterns of behavior which function to bring us the approval of those around us. Our behavior is thus based not on what we want for ourselves but on what will make us most accepted. The basis for these patterns, as in all distress recordings, is past hurtful experiences. Their effect is that our present wants and needs are overshadowed by the frozen need for approval. Let me illustrate this pattern with an example.

Dave is thirty-seven years old, married, and the father of three teenaged children. He considers himself to be happily married and loves his family very much, but he has a hard time being assertive in either his family or his job. He tends to be agreeable most of the time and seldom directly states a position contrary to that taken by someone else in his presence. In fact, Dave has a reputation as a friendly, easy-going sort of person, who never gets involved in conflicts. He clearly derives benefit from his behavior—that is, he is well liked—but he also suffers the cost of often feeling as though he doesn't know what he really thinks or wants. The roots of this behavior are evident in this condensed segment from a counseling session:

COUNSELOR: Dave, can you remember a time recently when you weren't able to say what you were really thinking?

DAVE *(pause)*: . . . It happened just the other day, at work. A couple of friends were laughing at this other guy who wasn't there, saying he was stupid and making wisecracks about him. I wanted to say something, but I just couldn't.

COUNSELOR: Why not? What is your first thought?

DAVE: I was scared . . . *(yawns)* . . . I was afraid they wouldn't like me.

COUNSELOR: Why not?

DAVE: Because I disagreed with them.

COUNSELOR: Can you remember a time when you felt that someone didn't like you because you disagreed with them?

DAVE *(laughs)*: . . . Sure, with my father all the time. He always used to laugh at me whenever I said anything. He didn't say I was stupid or anything like that. He just showed how everything I said was wrong. It got so that I worried about every word I said in front of him.

COUNSELOR: Can you remember a specific time?

DAVE: I remember once when we had some of my dad's friends over for dinner. I must have been about twelve or so. . . . Anyway, after dinner everyone was sitting in the living room talking. I forget what we were talking about, maybe the presidential elections. I think I said something that I had heard at school, and everyone laughed. Dad proceeded to tell me in front of everyone how what I said was stupid, and that I should know better.

COUNSELOR: What would you have liked to have said to him when he did that? What's your first thought?

DAVE: "Stop it!"

COUNSELOR: Tell him again, like you really are going to stop him ridiculing you.

DAVE: Stop it! Love me, don't laugh at me! *(After several minutes of focusing on his feelings, Dave eventually started crying over his hurt.)*

The incident that Dave is recalling is not necessarily the first or the most painful time that he was ridiculed by his father for sharing his thoughts. Nevertheless, it is one event in which his feelings of hurt, embarrassment, and fear were glued together with the actual circumstances of his being disparaged for being assertive. Because this kind of invalidation occurred repeatedly, attached to the same feelings, the distress recording based on these incidents was deeply ingrained. As a result, whenever Dave is in some way reminded of these incidents, the distress recording based on them is replayed. The fear that people are not going to like him if he disagrees with them prevents him from asserting himself. This fear is not based on the present situation; usually people are not disliked merely for stating their opinions, and they are certainly not disliked if they do so caringly and thoughtfully. Dave's need to be liked is not based on the present reality but on the fact that his past need to be liked and appreciated was not filled.

This is not to say that being liked is not important. What is most sensible is for Dave to choose what to say and do depending on what he deems most appropriate in the particular situation. Usually he will act in ways that other people will approve; but sometimes he will choose to do or say things as a result of which other people will have their painful feelings restimulated. In either case, his behavior is based on his best thinking.

Dave's approval pattern is being passive and not stating what he needs, wants, and believes. Other people's patterns are different, because the ways in which they have been hurt are different. Some people are overly friendly, others tell jokes, and others agree to have sex whether or not they want to. The important point is that all approval patterns are based on past, unfilled needs to be loved.

Another factor affecting our ability to maintain a strong sense of identity while involved in relationships is also based on the way many of us were hurt in the past. Unlike approval patterns, however, these tend to be found more in one sex than the other. These are what may be called *accommodation patterns*, and are more common to women because of their more oppressive conditioning. Through many different aspects of our culture, but primarily the home, women have been taught to put other people's needs and wants before their own. The positive part of this training is that women in our society are very effective at loving and caring about other human beings. The harmful aspect is that their own needs and wants are often not met. A person who gets up in the morning, wakes everyone else up, makes breakfast for the family, dresses the young ones for school, makes their lunch, cleans up after breakfast, does the laundry, cleans the house, goes shopping, babysits all afternoon, cooks dinner, cleans up afterward, babysits in the evening, puts the young people to bed, and in addition listens to and tries to take care of everyone's problems—this person does not have much space to think about or act on what she wants for herself. Part of the oppression of this role is that young girls are systematically invalidated for being assertive. The message is repeatedly transmitted to them that they will be accepted if they are cute, quiet, friendly, thoughtful, and don't make any trouble. When they act otherwise, that is, when they are strong, assertive, loud, and stick up for their own rights, they are ridiculed, beaten, ostracized, or just plain ignored or unappreciated. This is the mechanism by which accommodation patterns are instilled. The distress recordings contain the messages that "it is not okay to think of myself as being important," "men are more important than women," "my needs do not count." It is necessary to impose these hurts on young girls if they are to be forced into taking on the role of family nurturer/maid when they become adults. Being mother and nurturer is a very important and valuable function. It should be treated as such, and not forced on women by invalidating their intelligence and assertiveness.

Women's conditioning will be discussed more extensively later in this book, but for the present we can see what effect it must have on a person's identity in a relationship. In a world in which others are making demands on us, in which we have been trained to try to take care of their needs and ignore our own, it is going to be difficult to pay attention to ourselves and to see ourselves as strong, competent human beings. Unless partners make a concerted effort to go against this oppressive conditioning, women will continue to lose themselves in their relationships.

We are all in charge of our lives and aware of who we are and what we need to the extent that we are free of rigid behavior patterns. This is particularly true with respect to intimate relationships, which tend to remind us of our most painful experiences involving love and acceptance. As we act according to our best thinking and not to our patterns, so will we be strong and assertive in our relationships.

LOOKING AT OURSELVES

The hurt we incurred in the past cannot be removed by current relationships. We can never receive the love we did not get when we were younger. We can be loved and we can be made to feel better as a result of relationships, but we cannot be *made* to feel good about ourselves in a basic sense. In other words, being told we are okay can satisfy our present need for validation and approval, but it can never completely satisfy our unfilled past need. These frozen needs can only be removed by discharging the feelings related to the painful incidents upon which they are based.

If we do not feel good about ourselves as human beings, becoming involved in intimate relationships will not help. In fact, rather than our self-images being determined by our relationships, the opposite tends to be true: The quality of a relationship is in large part determined by how good both partners feel about themselves, their lives, and the things they do. If each of us likes ourself, feels good about our life, and enjoys the things we are doing, the task of maintaining a healthy relationship will be relatively easy. Our reasons for spending time together will be based on feelings of self- and mutual love and respect. We can enjoy each other, but will not feel that our whole lives depend on the relationship.

If, however, one of the major bases of the intimacy is that we do not feel good about ourselves and our lives, numerous difficulties immediately become apparent. If we are using the relationship to try to feel better about ourselves, then we must continually operate out of the fear that it might end. The question of "What would my life be without you?" cannot be answered without fear and trepidation. This imposes an unfair burden on the relationship, which it cannot bear and remain healthy. We cannot reasonably expect our partners to be our therapists. Although we were not at all responsible for the ways in which we were hurt in the past, it is entirely our responsibility to make our lives the way we want them to be in the present and future. Accepting this responsibility ourselves will not only improve our relationships but also allow us to change our lives so that we can be more satisfied.

Exercise 1 is presented to give you the chance to assess your life, to examine what is going well and what needs to be improved upon. Use this as an opportunity to think and reflect upon your present life and activities. Sit down in a quiet, comfortable place, take the phone off the hook, and relax. Take the time to meaningfully examine the different aspects of your life mentioned in the exercise, to evaluate how things are really going for you. You can use the questions to help discover how satisfied you are right now, apart from any intimate relationship. They will then also be a gauge to measure indirectly the extent to which you are relying on your relationship to provide you with a sense of joy and fulfillment.

EXERCISE 1   ASSESSING YOURSELF

Purpose: To give you the opportunity to look at and evaluate yourself and your life.

Task: Answer the following questions:

What are some of the qualities you like about yourself?
What do you do well?
What do you do for fun, pleasure, and relaxation?
What is your work? (This need not be a money-making job.)
Who are your close friends?
Fantasize about the most fulfilling work you could be doing. Is it possible? What is in the way of your doing it?

Assuming you could create yourself anew, what would you change about yourself?

What would you change about your work?

Your leisure time?

Your friendships?

Any other things?

What in your life is most difficult for you right now? Why is it hard?

On a scale of 1 to 5, how satisfied are you with your

	Not at all	Very		
Work situation	1 2 3 4 5	Friendships	1 2 3 4 5
Leisure time	1 2 3 4 5	Role in your	
Family life	1 2 3 4 5	community	1 2 3 4 5
		Overall life	1 2 3 4 5

What do you need to change in order to be satisfied with yourself and your life?

SETTING PERSONAL GOALS

One of the first steps in the process of taking charge of our lives is the act of setting goals. We can go against all the patterns that make it difficult for us to think about ourselves and our lives by sitting down and taking the time to decide what we want for ourselves. Exercise 2 is designed precisely to help us set short- and long-range goals for ourselves and for our intimate relationships. Think about what you would like to accomplish over the next week, month, year, and five-year period. Setting a goal does not mean that we *must* achieve it, or that we need to feel guilty if we do not. It is merely a good tool to help us to focus on what we want for ourselves and our relationships.

EXERCISE 2   SETTING PERSONAL GOALS

Purpose: To help you focus your activities by setting short-, medium-, and long-range goals for yourself.

Task: Fill out the following chart, choosing goals that are conceivable. Do not let your goals be diminished by your memory of or your feelings about past experiences.

Space is provided for setting both personal goals and goals for a relationship. One way of formulating goals for the latter is to answer the question, "How would you like the relationship to be in a week (or month)?" or "What would you like to have happen in the next week?" and so on.

Goals for:	Yourself	Your relationship
Next week	CALL SUSAN	
Next month	GO OUT w/SUSAN	
This year	MAKE OUT w/ SUE	
Next five years	FUCK THE BITCH!	IN THE GUTTER

Once we have a clearer idea of how we want things to be, we can then base our behavior in part on moving toward these ends. If we have a five-year goal of doing work that we really enjoy, then what do we need to do over the next year to help bring this about? What do we need to do over the next month? The next week? Today? Approaching our activity from this basis is quite different from facing each day with "What do I feel like doing today?" and will in the long run be much more satisfying.

YOU CAN TAKE CHARGE
OF YOUR RELATIONSHIP

We have all the intelligence and the capability to take control over our lives and our loves. It is entirely within our power to bring about the kind of future we want and deserve. It will not feel easy to do, and it will not always feel good. Grabbing the bull by the horns and steering it in the direction of our choice is bound to bring up some distressful emotions, because it directly contradicts our feelings of powerlessness and hopelessness. "I can't do that" the distress recording cries. "Maybe you can, but I'm not good enough" the pattern moans. "It's hopeless, that's all there is to it." These feelings will all come up as we go against our rigid patterns and move to take charge of our activities and relationships. It is fine that these feelings are being restimulated. It is a good opportunity for us to discharge them and remove ourselves from their constraints. Most important, we must not let ourselves be controlled by them and the behavior patterns associated with them.

Basically, we have two choices: We can either continue to operate out of rigid patterns resulting from how we were hurt in the past, or we can go against these patterns and call up every available resource to help us use our human intelligence to guide our behavior. Which shall we choose?

three
Evaluate
Your
Relationship

Fair Iris I love, and hourly I die
But not for a lip, nor a languishing eye,
She fickle and false, and there we agree,
For I am as false and fickle as she.

John Dryden (1631–1700)

The complications and convolutions of human love relationships are unrivaled in the animal world, with the possible
exception of crocodiles, who eat their young. Fortunately for
the human species, our cannibalism does not usually extend
beyond the verbal level. We may tell each other to die, drop
dead, go to hell, get lost, or in some other way disappear
from the face of the earth, but these death wishes seldom arc
fulfilled on the spot. Instead, we continue to battle for years
and years, until divorce or death does literally "do us part."

It sometimes takes a physical separation for us again to see
our partners as unique individuals rather than as something
to be taken for granted. Several years ago the woman with
whom I am intimately involved was in a foreign country for
several months while I stayed here in the United States.
Being apart was hard for each of us, and we both had feel-

ings of loneliness and abandonment. We corresponded by mail quite frequently, but had no physical, visual, or oral contact for almost six months. During this period I spent hours crying over "Why did she leave me?" "Why don't you love me?" "I need you so much," and other variations on the same theme. At the same time, however, I was going about living my life, working, spending time with friends, meeting new people, and so on. What happened was that I established an identity for myself completely apart from my love relationship.

When my friend returned from Europe, I was astounded. Why, here was another person! She was no longer someone whom I "needed" and without whom I would die, but she was a separate human being, who clearly had been functioning as a whole person by herself (as had I been). As she talked about what the six months had been like for her, I just sat and marveled. I still loved her as much as ever, but I was enjoying her more now than I had for a long time. In a way we were no longer "attached" to each other, but could instead appreciate each other as independent people whom we knew and loved very much. During that first conversation I remember thinking, "Oh, *that's* what I like about her, I remember now."

Another kind of experience that often yields the same awareness is watching our partners relate to other people. Have you ever been to a party and observed your partner participating in an animated conversation with another person? This person seemed to be excited to talk to your partner, and was very interested to hear about what your partner was thinking and doing. When this has happened to me I have often felt a little taken aback, and have wondered what was so fascinating. Then I am reminded of how I first saw my partner and all the things that I liked about her in the first place.

It is very difficult for us to stay in touch with our partners in this way, as unique individuals fully apart from ourselves. We take them for granted and treat them as if they were merely habitual parts of our lives. Our sense of them as exciting and important people gets lost in the midst of the routines and problems of everyday living. When was the last time you felt proud to know your partner? In the absence of painful feelings, we would feel this way all the time. It is the negative emotion and associated behavior of both us and our partners which interfere with knowing and appreciating each other as separate people.

Unfortunately, we do tend to stop seeing our partners' strengths and human qualities, and instead sometimes act toward them in ways that we wouldn't to our worst enemies. It is not that we want to act this way; usually we feel as if we "just can't help it." After we yell at them or laugh at them or ignore them, we usually know that it was wrong to do so. (We may not admit it to them, of course, and sometimes not to ourselves, either.) We are not responding to them as distinct people when this happens; we are instead responding rigidly out of our own painful emotions.

Some of the same factors that block us from feeling love for our partners also make it difficult for us to see them as separate, whole people. One of these factors is that our negative feelings and our rigid patterns of behavior are restimulated by our partners' rigid behavior, which is based on their old hurts. If we respond to this behavior with our own hurt feelings and it happens over and over again when we spend time together, we often stop seeing the person and see only the rigid behavior pattern. Let us illustrate this with an example.

Brad and Lisa are in their late twenties, and have been living together for several years. They have no children and are both pursuing independent occupations. In many ways they get along very well, but there are some areas in which their behavior patterns interfere with their relationship and affect how they see each other. One of these areas involves the feelings Brad has about making friends and initiating relationships with other people. Brad has a difficult time getting to know other people and almost never makes the first move himself. This pattern manifests itself in many little ways. He does not like to telephone friends, he seldom speaks up in a group, and he does not seem very friendly when meeting strangers. In all these situations he seems to freeze and be completely different from the way he is when he is feeling good and relaxed. The roots of this behavior are evident from this condensed portion of a counseling session:

BRAD: I don't know, maybe I just don't like other people. Like yesterday—Lisa wanted us to go out with some good friends of hers from work, and I just didn't want to go. It's not that I don't like them, it's just that I don't enjoy being with people very much. . . .

COUNSELOR: Did that situation yesterday remind you of anything?

BRAD: Yeah! *(laughs)* My mother used to try to get me to make friends all the time. She was always telling me to invite somebody over after school. *(yawns)* I never wanted to.

COUNSELOR: Why not?

BRAD: 'Cause I didn't have any friends, that's why. There wasn't anybody I wanted to bring home. I didn't think any of them liked me.

COUNSELOR: It must have felt pretty lonely back then, feeling like you had no friends.

BRAD: It sure did. I didn't have a single real friend until I got to college.

COUNSELOR: What did it feel like to you, having no friends?

BRAD: Pretty bad. It felt like I spent all my time alone . . . I don't want to talk about this, it doesn't feel good at all . . . *(tears come to his eyes)*. It was awful . . . nobody liked me. . . .

COUNSELOR: It must have felt pretty bad, feeling alone all the time.

BRAD: Yeah, it sure did . . . *(starts crying)*. It felt awful . . . *(continues crying)*.

It is clear from this exchange that Brad's present behavior around people is directly related to feelings and events from his past. Although the counseling session did not focus on the earliest hurtful experiences that resulted in his not having friends, it did get to the feelings that must have continually reinforced the initial hurt. The feelings that "Nobody likes me" and the physical and emotional withdrawal which accompanies the feelings are restimulated whenever Brad is in some way reminded of those painful incidents.

One way this interferes with Brad and Lisa's relationship is that Lisa starts treating Brad as if he were just his rigid behavior pattern. She starts thinking that "Brad just does not like other people" and that "He's just a timid person." She assumes that "This is just the way he is, and this is the way he always will be." Brad may act timid and fearful around other people, but he would rather be outgoing and relaxed; in fact, this is exactly how he would act if he had not been hurt over and over again in the past. However, as with most of us, he did not have the opportunity to get rid of the painful feelings connected with the hurt. To accept that Brad wishes to remain a timid and fearful person, to accept the pattern of behavior he has developed, is equivalent to saying that we can never change, that we must always remain in the grip of the negative things that happened to us as children.

If someone has been told his or her whole life that s/he is no good, does that make the person no good? Of course not. Hurts have been imposed on human beings, and their effects can be removed by the discharge process. If we see our partners as only being their patterns, we are ourselves reinforcing the rigid patterns by playing into them. Instead of encouraging the person to act outside the pattern and to release the hurtful feelings related to the pattern, we often try to accommodate the pattern—which only reinforces it. When Lisa makes all the social arrangements and does the talking for both of them, Brad's feelings that "I am alone-nobody likes me-I don't know what to say-I hate people" are only encouraged. This is anything but the effect that Lisa would like to have.

Lisa accommodates or accepts Brad's pattern because of her own distress. Upon first meeting Brad she did not see him as this bundle of fear and timidity. What she immediately appreciated about him was his sense of humor, his intelligence, his social concerns, and his ability to motivate himself (among other things). While living together, however, many of her positive feelings became overshadowed by the feelings that were restimulated by having to deal with Brad's timidity pattern every day. Because she did not take the opportunity to discharge her feelings and frustrations about Brad's patterns, her own painful emotion and rigid patterns come into play and prevent her from thinking effectively about Brad and what support he needs to free his behavior from the effect of past distress.

This kind of seesaw of patterns is a normal occurrence in most relationships. One partner exhibits patterned behavior based upon his or her own hurt, and the other responds out of his or her own rigid patterns. Thus each of us loses sight of who our partner or friend really is.

Another factor making it difficult for us to see our partners as separate individuals is that often we use them to try to fill real and imagined needs. This was well exemplified in the first chapter, when Frank did not want his girlfriend to spend time with other people because he "needed" her to be with him. It is definitely in Gloria's interest as a person to have social communication with more than one human being. When Frank is not being controlled by his pattern he is aware of this, but while in its grip he is not thinking about her at all.

It is crucial for good relationships that we work to maintain the sense of ourselves and our partners as separate, unique individuals, who have different wants, needs, and concerns. The myth of oneness in relationships, that marriage or love involves merging ourselves with another person, can only be actualized if at least one of the people involved subjugates him- or herself to the other person. The "harmony" seen in such relationships is usually the result of one person completely denying his or her own needs and wants and trying to assume those of the partner. Because of the dynamics of sexism, it is usually the woman who gives up herself for the relationship.

EXERCISE 3   LOOKING AT YOUR PARTNER

Purpose: To give you the opportunity to see your partner as a separate person and to help you think effectively about him or her.

Task: Answer the following questions:

What are some of the things you liked about your partner when you first met?

What are some of the other things you like about your partner now?

What are some things that you notice other people like about him or her?

What do you think s/he likes about him- or herself?

What are the things that are going well in his or her life?

In work?

In friendship?

In leisure time?

In relationships with family?

In social and political communities?

In other areas?

What things are not going well in these areas?

Work

Friendships

Leisure time

Family relationships

Community activities

Other areas

> How would you like to see your partner change for his or her own sake?
>
> What can you do to support him or her to move in positive directions toward these goals?
>
> How is it hard for you to support him or her?
>
> What helps you to do it anyway?

Exercise 3 is presented here to provide each of us with a chance to look at our partners or loved ones as individuals, apart from any relationship they have with us. Use this time to really try to think about your friend—what is going well for him or her, what is difficult, how s/he can move against the difficulties, and what you can do to support him or her. In reality our partners *are* separate and distinct from us. The better we can think about them, the better their lives will be. And isn't this what we want for the people we care about?

IDENTIFICATION CHECKS

The physical process of how we are reminded of past distressful events is not well understood at this time, as we do not yet know very much about how the brain actually functions. It is clear, however, that what we call restimulation is a very real phenomenon. In a countless number of counseling sessions people have been asked what a current distressful situation reminds them of, and almost always they recall a past experience in which they were hurting and exhibited similar feelings and behavior to those in the present. This process seems to work best when the person is asked to verbalize his or her first thought immediately after being asked of what s/he was reminded, thus eliminating a kind of "second guessing" and musing which is often based on the person wondering what s/he *should* be reminded of by the incident in question. By focusing on the first thought we get right to the source or one of the sources of the rigid behavior pattern.

Concerning relationships with other people, particularly those involving much intimacy and contact, it is often useful to examine another aspect of the restimulation process. Rather than finding out what *situations* are being restimulated, we can discover what *people* we are being reminded of by those currently in our lives. Almost always the question "Whom does ―――― remind you of?" is answered with the name of a person with whom we have retained some past distressful feelings.

An incident occurred in one of the courses I taught that beautifully illustrated this point to the whole class. One of the women, let's call her Sally, came up to me after one class and told me that she just could not stand to be in the same room with Donna, another woman in the class. Donna is a very forceful woman and has a loud and somewhat harsh voice. She had good things to say in class, but sometimes took up more than her share of the discussion time. This bothered Sally tremendously, and she was thinking about dropping out of the course as a result. Because I thought it would be good for her and the whole class, I asked her if she would be willing to do a demonstration in front of the class on her feelings, and after a little discussion she agreed. It was a scary thing for her to do, and I continue to appreciate her courage. The demonstration went approximately as follows:

ME: Okay, Sally, you told me yesterday that you're having feelings about Donna. Right?

SALLY: Right.

ME: I would like to spend a little time focusing on this, both for your sake and because it will illustrate to everyone what we have been talking about in class. Okay?

SALLY *(with a nervous laugh)*: Okay.

ME: All right. Who does Donna remind you of? What's your first thought?

SALLY *(starts laughing)*: Oh, that's silly.

ME: What's silly?

SALLY: I'm thinking about a woman who was my supervisor a couple of years ago.

ME: What was her name?

SALLY: Miss Ryan.

ME: How are Donna and Miss Ryan similar?

SALLY: Well, they both have loud voices. . . . They are both about the same height, and have brown hair. . . . They both talk like they are always right. . . .

ME: Any other ways?

SALLY: Well, they are both women . . . *(laughs)*. Their voices are both nasal in quality. . . .

ME: Okay, how did you feel toward Miss Ryan?

SALLY: I hated her! *(laughs, as does the rest of the class)* She had this holier-than-thou attitude, and was always telling me that I wasn't doing well enough. This is so embarrassing . . . *(continues laughing)*. I had a horrible time. I used to go home with headaches every night, and that's all I wanted to tell my husband about. . . .

ME: What would you have liked to have said to her back then? What is your first thought?

SALLY *(laughing)*: Go away. . . . This is so embarrassing!

ME: Tell her again, and stamp your foot at her this time when you say it. Here, I'll demonstrate. *(I stamp my foot and yell "Go away!")*

SALLY *(now laughing loudly and continuously, as is the rest of the class)*: Go away! *(continues laughing)*.

ME *(after the laughter had died down)*: Let's move on to the differences between Donna and Miss Ryan. How are they different?

SALLY: Well, Miss Ryan was my supervisor and Donna is not . . . Miss Ryan was heavier than Donna is. . . .

ME: When you point out the differences, try to use separate

clauses for each person, like "Miss Ryan was a heavier person, and Donna weighs less." By saying it this way we may actually be separating these two people in our brains.

SALLY: Okay. . . . Well, Donna, is really a nice person, and Miss Ryan was not very nice at all. . . . I knew Miss Ryan two years ago, and I just met Donna this term. . . .

ME: How are their voices different?

SALLY: Miss Ryan's voice was very nasal, and Donna's voice is less so. Also, Donna's voice is high-pitched, while Miss Ryan's was a little lower-pitched. . . .

After this demonstration was over, Donna had a chance to talk about how it felt to listen to these feelings that Sally had about her. Because it was clear that the main source of Sally's feelings had nothing to do with her, she had not been too uncomfortable.

This demonstration clearly points out the value of doing what we call *identification checks*. To a large extent Sally's feelings toward Donna had nothing to do with who Donna is as a person. They are almost entirely due to Sally's being reminded of Miss Ryan by the similarity between their voices. Sally's undischarged feelings over what happened with Miss Ryan came to the fore. Sally herself was not even aware of the connection until she was asked whom Donna reminded her of. One of the benefits of the demonstration was that Sally felt a big sense of relief over understanding why she felt the way she did toward Donna. Afterwards she felt noticeably more relaxed around Donna, and their relationship greatly improved.

Identification checks serve a number of functions, First, they let us know how our behavior around people in the present is affected by distressful experiences from our past. Second, they help us to get back to and discharge the feelings related to those past incidents, so that we can be free of them in the present and future. And third, they help us to clearly separate the people with whom we are now relating from the figments from our past—which helps us to think and act more creatively and less rigidly.

Because we are so prone to using our love relationships to fill frozen needs which were not filled in our childhood, they are particularly susceptible to being influenced by our feelings about people with whom we were close while growing up—namely, our parents and siblings. This kind of restimulation can wreak havoc on a relationship! The following segment from a session provides an example of how identification checks can be used successfully. Mary and Rick have been living together for fifteen years and have two children.

COUNSELOR: What's been going on?

RICK: Mary's been getting mad at me a lot lately. Yesterday she blew up at me for forgetting to mail some letters. It really gets me upset.

COUNSELOR: How so?

RICK: It makes me feel bad. I just feel hurt when she yells at me for no reason. Or that's what it feels like.

COUNSELOR: Who does she remind you of when this happens?

RICK: My mother *(laughs)*.

COUNSELOR: How is she like your mother?

RICK: They're both women . . . *(laughs)*. They both love me . . . I've lived with both of them a long time. . . . They both have soft voices. . . .

COUNSELOR: How are your feelings about them similar?

RICK: I love them both . . . I feel like I need their love and approval.

COUNSELOR: What are you reminded of about your mother when Mary yells at you?

RICK: Mom used to yell at me a lot when I was younger. It seems like she was always yelling at me to pick up my room, take out the garbage, walk the dog, wash the dishes. . . . Sometimes she got *really* mad.

COUNSELOR: Can you remember a time?

RICK *(pauses)*: . . . One time I remember well. I guess I was about six, and I was trying to help Mom straighten the house. Maybe she was expecting company, or something like that. I wanted to help out, so I started rearranging the living room furniture *(laughs)*. I was really pleased with the work I had done, and expected her to be really pleased with me. But she wasn't *(laughs)*. When she came into the room she was furious. She started yelling at me and grabbed me and started hitting me. I didn't know what I had done wrong. I was only trying to help . . . *(starts lightly sobbing)*.

COUNSELOR: Go on.

RICK: She kept hitting and hitting me . . . *(starts crying more heavily)*. I was only trying to help. . . .

The session continued like this for quite awhile, with Rick crying and talking about this incident. When fifteen minutes or so were left in the session, we moved on to the following:

COUNSELOR: Let's move on to the differences between your mother and Mary. In what ways are they different?

RICK: Well, my mother is sixty-one and Mary is thirty-five . . . Mom I've known my whole life, and I've only known Mary for about half of it . . . *(laughs)*. Mom is my mother, and Mary is my lover and friend, and the mother of our children . . . I live with Mary now, and I lived with my mother a long time ago. . . .

COUNSELOR: How is the way they love you different?

RICK *(laughs)*: My mother loves me as her son, and Mary loves me as her spouse and mate. . . . Mary is supportive of me as an adult, and my mother took care of me as a child. . . .

COUNSELOR: How are your feelings toward them different?

RICK: Well, I don't need Mary the way I needed my mother back when I was younger. I'm not really dependent on Mary for getting my needs met the way I was dependent on Mom when I was a boy. . . . It just feels this way . . . *(laughs)*. And when Mary gets angry at me, I'm not in a helpless position. With my mother, I was in a much more powerless situation. Also, my mother got mad at me more, and Mary gets angry less often.

COUNSELOR: What are some more of these differences?

RICK: Mom paints and does nice artwork, and she has a great artistic sense. Mary is really good around other people . . . She is really friendly, and lets people know that she cares about them. She also is an excellent mother to our children. . . .

COUNSELOR: And how are their voices different?

RICK: Actually, Mom has a very soft voice, and Mary's is a little higher and a little louder. . .

This identification check provided Rick with much insight into his present relationship with Mary. It became clear to him how much his feelings about his mother are transferred to Mary. Of course, this is not at all helpful to their relationship. By discharging the painful feelings attached to his mother, Rick is getting rid of them, and his behavior will be less controlled by them in the future. Another result of the identification check is that he is more conscious of the distinction between Mary and his mother, and aware that many of the feelings he is experiencing in his current relationship have little to do with the actual dynamics of it.

Exercise 4 is an identification check, which you can do on your partner or best friend or parents or whomever. It is probably best done when you are asked the questions by another person (not your partner), but it is valuable when done alone also. Be sure to do your best to not censor your thoughts. It may feel embarrassing to discover that your friend reminds you of your father or brother or mailman, but if this is the source of your restimulation you may as well acknowledge it—hiding it from yourself will not make it go away! Go over all the similarities you can think of between the two people, and then try to recall what things happened

EXERCISE 4   IDENTIFICATION CHECKS

Purpose: To help you mentally and emotionally separate your partner or friend from people s/he reminds you of.

Task: Answer the following questions. Do not censor your thoughts, and acknowledge your first impressions.

Whom does your partner or friend remind you of? What is your first thought?

How are your friend and this person similar physically?
   Emotionally?
   In what they do?
   In ways they relate to you?
   In their rigid behavior patterns?
   In any other ways?
How are your feelings toward them similar?
Do you remember any distressful incidents with the person of whom you are reminded?
What feelings are associated with these incidents?
How is your friend different from this other person? (Particularly emphasize differences within the above similarities; for example, if they are both heavy-set men, how are their body structures different?)
   Physically?
   Emotionally?
   In how they relate to you?
   In what they do?
   In their behavior patterns?
   In other ways?
   How are your feelings toward them different?

Evaluation:

What insights did you gain about your relationship with your friend or partner as a result of this exercise?

between you and the person of whom you are reminded. This will help you discover what feelings you are transferring to your friend because of the restimulation. Then, go over the differences between the two people, including how they are different in the areas in which you saw similarities earlier. In the above example, the counselor asked Rick to distinguish between Mary's and his mother's voices, because earlier he had said that their voices were similar. You may be surprised by what you find.

The ways in which we are restimulated by our partners are exactly the ways that we are not seeing our partners as separate individuals. Allowing our behavior to be controlled by our feelings from the past has the effect of both hurting ourselves and our partners. It also prevents us from having the kind of relationship we deserve.

ARE WE EFFECTIVE PARTNERS
FOR EACH OTHER?

My vision of a good relationship between two human beings is one in which they are meaningful allies for one another. They enjoy being with one another and get one or more of their real human needs met through the relationship. The relationship is not used, however, to try to fill false or frozen needs, and they see and treat each other as whole individuals in their own right. Their love for each other grows all the time, but it does not interfere with their loving other people. They accept and give love freely, and do their best to support and encourage each other to live as meaningful lives as possible. When one of them is hurting, the other listens respectfully and helps him or her get rid of the painful feelings. To sum up, they like each other and help each other the best they can.

We cannot directly measure the extent to which we can be

effective partners in love relationships, but we can pinpoint the areas in which we are doing well and the areas in which we need to improve. Exercises 5 and 6 are presented here for just this purpose. The first is about ourselves as partners, and the second has to do with our friend's ability to be an effective partner. Both exercises are questionnaires, and the answers to the questions should provide you with a sense of how you and your partner need to change to make yourselves better participants in intimate relationships. You may also gain a sense of how well you are already doing.

The purpose of these exercises is not to provide us with reasons to castigate ourselves or our partners for any sup-

---

EXERCISE 5   ASSESSING YOURSELF AS A PARTNER

Purpose: To help you evaluate where you are doing well and where you need to improve as a partner in a relationship.

Task: Answer the following questions:

How openly do you express your caring?
  Physically?
  Verbally?
  By your actions?
Do you share your thoughts and feelings with your partner?
How often do you check in with your partner about what s/he is thinking or feeling?
How well do you pay attention to your partner's thoughts, feelings, concerns, and goals?
How well do you listen to your partner without interrupting with your own concerns?

How often do you think about and help your partner achieve his or her goals?

How do you deal with your hurt and angry feelings with respect to your partner? Do you avoid taking out your painful feelings on him or her?

Do you enjoy spending leisure time with your partner?

Do you encourage your partner to spend time with other people and feel good about doing so?

How often do you invalidate your partner by disparaging him or her, either subtly or grossly?

How well do you let yourself accept love and affection, both physically and verbally?

How committed are you to the relationship?

Evaluation:

What insights have you gained about yourself as a partner?

In what areas do you most need to improve?

What can you do now to bring these improvements about?

**EXERCISE 6   ASSESSING YOUR LOVED ONE
AS A PARTNER**

Purpose: To help you evaluate where your close friend is doing well and where s/he needs to improve as a partner in your relationship.

Task: Answer the following questions:

How openly does s/he express his or her caring to you?
  Physically?
  Verbally?
  By his or her actions?

How often does s/he check in with you about what you are thinking or feeling?

Does s/he share his or her thoughts and feelings with you?

How well does your partner pay attention to your thoughts, feelings, concerns, and goals?

How well does your partner listen to you, without interrupting with his or her own concerns?

How often does s/he think about and help you achieve your goals?

How does your partner deal with his or her hurt and angry feelings with respect to you?

Does s/he enjoy spending leisure time with you?

Does s/he encourage you to spend time with other people?

How often does your partner invalidate you, either subtly or grossly?

Does your partner let him- or herself accept love and affection, both physically and verbally?

How committed is s/he to the relationship?

Evaluation:

What insights have you gained about your loved one as a partner?

In what areas does your partner most need to improve?

What could s/he do now to bring these improvements about?

posed inadequacies. It is not at all helpful to feel guilty and despondent over the ways in which we are not the best partners we could be. What we need to do is meaningfully to assess our behavior, and work to change it where necessary. Nothing is in the way but feelings and leftover behavior patterns.

HOW GOOD IS YOUR RELATIONSHIP?

Intimate relationships can be a place for people to grow, a supportive environment for working toward our goals, a place of both safety and struggle. One of the things I am suggesting in this book is that we not take our relationships for granted, but rather take the time to *think* about our close friends and our relationships with them. This can make an enormous difference in the quality of our relationships, which in turn can affect just about every area of our lives: our work, our leisure time, our social activities, our involvement with improving the world, and how we feel about ourselves.

One of the first steps toward improving our relationships is to assess accurately and evaluate what they are like now. Just how good is this relationship? Is it helping me get what I want in my life? Where is it not giving me the support I need? How supportive is the relationship to my partner? Is s/he getting what s/he needs?

Exercise 7 is a chart which has been found to be very useful in helping people evaluate their relationships. In it are three columns, the first for listing what is going well in your relationship, the second for what is going poorly, and the third for what needs to be improved. Take several minutes on each column, and be sure to avoid focusing entirely on the negative aspects. For every thing that is not going well, there should be a way to improve it. Also, if it feels difficult to think of good things to write down, spend more time on this category; there *are* good things about your relationship, and if you are having trouble listing them it is only because painful feelings are interfering. Filling out this chart will in this case also help you push past some of your feelings to enable you to see more accurately your relationship as it really is. (There is *something* good about almost every relationship.)

Relationships are not good or bad in the sense that we should feel guilty if the negatives outnumber the positives. If things are going fairly well, great! How can we make them even better? If things are not going so well, let us fix them. However bad it might feel, it is never hopeless. Perhaps it seems as if the task is overwhelming, and that there is no place to start. This is one of the main functions this book is meant to serve. The tools and exercises in the following chapters will be applicable to almost all human relationships, and their use will facilitate the changes necessary to improve even the "most hopeless" of them. Just consider the possibility of having a real ally and being a real ally for another person. We deserve no less.

EXERCISE 7   EVALUATING YOUR RELATIONSHIP

Purpose: To help you think about what is positive, what is negative, and what needs to be improved in your relationship.

Task: Fill out the following chart with as many things as you can think of.

What has been good about your relationship?	What has been negative about your relationship?	How does your relationship need to improve?

---

four
The
Amazing Effect
Of Validation

Vast intelligence, zestful enjoyment of living,
loving cooperative relationships with
others—these seem to constitute the
essential human nature.[1]

When I work with couples or any two people on problems they may be having in their relationship, I usually begin by asking them each in turn to tell the other what they like about him or her. Very often this is the way it proceeds:

COUNSELOR: Bruce, what do you like about Allen?

BRUCE *(laughs)*: ...He's smart ... he's a friendly person. ...

COUNSELOR: Say it directly to him, using "you" instead of "he."

BRUCE: Okay ... *(laughs, turns to look at Allen)*. You are smart, you're a friendly person, you're good-looking, you're ...

COUNSELOR: Please leave a little space between each validation

---

[1]Harvey Jackins, *The Human Side of Human Beings* (Seattle: Rational Island Publishers, 1965), p. 27.

to give Allen time to hear each one. *(turning to Allen)* These are all true, you know *(Allen laughs)*.

BRUCE: All right. . . . You are smart . . . you're a very friendly person . . . you show your caring about other people well, and I know you care about me . . . *(Allen laughs)*. You're a gentle, sensitive man . . . you usually say exactly what you think . . . you're good-looking . . . *(both laugh)*. You seem to know what you're doing, and have a good sense of who you are. . . . I love the way you dance. . . . You're a good man . . . I love you . . . *(Allen starts crying)*.

COUNSELOR: Anything else?

BRUCE: That's it for now.

COUNSELOR *(turning to Allen)*: You can take some time to cry *(Allen sobs for several minutes)*. What were some of the things Bruce appreciated about you?

ALLEN: I don't remember.

COUNSELOR: Yes, you do. They're all true.

ALLEN: They don't feel true at all. It feels like he's just making it up.

COUNSELOR: No, he's not. What did he say?

ALLEN: He said I was good-looking . . . that I say what I think . . . that I'm smart . . . *(starts crying)*. I don't feel very smart. . . .

COUNSELOR: You are . . . What else did he say about you?

ALLEN: That's all I remember. . . . Oh, he said I'm a good dancer. . . . That's true . . . *(laughs)* . . . I'm a good dancer. . . . That's all.

COUNSELOR: Didn't he also say that you're a gentle and sensitive man? And that you care very well about other people?

ALLEN: Oh, yeah . . . *(laughs)*.

COUNSELOR: And that he loves you?

ALLEN: Yeah . . . *(starts crying again, and continues for several minutes)*.

COUNSELOR: Okay, let's give Bruce a chance to hear what you like about him. Go ahead, and tell it directly to him.

ALLEN: Oh good, it's your turn . . . *(both laugh)*. I like your sense of humor. . . . You seem to be able to lighten up almost any situation, no matter how serious it feels. . . . You're a really creative person, with your music and your painting. . . . You know how to listen to other people very well, and still make yourself felt. . . . You're also good-looking . . . *(both laugh)*. You're a really strong person, and you know how to work with all kinds of things. . . . You're also an excellent dancer. . . . I also like the way you think very carefully about what you say before you say it, so that what you say is well thought out. . . . You're a good friend to have, and I'm glad I know you. . . .

COUNSELOR: Anything else?

ALLEN *(pauses)*: No.

COUNSELOR: Okay, let's give you some time now, Bruce. How are you doing?

BRUCE: Fine. I didn't hear a thing . . . *(laughs)*.

COUNSELOR: What's in the way of you hearing how good you are?

BRUCE: I don't believe it. . . . I mean, I believe it, but I can't feel it at all. . . .

(The session continued with Bruce trying to remember what Allen appreciated about him, and his discharging some of the painful feelings which this evoked.)

Why is it so difficult to give and especially to receive validation? People seem to treat it as if it were some dreaded disease—one mention of it and they change the subject. And, if they really hear what you are saying to them, they may burst out in tears. Confusing, isn't it? It seems to be very difficult for almost all of us to accept validation completely. We laugh it off; we politely say "thank you"; we say "Oh, that's nothing"; we immediately tell the other person what we like about him or her; or we discount the validation: "You like this dress? This old thing? It's just an old hand-me-down from my sister." We do anything but accept and believe what people are saying.

It is not from free choice that we have consistently rejected validation. The main reason we dismiss other people's appreciation of us is that it makes us feel uncomfortable. Often we feel embarrassed, and attempt to divert attention away from us. Laughter is the natural human response to the feeling of embarrassment. That this mode of discharge is common when we are told good things about ourselves is evidenced in the previous session by the number of times Bruce and Allen laughed. Nothing funny was said by either person throughout the validations; the laughter was, a way of releasing their embarrassment.

Often validation brings more painful feelings to the surface. It is not unusual for deep feelings of grief, fear, and anger to come up as a result of being warmly and genuinely appreciated. (An example of this response will be presented later in this chapter.) One reason these painful feelings arise as a consequence of validation is that the good things other people say usually do not feel true. Each of us feels as if we have rotten parts of ourselves we need to hide from other people, and when they begin appreciating us, the feeling is "Ah, but if you *really* knew me, you wouldn't think that." The response that both Allen and Bruce displayed in their session was typical. How we see ourselves is sometimes so much at variance with what is being said that we cannot accept it. Under these circumstances we come face to face with how bad we feel about ourselves.

In the first chapter we discussed some of the reasons we do not feel like good, worthwhile human beings. In every case, we can trace our painful feelings and negative self-images to hurtful things that happened to us in the past. Because the feelings about these invalidating experiences were not discharged, we did not evaluate these incidents as they happened. So the message we were left with was "I'm no good—why else would this be happening to me?" If we had been able to evaluate the experience we would have known that we were hurt because the other person was upset and not thinking clearly, rather than because we were "bad." We would have known that our schoolmates laughed at us, not because we were ugly and therefore no good, but because they were themselves distressed. Our pain then was very real and needed to be released; when it wasn't, our mental processes of storage and evaluation were inhibited. One of the things that happened was that we took the responsibility for the hurt on ourselves. Not only were we hurt, but it felt, and feels, as if it was our fault that we were hurt. This is the component that has the most drastic effect on our self-images—that we are bad for having been hurt. Because literally thousands of major and minor invalidating incidents have occurred in each of our lives, it is no wonder that we do not think well of ourselves.

When we have been disparaged in the same way over and over again, without discharge there is no way we can avoid internalizing the hurtful things that were said and done to us. And unless we can evaluate or reevaluate those past experiences, we will continue to believe and feel that we are ugly or stupid or silly or selfish or rotten. The reality is that no human being is *essentially* any of these things. We may act irrationally, in a stupid or silly or selfish way, or be hurtful to others, but only because we ourselves were hurt. These hurts were imposed upon us, and with discharge their effects can be removed.

Here is an example of how invalidation can be inflicted and the effect it has on the way a person sees him- or herself. Sandy is about thirty, the mother of two children, and a worker in a day-care center in a large metropolitan area. I know that she is an intelligent person; when we have conversations she is articulate and coherent, and the things she says are almost always well thought out. I enjoy talking to her, and our discussions usually change my thinking in some way.

It sometimes seems incredible to me, but Sandy "thinks" or rather feels herself to be stupid, because thinking has nothing to do with the way she feels about herself in this area. Her feelings about being stupid are directly traceable to early painful experiences. One of the effects of these experiences is that she freezes in a group and does not express herself clearly; hence, her feelings about being stupid are reinforced. Consider this segment of a counseling session:

SANDY: I just can't think. I just freeze up, and the words won't come.

COUNSELOR: I know it feels that way, but it's not true. You can think, and you're a very intelligent person.

SANDY: No I'm not . . . *(starts crying)* . . . I've never been able to . . .

COUNSELOR: Sandy, would you be willing to try something?

SANDY: What?

COUNSELOR: Think out loud to me about something that you feel you just cannot think about. How about explaining to a man why he shouldn't keep asking his wife to get him food and drink whenever he wants it.

SANDY: I can't . . . *(starts crying heavily)*.

COUNSELOR: Yes you can. Take your time.

SANDY *(after crying for several minutes)*: Well, it's not . . . I mean, you shouldn't do that. . . . Oh, I just can't do it . . . *(bursts into tears again)*.

COUNSELOR: Yes you can . . . you're doing fine. Keep at it.

SANDY *(after crying for awhile)*: Well . . . it isn't fair for you to expect that.

COUNSELOR: Why not?

SANDY: It just isn't . . . *(starts crying again, and cries for several minutes)*. It's not fair to another human being to treat them as if they are just there to do what you want them to.

COUNSELOR: Well said.

(Sandy continued crying for awhile.)

COUNSELOR: Whoever made you think that you were stupid? What's your first thought?

SANDY: My father . . . *(starts crying again)*. He used to laugh at me all the time. . . . It seemed like anything I said was wrong. . . .

COUNSELOR: Can you remember a specific time?

SANDY *(pauses)*: I remember how he used to say a lot, "It's a good thing you were born pretty, 'cause you haven't got much in the brain department."

COUNSELOR: How did that feel?

SANDY: Awful, just awful . . . *(starts crying)*.

Sandy is not stupid, and never was. Her ability to think clearly and express herself is intact. Her undischarged distress, however, has prevented her intelligence from operating at its full potential. That she was hurt in this way does not diminish her value as a human being, nor does it mean that she will "always be that way." She *can* think well, and given the opportunity to discharge the feelings that come up, will be as coherent as any other person.

One of the harmful consequences of feeling bad about ourselves is that it keeps us from taking charge of our lives. We will rarely take positive actions to improve our lives when we are feeling worthless and powerless. Just as Sandy's thinking froze in the previous example, so our behavior and our creative thinking freezes when we are feeling bad. After all, we don't deserve any better than we already have. Right? This is of course an old recording talking, not an alive, zestful human being.

WHY SO MUCH INVALIDATION?

The reason so many people feel worthless is that we have been consistently invalidated and have not had the chance to discharge. This thought leads to the question of why there is

so much invalidation in our culture. Why is it that we disparage each other so frequently?

One reason is that invalidation tends to be a self-
perpetuating process. Very often people hurt others in the
same way that they themselves were hurt. Although this response may seem strange on the face of it, it is understandable when we think of it in terms of rigid behavior patterns.
To reiterate, when people are hurt and do not discharge, the
feelings and everything that happens at the time are recorded together without any evaluation. When people are in
some way (usually not consciously) reminded of the distressful incident, the recording plays back as a rigid behavior
pattern. When the pattern is restimulated in the present,
however, people often play the role of the abuser rather than
the victim. In the present situation, the feelings are restimulated, and the person once again feels out of control, powerless, unable to think, and so on. If there is someone around
with even less power, perhaps a child, an employee, or a wife,
the restimulated person often acts out the original hurt, only
this time they get to wield the power. The distress recording
itself is essentially unaltered. To illustrate, a woman describes
how her own behavior around her son was affected by the
way she was mistreated by her own mother:

> Jim [her son] went through a period when he was five or six when
> he needed everything exactly in order. If he left something
> under the bed, by the baseboard, he would become very, very
> upset if it had been moved. [This was right after his father left
> for the last time, and it was clear Jim was attempting to create
> order in his life.] What would happen is that he would come
> raging down the stairs screaming, and head straight toward me
> and begin hitting me and demanding to know where such and
> such was. Most often, I would have no idea, either because
> Helen [his sister] had moved the object or Jim himself had mis-
> placed it. But what would happen is that from the first blow Jim
> laid on me, I would begin screaming at him, often hitting him on
> the rear, pushing him away, demanding that *he* listen to *me*. I was
> often left stunned afterwards, because I had sworn never to hit

my kids after what my mother did to me. I also felt guilty and awful that I simply didn't know what to think or say or do with him. If he cried, it drove me crazy; if he screamed, it drove me crazy. There was no space in my head to deal with his emotions. As I discharged on it, I suddenly realized that the situation was an exact duplication of what happened with my mother: I'd be sitting peacefully reading and she would come storming into my room and scream and begin pulling me up by my hair, hitting me in the face, for some infraction—where was her hairbrush, she knew she left it in the bathroom, what had I done with it? Or "Why didn't you do the dishes?" when she hadn't told me to. I, of course, had no opportunity to discharge. When put in a similar situation with Jim, I was massively restimulated, but this time, I could talk and scream and hit back, and I did. He was powerless to stop me, and so I used him to dramatize and "discharge" on what had happened to me when *I* was a child.

This story exemplifies why we invalidate others; we ourselves were invalidated, and when we are restimulated we often treat others as we were treated. In other words, if a person internalizes invalidation, which is what happens when there is no release of feelings, it is taken out on some undeserving target. Invalidation thus gets passed around from one hurt person to another.

Another part of the explanation for the phenomenon of invalidation lies in the crucial role it plays in the functioning of our social and economic system. As everyone who has gone through junior high school knows, our economic system is based on competition. What is important is winning, not how you play the game. People are rewarded, not for cooperating well with others or for doing their best, but for getting ahead, doing better than others, and beating the opposition. In this competitive atmosphere, validation is reserved for those who win. We have all taken in the message that we are good if we win, and we are worthless if we lose. In sports, finishing first is all that counts. In school, only the A-students are validated; the implication is that the rest of us are just not good enough. It does not matter whether we are trying our best or whether we are actually learning a tremendous amount in comparison to what we knew before; what counts is whether or not we are better than the other students. This method of determining our own value as people by comparing ourselves to others pervades almost every aspect of our culture, from politics to entertainment, from health to business. It even directly affects our relationships: "Hmmm . . . her husband is the life of the party. Look at those people around him. Why isn't Harold like that? Why isn't he as good?"

The invalidation inherent in a competitive environment such as ours is not there by chance. It is rather an important part of a system that gives a few people a tremendous amount of wealth and privilege at the expense of the many. Invalidation functions in such a way as to keep the many "losers" feeling bad about themselves and each other, and to keep them thinking of the few "winners" as being better people who therefore deserve their privileges and power.

Also, different ethnic, racial, and sexual groups learn to invalidate members of other groups. Through ethnic jokes, movies, television, and derogatory comments of family members and friends, whites "learn" that people of color are inferior, men "learn" to look down on women, Christians "learn" that Jews are inferior, middle-class people "learn" to put down working-class people, Protestants "learn" that Catholics are not as good as they are, blacks and Puerto Ricans "learn" to invalidate each other, and so on. A large part of the invalidation directed at different groups is the result of cultural stereotyping. These stereotypes, manifest throughout the culture, imply that all members of a particular group are alike, and that their uniformity is based on some distressed or negative or otherwise undesirable quality. Thus members of one group are thought to be "lazy," those of another, "stupid," another, "cheap," and so on.

Because these stereotypes are widespread throughout our culture and are passed down from one generation to the next, we have all been inculcated with them at some conscious or unconscious level. Whether or not we can remember them, incidents occurred which communicated the stereotypes to us. Sometimes the message was direct— "Those ——— sure are stupid"—and sometimes it was more subtle, as in the case of news broadcasts of crimes in which the race of the perpetrator was unnecessarily emphasized.

The effect of this stereotyping is that the members of these groups are in some way invalidated. The form the invalidation takes may be as vicious as physical attack or rape, or it may be as subtle as a semiconscious avoidance by others. In any case, the result is that hurt is inflicted on the individuals involved, and unless the feelings are released they will internalize the invalidation; they will feel themselves to be bad or worthless. Because the stereotyping is so widespread, these feelings are constantly reinforced by daily interactions.

As a consequence, with respect to this kind of sexual, racial, and ethnic invalidation, we need to not only discharge the feelings connected to our past hurts, but also stop the *ongoing* invalidation—stop the catcalls at women, the racial slurs, and the economic disadvantage of all minorities. Only then will the invalidation cease and all people be treated with the respect and care they deserve.

SELF-APPRECIATION

We do not have to wait for our society to change before we can feel good about ourselves and other people. *Right now* we deserve to fully appreciate ourselves and know how good we are. I am not saying that everything we have done in the past has been rational and sensible. Every one of us has done hurtful things to other people, things we now know (and probably then knew) we should never have done. However, we only did those things because we ourselves were hurting. We need to release our grief over having done them, and we need to stop doing them in the future; but having done those things does not make us "bad" people. In fact, telling ourselves that we are not good only reinforces the rigid patterns that make us act irrationally.

Knowing that we are good, in contrast, makes us more powerful and in charge of our lives. As good people we can relate to others as our friends and allies. We can expect, and when necessary, demand that we be treated with all the respect due any good person. We can also take action to make our lives as fulfilling and rewarding as possible. A person controlled by feelings that s/he is worthless will have a more difficult time with all these things.

As young people, we naturally validated ourselves a lot. We were proud of our accomplishments, from learning to walk to painting our first picture to learning to blow our first bubble. For the first few years of our lives, the adults around us generally treated this self-validation, or "bragging," as being very cute. At some point, however, taking pleasure in ourselves was cut short by ridicule and invalidation, with remarks like, "Well now, don't you think *you're* a hot shot," "It's not polite to brag," and so on. So we learned to stifle our legitimate pride in ourselves, and in addition, felt guilty for feeling proud in the first place. As our natural self-appreciation was inhibited by those around us, we began to rely more and more on validation by others. As a result we have lost touch with what we know about ourselves: what we do well, what pleases us about ourselves, what we are proud of, and so on.

EXERCISE 8   APPRECIATING YOURSELF

Purpose: To give you an opportunity to appreciate yourself completely, without reservation or qualification.

Task: This exercise is most effective when done in the presence of a friend who will encourage and support you, but it also can be done well by yourself. Do it while looking at yourself in a mirror, while driving your car, while taking a walk, and so on.

To do it, simply brag about yourself—how good you are, how good-looking, how smart, how well you do things—whatever you think of. Stay completely positive. Other thoughts will come up, such as you're not *really* smart or you are really pretty ugly, but do not verbalize them now. This time is for acknowledging how good you are, and nothing else. If you run out of things to say in a short time, start saying things that might be true but do not feel true, for example, "I'm really likable." If you again run out, start over again. Maintain a physical posture and verbal tone consonant with your total self-appreciation. (If this is very hard for you, it is an indication how little time you spend noticing how good you are.)

If doing it with a friend, it works best if you take turns. The person who is listening can encourage the other by maintaining a delighted attitude and saying "What else?" after each self-validation. Try it!

Evaluation:

What was good about you appreciating yourself?

What was hard about it for you?

What feelings came up?

What insights did you gain about yourself?

Exercise 8 will give us the opportunity to pay attention to and appreciate the good things about ourselves. By yourself or to a friend, simply say everything good you can think of about yourself. Use the proudest tone you can, and stand up or sit proud and tall while you do it. We are aiming for total appreciation of the wonderful person each of us is. Due to the invalidation imposed upon us, this exercise may be hard to do: "I just can't think of anything good," "This feels uncomfortable," and so on. Pay these patterns no respect, and prod yourself to come up with things, even if they do not feel true. They usually are true, despite the feelings. If you continue to do this exercise, your life will improve. It will not solve all your problems, but it will enable you to think more clearly about them. Aside from the discomfort you will feel doing this exercise, other feelings will probably appear, including anything from giggles to tears. With these feelings and their release will eventually come the realization that just maybe we *are* good, and worthy, and smart, and kind, and. . . .

VALIDATING OTHERS

When we appreciate ourselves it has a ripple effect on most areas of our lives. As we might expect, appreciating others has a similar effect on their lives. Further, using validation can immeasurably improve human relationships, particularly those that involve much intimacy.

We have every reason to appreciate our friends and partners openly and unequivocally. First, like ourselves they are good people and deserve to hear it. Despite whatever rigid behavior patterns they act out, they are still essentially good. Whether or not they can accept or believe it, it is good for them to hear how good they are. Besides, you really do like and love them.

Second, validation makes people feel good. Other feelings may also surface when people are openly appreciated, but it fills a real human need to be loved and to have this love expressed. We all know how good it feels when somebody says to us, "Wow, I really like you! You're a wonderful person!" It feels nice, doesn't it?

Third, letting our partners and friends know how good they are contradicts their negative feelings about themselves and puts them at least a little more in touch with the reality of their essential goodness. We cannot talk them out of their painful feelings, but we can help them remember that they are worthwhile. 'No matter how rotten they feel, the fact remains that what is preventing them from feeling good about themselves are exactly these rotten feelings.

The fourth reason for validating our friends and partners

is that it enables them to think more clearly about themselves and their lives. As we mentioned earlier, people function much more effectively and can take more charge of their lives when they know that they are okay than when they are feeling weak and worthless. Everything we can do to help our friends and partners feel strong and worthwhile also will help them be more competent, thinking human beings.

It also often contradicts our own feelings and behavior patterns to appreciate others openly. While operating from our own hurt, it is difficult for us to give other people our undivided attention and to tell them what we appreciate about them. When we are feeling lousy ourselves, how can we be enthusiastic about how great someone else is? To do so we must to some extent admit the possibility that we may be worthy ourselves.

The final reason that validation is so productive is that it tremendously benefits relationships. If our friend or partner knows that s/he is loved and feels good about him- or herself, s/he will act much more positively with respect to us and to our relationship. S/he will be better able to think about us and what we need as individuals, and will also be more likely to share with us what s/he appreciates about us.

Validation is particularly valuable in long-term relationships, in which we and our partners often lose sight of one another in the midst of the constant restimulation we experience dealing with each other's rigid behavior patterns. The act of validation cuts through some of the restimulation and again puts us in touch with why we liked the other person in the first place. Thus, I begin counseling sessions by asking each person to tell the other what s/he likes about him or her, which establishes why they are both there in the first place: that they like and love each other, and are committed to trying to make things better between them. It also enables each of them to hear and understand what the other is saying about him or her with fewer defensive feelings.

This last point is crucial. In all kinds of situations it is common for us to interpret any criticism as meaning that

"I'm no good" or "You don't like me." With this response, the criticism, no matter how well intended, will produce little positive result. We either dismiss the feedback ("He never liked me anyhow") or make it another "reason" that we are rotten ("She's right, she's completely right—I *am* bad"). In either case we do not use the criticism to change our behavior. Validation can prevent both these things from occurring. In fact, each of us would like nothing better than to be encouraged thoughtfully to act more humanly and rationally. Validation serves as a vital part of this process.

In order for people to hear and accept validation it must be genuine and done thoughtfully. When it is not done with awareness, it may be worse than saying nothing. A good example of an unaware validation occurred with an acquaintance of mine several years ago. A friend had just introduced me to her fiancé, who, without so much as even the most preliminary steps of getting to know me, clasped my hand tightly and said, "I love you. I don't know you, but I *love* you. You're an awfully nice person. You're Judy's friend and that's good enough for me." This left me a little taken aback. Rather than help us develop a relationship, this "validation" served only to make me wary of this person. His appreciation of me was more the product of his own anxiety than it was of his thinking.

The usefulness of validation for facilitating effective communication in human relations has been demonstrated over and over. Below are several cases in which people went home from a class I was teaching and tried to use validation as a part of their interactions. Some of the things that happened are quite instructive.

1. One person came back to the class the next day and reported "great success." He had told his wife how much he loved her and all the things he liked about her, and she had started crying. He let her cry, and later she told him how

much she loved him. He said in class that they felt closer than they had in years.

This case exemplifies how validation can bring to the surface other, painful feelings. This effect is not wrong or harmful, however. These feelings need to be discharged if the person is to become free of them. By really being there for his partner, this man demonstrated his love and his caring very effectively.

2. Another person said that she had told one of her teachers how much she liked her. The teacher seemed very pleased, and responded by telling her what a good student she was. In this case, validating the teacher enabled her to feel good and to think about and return a validation to the student.

3. One woman came back and talked of her "defeat." She had gone home and validated her husband, and he replied, "What do you want? Why are you saying these things to me?" She told him that it was an exercise for this class she had, and he then said that he wasn't interested.

In this instance validation brought immediate suspicion. Her appreciating him was so different from their normal behavior and so at variance with his self-image that he did not trust it. It was pointed out in class that she could have stuck with it and said, when asked why she was saying those things, "I've just been thinking how much I like you, and I was reminded of it in class today." Instead, in her own embarrassment she implied that she was only doing it because it was an assignment. Her husband used this as an excuse to dismiss the validation. Here it is clear that her own feelings got in the way of her communicating effectively with him.

Although it might seem strange that someone would go out of his or her way to reject appreciation, we must remember that accepting it goes against much of our conditioning and all our hurtful experiences. The woman in this example did not necessarily make a mistake in the way she

validated her husband. However, her own timidity prevented her from persisting.

At the last meeting of the course from which the above
examples are presented, we used validations to close the
class. Everyone in the class shared something we liked about
each person in turn. It was a particularly moving experience
for all of us, with several people crying over the positive
things that were said to them. Not only did this exercise
break down many of the barriers that ordinarily exist among
students, but it also enabled the people in the class to see me
as a person rather than just as the teacher. It also helped me
see them as human beings and not just as students.

One trap we want to avoid is that of validating people only
for their good deeds. It is not helpful to communicate the
message, "You are good because you've done a good thing."
They *are* good, and they *have* done good things, but their
essential worth has nothing to do with their performance at
particular tasks. To equate worthiness with ability is to say
that A-students are "better people" than B-students, which is
of course not true.

If we only appreciate people for doing well, they will usually develop a fear at some level that their self-worth is dependent on both their continuing to do well and our continuing to approve of their work. This fear defeats the main
purpose of validation, which is to communicate our *uncondi-
tional* love and acceptance. We can still appreciate good
deeds, but only within the context of an appreciation of the
whole person.

Exercise 9 provides a chance for us openly to appreciate
another person. Simply tell your partner or friend what you
like about him or her. Avoid the temptation also to tell the
things you do not like or the things that you wish s/he would
change. You may need to be persistent to get your friend to
listen to you; do not be surprised if s/he tries to change the
subject or say something funny or start telling what s/he likes

EXERCISE 9 VALIDATION

Purpose: To give you the opportunity to verbally appreciate a friend directly and to notice what happens.

Task: In a relaxed situation say what you like and appreciate about your partner or another friend. Say the things you genuinely believe, and say them slowly to give him or her a chance to hear what you are saying. Be specific as well as general, but keep it to the positive things—save your criticisms for another occasion. It may feel embarrassing to you or to your friend, but do it anyway. (There is nothing wrong with feeling a little embarrassed.) If any other feelings come to the surface for either of you, it is fine to just let them happen.

One cautionary note is that if your friend asks why you are saying nice things to him or her, do not say that this book told you to! The fact is that there are many positive things you appreciate about your friend. (Why else would s/he be your friend?) You are simply taking this opportunity to begin expressing them.

Evaluation:

What happened?
What was your friend's reaction to validation? Was s/he able to hear and accept it?
What feelings did it bring out in your friend?
In you?
How will you do it differently next time?

about you. Give him or her your undivided attention, and if any painful feelings come up, treat them as if they were perfectly all right. This validation may have a very positive effect on your friend and your relationship with him or her. You can be sure that it will not hurt.

ELICITING VALIDATION

As much as our friends and partners deserve to hear how much we like them, we deserve to hear about how much they like us. Our receiving validation will have a similar positive effect on us and our relationships that their receiving validation has on them. It will make us feel good, help us know that we are loved and thought about, contradict our negative feelings about ourselves, and help empower us to take charge of our lives. It will also help us to see our partners as caring human beings rather than as bundles of distress.

Of course, in one way it is more difficult to receive appreciation than to give it. That is, if it does not occur to our friends to tell us what they like about us, then we are going to have to initiate it ourselves. This solicitation can be a little embarrassing; you may feel as if this kind of thing is never done and you are breaking some taboo. "Focus attention on myself like that? Never!"

Is there any valid reason for not asking our friends and partners how and in what ways they appreciate us? "Yes," a little voice in our heads answers. "It's embarrassing! That's not the kind of thing people do!" These reactions can be chalked up to those old experiences in which attention focused on us was accompanied by laughter and derision. Letting this embarrassment prevent us from hearing why we are valued is tantamount to agreeing that our past hurt will always control our present behavior. It is also going along with all the invalidation in our culture which has made us feel worthless in the first place. By asking that our friends verbally appreciate us, we are in fact taking a stand against the kind of hurting rampant throughout our society.

In the final analysis, the only reason it is difficult for us to ask for validation is the same reason it is hard for people to accept it once it is given—it restimulates our painful emotion. Often, the mere thought of asking is sufficient to bring many feelings to the surface. Consider the following segment from the middle of a counseling session:

COUNSELOR: Why don't you ask Nick what he likes about you?

KAREN *(laughs)*: I couldn't do that . . . *(laughs)*.

COUNSELOR: Why not?

KAREN: I just couldn't . . . *(continues laughing)*.

COUNSELOR: Why don't you try it right now. Pretend that I'm Nick. Ask me to tell you what I like about you.

KAREN *(laughing loudly)*: No.

COUNSELOR: Aw come on.

KAREN: Can I tell you what I like about you instead? *(continues laughing)*. . . .

COUNSELOR: Nope.

KAREN: All right . . . Nick, would you . . . I can't do it . . . *(starts crying)*.

COUNSELOR: Why not? What's your first thought?

KAREN: I'm scared . . . *(continues crying)*.

COUNSELOR: Of what? Your first thought?

KAREN: That he won't like me . . . I don't ever remember people saying nice things to me. . . . It was always "You don't do anything right," "You're stupid," "You're crazy" . . . *(continues crying)*.

Karen's fear, hurt, and embarrassment all play a part in her not wanting to ask for validation from her friend. What happens to each person is of course different, so we cannot generalize from Karen's particular experience. We can say, however, that our own painful experiences are what prevent us from asking for and getting the support we deserve.

Exercise 10 is one in which each of us is encouraged to ask a friend what s/he likes about us. Do it while sitting over a cup of tea at home, while taking a walk, or whenever it seems appropriate. Be sure you have enough time and you are in a relaxed atmosphere. Otherwise, the tension either of you is feeling will make it difficult for you to have all the attention you should. Do your best to enjoy being told nice things about yourself—try to remember that they are all true.

EXERCISE 10   ELICITING VALIDATION

Purpose: To arrange a situation in which you are the recipient of validation, which of course you deserve to hear.

Task: In an appropriate situation, ask your partner or another friend what s/he likes about you. This may feel embarrassing to either or both of you, but do not let it stop you. Feel free to ask your friend to be more specific, to elaborate, and to say more. Be sure to be receptive and to let the appreciations sink in one at a time. When your friend is finished you can thank him or her for sharing his or her thoughts and feelings with you.

Evaluation:

Was it a good experience for you?

What do you remember of what your friend appreciated about you?

How did you feel while being verbally validated?

What thoughts came up for you at the time?

Was the experience good for your relationship? How so?

Validation is not a gimmick or a tool. It is rather a natural aspect of human relations, part of the way two people who love each other relate to one another; that is, they express their love and caring to each other physically, verbally, and by their actions. We are all good; there are no "bad" people, only good people controlled by rigid patterns based on how they were hurt. The way to help all of us emerge from these patterns is not to chastise us for having them, but to validate and encourage us as the human beings we really are. It is from a position of strength and goodness that we will work to improve ourselves, our relationships, and the world.

five
Learning To Listen To Each Other

Gosh, did I have a lousy day today.

You think *you* had a bad day today. Mine was awful. I woke up with a headache, and it's gone downhill from there.

Yeah, well, I had a horrendous day at work. I didn't have any time to think, let alone take a break.

I had a fight with Paul on the phone today, and it was awful. He hung up on me. You know what happened? He said that . . .

Listen, I don't want to hear about your troubles. I've had a hard day myself.

Do you think I want to listen to you spout off? I came home to relax.

All right, just go ahead and relax! Sorry I bothered you, *Sir*!!

You don't have to get sarcastic about it.

(And so on.)

Are these two "psychotic" people, human beings who are just unable to cope with life? If they are, then so are most of us, for conversations such as this occur thousands of times every day, in couples of all racial, ethnic, and class backgrounds. People who love each other and want to be with one another get themselves into the most tangled emotional messes imaginable. The result of the above interaction might be that the two people will not speak to each other for several hours, or even days.

One of the main things happening here is that early in the conversation each person is indirectly saying to the other, "Listen to me, I'm feeling bad." Neither of them is listening to the other, however, because their own need to be listened to is paramount. As a result, they both feel more and more frustrated, finally taking out all their accumulated feelings on each other. What was originally bothering them no longer seems important and has been replaced by their mutual animosity.

Despite appearances, the inability of each person to listen in such cases is not due to lack of interest or concern. In fact, when we care about people most deeply it is often hardest to listen to their problems and difficulties. Many of us have had the experience of telling complete strangers things about ourselves and our lives that we would never tell those who know us well; it somehow feels safer, and they seem to be able to listen better.

We have trouble listening to other people, not because we do not care, but because our own feelings and behavior patterns interfere with our giving them our full attention. It is like trying to listen to a friend tell you about something that happened to him or her a few hours after you have received a painful sunburn at the beach. Our attention is focused on our pain. As much as we may love and care about our friend, it feels as though we simply cannot take our attention off ourselves and our physical hurt.

A similar thing occurs when what we are feeling is painful emotion. When we are feeling grief, fear, anger, or embarrassment, it is difficult for us to pay attention to others and not focus on or act out of our own distress. This reaction is not a conscious decision on our part; it seems to be the natural effect painful emotion has on our mental functioning. We can illustrate this phenomenon with a segment from a counseling session with someone who had just come from an encounter with her partner similar to the one beginning this chapter.

COUNSELOR: What happened?

VIVIAN: Oh, George came home upset, and I was upset, and inside of five minutes we started fighting with each other. The first thing he did when he got home was to complain about the traffic. Then it was how I was on the telephone when he tried to call me several times today. I was feeling bad enough without him yelling at me, and I really let go at him. I just didn't want to listen to his problems.

COUNSELOR: Why not?

VIVIAN: I have enough of my own.

COUNSELOR: What was your day like today?

VIVIAN: Awful. At work we are operating under this deadline, and everyone is all tense. I hate it when it's like this. It's just no fun being there. And then I get home and George wants me to listen and be there for him.

COUNSELOR: What would you like to say to him? What's your first thought?

VIVIAN *(in a pleading voice)*: Listen to me . . . *(starts crying)*.

COUNSELOR: Tell him again, only this time demand that he listen to you.

VIVIAN: Listen to me! . . . *(cries heavily)* . . . Listen to *me*. . . .

Whenever we find it hard to listen to others, either we are feeling bad in the present or what is being said or done recalls painful feelings from our past. There is no general rule to explain why any of us has difficulty listening to any particular thing, because our restimulation is the result of our own unique experiences.

An additional factor affecting our ability to listen to our partners is that the ways we relate to each other tend to become fixed and inflexible. Unless at least one of the partners gets rid of his or her painful feelings that arise while relating to the other, it is almost inevitable that each person's rigid behavior patterns will be reinforced by the relationship. Let us take, for example, a situation of a man and a woman in their late fifties, who have been living together for over thirty years. The man has a pattern of finding fault with everything the woman does, and the pattern operates whenever he is feeling upset or frustrated over anything. This pattern is of course hurtful to the woman, who is consistently invalidated by it. She responds to it usually by saying nothing, and occasionally by snapping back at him.

Their responses to one another are set and nonthinking. By now their rigid patterns are caused almost as much by hurts inflicted during the thirty years of their intimate relationship as they are by those received in childhood. The experience of relating in patterned ways and not discharging the feelings has had the effect of adding more grooves to distress recordings which had already begun by the time their relationship started. The man's pattern of finding fault can be traced back easily to earlier experiences. Because this pattern has been allowed to continue to operate in the relationship, however, it has gotten further rigidified.

When people become so set in the ways they relate to one another, we cannot expect them to listen well to each other without some facilitation from outside the relationship —either a friend, a counselor, or perhaps this book. It is not that they cannot listen to each other, it is merely that the ways they act around each other are too inflexible for them to see and respect each other as separate, intelligent people who deserve their support.

Another factor that makes it difficult to listen to those we love is that we feel bad when they are hurting; we feel scared, we are angry if they are in any way mistreated, we grieve when they feel physical or emotional pain. This is a natural human response to seeing those we love hurting, and is by no means something to feel guilty about. When we let our behavior be controlled by these feelings, however, it often has the effect of interfering with our ability to be good listeners.

DAUGHTER: Mom, I just got a D in biology. I feel awful. I just don't understand it, I don't know what to do . . . *(starts crying)*.

MOTHER: Okay, now, don't get upset. It's going to be okay, it's all going to be all right. I'll call up your teacher tomorrow, and we'll see what we can do. Just don't worry about it, it will be okay. All right?

DAUGHTER: Oh, I don't know. . . . I thought I was going to do better than that . . . I feel so stupid.

MOTHER: That's enough of that talk. Would you like something to drink?

DAUGHTER: Okay.

This woman clearly cares about her daughter and her daughter's welfare. She nevertheless has great difficulty listening to her talk about her problem. First the mother tries to fix the problem herself, and when that does not make the daughter feel better, she tries to change the subject. Whether or not she is successful, she is not giving her daughter what her daughter most needs at this time, that is, her loving, aware attention. If she could temporarily shove aside her own feelings, she could give her daughter better support.

This dialogue points out another common factor interfering with listening, which occurs when the listener starts owning or assuming responsibility for the other person's problems. The feeling is that *we* have to solve their problems, that it is up to us to stop them from hurting. Although our intentions are good, acting to solve others' problems is usually ineffective and seldom helps them take control for themselves. Often it has the opposite effect, making them feel even more powerless.

We all deserve to be listened to and understood. Having someone there to listen can make an enormous difference in how well we function. It can help us release our feelings, think better, and generally take charge of our lives. Each of us has the ability to come up with good solutions to our problems. The best support other people can give us is to listen to us and to act in such a way as to help us think clearly and act on this thinking.

In the long run it does not help us to have other people try to solve our problems for us. It may help us resolve a particular situation, but it will not teach us how to deal with the next problem that comes up. Further, often people's advice is based on their own distress, and not on their thinking about what is best for us. Here are some examples of "advice" that I have heard people give:

> If I were you I'd go back there and bust his face.
>
> Here, have another drink.
>
> Why don't you leave her. It's more fun being single, anyhow, like I am.
>
> Yeah, there's really nothing you can do. I guess you'll just have to put up with it.

Each of these gems is coming directly from the distress of the person giving the advice. Because they are not based on good thinking about the person being advised, they are in fact more harmful than saying nothing at all. For if the person follows this advice, s/he may be worse off than s/he was before.

What is helpful in both the short and long term is for other people to encourage us to do our own best thinking about our problems. This encouragement will not only enable us to solve the immediate issue but will also increase our ability to think in all kinds of situations. To think well about the present we must push past feelings and patterns from our past. These same patterns and emotions make it difficult for us to think at other times, also, and working through them now will make it easier for us to work through them in the future.

Listening is one of the most vital steps in helping people think about and solve their own problems. One reason is that having the attention of another person contradicts the conditions of the past when we were hurt and were ignored or left alone. Having this attention seems to help us discharge and think more clearly in the present. Also, aware listening tends to give us confidence in ourselves, that our thinking is good, that we are loved, and that we are okay. We all know that human beings function best when they feel good about themselves, and good listening makes people feel good and worthwhile.

WHAT CONSTITUTES AWARE LISTENING?

Listening well involves more than just being around other people while they are talking. We have all had the experience of talking to people who did not understand or care, and feeling frustrated as a result.

A number of different things are necessary for aware listening. To the extent that these elements are present, our listening will have a productive effect on other people. We can think of these elements as messages we communicate while listening.

1. "I'm here." This is perhaps most important, and involves the crucial element of *attention*. Listening well means paying attention to other people and not shifting the attention onto ourselves or away from them in any other way. Looking at them, not changing the subject, not thinking about something else while they are talking—these are all attributes of attentive behavior. What is *not* good attention can illustrate what is.

A: Ow, I stubbed my toe!
B: Shhhh . . . I'm watching this show.

Or

A: Ow, I stubbed my toe! It really hurts!

B: Yeah, I did that yesterday. I was walking into the bedroom, and. . . .

Or

A: Ow, I stubbed my toe!
B *(reading the paper)*: Uh huh . . . *(continues reading the paper)*.

Being interrupted is another good clue that the listener's
attention is somewhere other than with the person talking.
The effect of this inattention is that the listener is less able to
think effectively about the other person, and the person talking feels less safe and less understood.

2. "I care about you." In order for people to feel supported, they must know in some way that we love and care
about them. This feeling is communicated by what we say,
how we say it, our facial expressions, and our general de-
meanor. There is no rigid formula to follow; we can only
determine what behavior is appropriate by the particular circumstances. Sometimes it makes sense to touch people; other
times it makes sense to smile at them. Whatever we do in this
regard, we need to think about how to communicate our
caring most effectively.

3. "I understand." We can let people know that we understand what they are saying in a number of different ways.
Sometimes it is sufficient to say nothing and just keep looking at them. Sometimes it suffices to say "Uh huh" every
couple of minutes. On some occasions we need to feed back
to people what we have heard in order for them to feel
understood. If we successfully communicate that we understand, using whatever responses are appropriate, we both
validate other people and encourage them to continue to
share their thoughts and feelings and find solutions to their
problems.

4. "You are good." Communicating through our listening
that the people talking are worthwhile and have real and
important concerns will help them think about their lives

and their problems. It will contribute to their dealing with situations from a position of confidence and strength, rather than from feelings of weakness and despair. Again, there is no one correct way to share our knowledge that they are okay and are wonderful human beings. This message can be told with looks, words, or actions.

Telling people that they are good can be difficult to do. First, we must push past any feelings that prevent us from seeing their goodness. We need to recognize that any thoughts we have otherwise are due to our own painful emotion and not to any lack of worthiness on other people's part. People are basically good no matter what they do; any irrational behavior on their part is the result of how they were hurt and has nothing to do with their inherent worth. If our negative feelings are restimulated by things they do, then we need to discharge these feelings, and not let them prevent us from reaching out to these people.

Second, we must ignore or in some way move around our embarrassment over telling people that they are good or that we like them. If we can manage to communicate validation despite our embarrassment, the quality of our listening will greatly improve.

5. "You are in charge." By maintaining an understanding and awareness that they are fully capable human beings who can take complete charge of their lives, we can by our listening help other people achieve this potential. It is very important that we think and communicate that it is possible for them to do so—which leads directly to the next point.

6. "It's not hopeless." The feeling that everything is hopeless and nothing can be done is one of the biggest stumbling blocks in taking positive action in our lives. This feeling is the natural result of having been hurt over and over while growing up and having had no chance to discharge the feelings. It is not at all our fault that we feel hopeless, but its effect is that sometimes it does not even occur to us that things could be different or that we could act to change things.

It is important that as listeners we not be sucked into

people's patterns of hopelessness. Every way we contradict this feeling by our thinking and practice, we help them move beyond their hopelessness to feel and act constructively. This help can be merely saying, "It's not hopeless," or it might involve our maintaining a light, positive attitude. Again, there is no standard way to communicate that there is hope and that change is possible. We must think about what is most appropriate to say and do for the particular situation.

7. "It's okay to feel bad." Aware listening must include the acceptance of painful emotion as being perfectly all right. It is fine to cry, to feel grieved or angry or scared. Any indication that we feel uncomfortable with the release of feelings will make the people to whom we are listening feel it is less safe to do so. And unless the painful feelings are acknowledged and discharged, they will continue to impede their mental processes, and thus, their ability to think and act most sensibly. To be effective listeners we must temporarily shelve our own feelings and act as relaxed and accepting as possible. As we discharge our own feelings of pain and embarrassment, this will become easier to do.

The more our behavior includes the seven points just mentioned, the better we listen. As we have repeatedly said, however, there is no formula for bringing these elements into our interactions. We must think for ourselves and respond to each situation and each person as is warranted at the time.

Let us now look at examples of people listening well to others in two different situations. We must remember that what these people say and do may be different from what other people who are listening just as well might do in the same situation.

I. Mark, a seven-year-old boy, has just come into the house crying, and Doug, an adult, is in the living room when Mark rushes in.

DOUG: Hello, Mark.

(Mark cries and runs upstairs to his room. Doug follows him and sits by the bed on which Mark is crying.)

DOUG *(gently)*: What happened?

(Mark says nothing, and continues crying. Doug moves over and places his hand on Mark's back. After several minutes Mark's tears begin to subside.)

DOUG: Something bad happened outside.

MARK: Yeah, Johnny hit me. I'll get him.

DOUG: You're pretty angry at him.

MARK: Yeah, I'll get him.

DOUG: What would you like to do to him?

MARK: Kick his head in.

DOUG: If this pillow were his head, what would you like to do with it?

(Mark takes it and throws it on the ground and starts jumping on it, and starts laughing.)

MARK: I'm going to call Johnny up and tell him that he better not hit me any more, or else I won't be his friend . . . *(leaves the room)*.

Let us compare this interaction with one in which the adult does not listen well, in which some of the necessary elements of aware listening are absent.

DOUG: Hi, Mark, what's wrong? Why are you crying?

(Mark runs upstairs to his room. Doug follows him and stands next to the bed on which Mark is crying.)

DOUG: Hey, Mark, don't cry, what happened?

(Mark continues to cry.)

DOUG: What happened? *(starts to get a little irritated)* How can you expect me to help you when you won't tell me what happened? Come on now, let's shape up. *(Mark stops crying, but hides his face in a pillow.)* Well, if you want to be that way, go ahead. *(Doug leaves the room, and Mark stays in bed, feeling hurt and angry.)*

When the support and attention were not there, Mark was not about to open up and talk. Further, Doug's unease with feelings had the effect of keeping Mark from crying, which he needed to do. In the earlier interaction, Doug's support both encouraged Mark to talk about and discharge what happened and helped him to think about what he needed to do.

II. Two women, Jill and Chris, are talking about their days at work.

JILL: I had a horrible day today. I'm exhausted.

CHRIS: Bad, huh?

JILL: Oh, it was awful. This was one of those days when the customers make nasty cracks all day long. You know what one of them said to me today? He said I had no business going to work and taking away the job from a man. Ooh, that made me so angry.

CHRIS: I bet it did.

JILL: I try to be friendly and understanding, but I have my limits, too.

CHRIS: You have every right to stick up for yourself.

JILL: Yeah. I wish I had told him just what I thought of him.

CHRIS: What would you have told him?

JILL: Oh, I don't know, maybe to just keep quiet. Anyway, things like that seemed to keep happening all day long. And am I wiped out. How was your day?

This interaction might have taken a different turn if Chris had not listened so well.

JILL: I had a horrible day today. I'm exhausted.

CHRIS: That's too bad. I had a good day today.

JILL: For me this was one of those days when the customers make nasty cracks all day long. You know what one of them said to me today? He said I had no business going to work and taking away the job from a man. Ooh, that made me so angry.

CHRIS: Yeah, something like that happened to me last week. I was installing a telephone at this one apartment, and this guy was there who gave me a hard time the whole time I was there. He was obnoxious. I wanted to kill him. Say, let's go out to dinner tonight, I'm starved.

JILL: No, Chris, I'm too tired. I think I'm going to go to bed early tonight.

CHRIS: Okay, I'll see you later.

Jill received no satisfaction from this conversation because Chris did not seem interested in hearing about her day. When Jill started talking about her upset, Chris immediately changed the focus to a time when a similar thing had happened to her. The result of this conversation was that Jill felt just as drained and upset as she did before the conversation began. In contrast, the previous conversation between them ended with Jill knowing that Chris cared and was interested in her concerns; then Jill felt better enough to be able to listen to how Chris' day had been.

When people have difficulty listening to others, we can be sure that they themselves are hurting and need to be listened to. In general, we can expect to find that those people who seem never to be able to listen well were never listened to when they were younger. Although it is impossible to measure how much people have been hurt, we can directly trace people's lack of attention for others to things that happened to them earlier, usually in their childhood. Because of the way we recorded information when we were hurt and did not discharge, our ability to listen to others was impaired precisely to the extent and in the way that others failed to listen to us. When other people are hurting it reminds us of how we were hurting, and the recordings which were made at the time of our hurt are then played back. If the people listening to us back then were not comfortable with feelings, then probably we will also not be comfortable with feelings.

For the same reasons, we do not usually expect to be listened to. "I was never listened to before, so why should I expect to be listened to now," the hurt recording says. Clearly the hurt inflicted upon us in the past limits our thinking about what is possible in the present and future.

USING OUR ABILITY TO LISTEN

Realistically, we are going to have to listen to other people first before they will be able to listen effectively to us. We can help them deal with some of their distress through our listening, and they will then have more attention for us and our concerns, and for others also. Of course often we must temporarily push aside our own feelings in order to start this listening process, but the benefits of doing so can be great. The following is an example of one couple's successful experience.

Steve and Debby have been married for about twelve years and have two children in elementary school. Debby had taken some college courses before they were married, but had dropped out before she met Steve. Over the last few years she has become more and more bothered about not having what seems to her a life of her own; Steve has his job, the children have their school, but all she has is taking care of other people. In the past when she raised her concern with her husband he responded negatively and was unable to understand what was bothering her. While discussing it together, her frustration got the better of her on a number of occasions, and these encounters ended with nothing resolved and both people feeling upset.

Over his strong objection, Debby enrolled in two courses at a local college, one of which was a course I was teaching on

Resolving Conflicts. One of the first things from the course she integrated into her life was the value of aware listening. The effect on her relationship with Steve was tremendous. The next time they talked, she restated her concerns and desires to him and listened to his thoughts and feelings on the subject. She worked hard to understand what he was saying and did her best to let him know that she had heard him. Then, she asked him just to listen to her and try to understand exactly what she was thinking and feeling. This conversation was the beginning of their being able to listen to each other and constructively deal with the issues between them. One of the results was that Steve first accepted and later supported Debby's desire to continue her education.

In this course I had suggested to everyone that they go home and listen to someone as best they could. I had instructed people to say little, if anything at all, and to give the person to whom they were listening their undivided attention. They were warned particularly not to take the focus off the other person by turning it on themselves or some other subject. Although the results were not generally as spectacular as in the previous example, they nevertheless illustrate the value of good listening.

1. Sarah went home and asked her babysitter, Fran, to have a cup of tea with her. She then asked Fran to talk about herself. Fran proceeded to tell her about some of the difficult things that were happening in her life, and to Sarah's surprise, began to cry. Sarah continued to listen, saying almost nothing and letting Fran cry. Fran talked and cried for over an hour, and when it was over felt much better. She told Sarah that she really liked her and was glad she had made a new friend.

2. James happened to give a ride to a woman who worked at the same agency as he did but whom he didn't know. He invited her to tell him about herself and worked hard to avoid interjecting his own comments and opinions (which

was quite difficult for him). He reported that she talked about her job and her boyfriend and troubles that she was having at home, and seemed very willing to open up to him. He was surprised to discover that his refraining from flirtatious behavior resulted in his being able to relate to the woman as a whole person, rather than as a potential mate or sex partner.

3. Sharon went home and asked her father how things were going at work. He told her about his concern that he might get laid off because of budget cutbacks. Sharon listened attentively without judgmental comment. He seemed to appreciate the chance to talk to a member of the family who did not impose her own fears and worries about the situation. A larger effect was the easing of tensions in the household.

4. Bart realized that he spent little time finding out what was going on in the life of his nine-year-old son, Tim. He asked Tim how this could be changed, and his son suggested that they spend time simply playing together. To Bart's surprise, he had a delightful time giving Tim that kind of attention. They ended their time together feeling warm, loving, and much closer than they had for awhile. In addition, Bart realized that it was important to continue setting aside time he and Tim could spend alone together.

If we really listen, people will tell us exactly what is going well with them and just what is hurting. They may not tell us in so many words, but the information will be communicated in some way—by tone of voice, facial expression, body posture, and so on. Initially we may have difficulty deciphering the message, but we will certainly improve with practice. In any case, the most important step is listening, making a concerted effort to give people our best attention and to communicate the elements of aware listening elucidated earlier. Exercise 11 provides an opportunity to practice listening well.

EXERCISE 11   LISTENING WELL

Purpose: To help you improve your listening skills, and thereby build a more supportive relationship.

Task: When you have some relaxed time together, ask a friend what is happening with him or her (in your own words). Listen attentively while looking at your friend. Do not interrupt, and do not divert the attention to yourself (e.g., "That same thing happened to me last week. I was at the store and . . ."). Restrict your comments to those that encourage your friend to continue to talk about him- or herself. These include feeding back what you are hearing ("You were really angry about that"), validation ("You handled that well"), and simple encouragement to continue ("What happened next?"). If your friend starts laughing or crying while receiving your attention, continue to listen respectfully, and do not try to stop the emotional release.

Evaluation:

What happened?
How did it feel to you?
Was it helpful for your friend? How?
Was it good for your relationship? How?
How can you listen better next time?

Listening is especially crucial to the ongoing functioning of healthy, intimate relationships. We and our partners must listen if we are going to be able to support one another to grow and develop as whole human beings. The benefits are twofold: First, it provides each of us with the chance to think out loud, to release our feelings, and to figure out what to do in our lives. Second, it provides the listener with accurate information about how to best support his or her partner.

A good example of the necessity of aware listening is one

in which one partner is trying to quit smoking. However good the other person's intentions, s/he can easily get locked into an adversary or parental role. Interactions such as the following are not rare:

A: Are you sure you want that cigarette?

B *(trying to quit)*: Of course I'm sure. Who do you think you are, my mother or something?

This kind of discord can be avoided by asking our partners what kind of support would be most helpful, and then doing what they say (if it makes sense to us). By not telling them what to do, we are clearly their allies, not their enemies.

One good way both partners (or any two people) can ensure being listened to is to take turns listening to each other. First one person talks and the other listens for a specified length of time; then they switch roles for the same amount of time. It usually makes sense for the person who is least upset to listen first, because s/he will give better attention. Then the other person, having had an opportunity to get rid of some of his or her distressful feelings, can listen more effectively and attentively. Exercise 12 is presented to help people experiment with exchanging listening time as described here.

EXERCISE 12   EXCHANGING LISTENING TIME

Purpose: To help both you and a friend think more clearly about important things in your lives.

Task: With your partner or another friend, take turns listening to each other for from five to fifteen minutes each. When it is your turn, talk about something important in your life, a problem you are having, a minor upset, or something that is going well; that is, use the time to talk about what you need to. In the other role as listener, listen respectfully without interruption, giving your complete attention. Look at your friend, and do not divert the focus from him or her onto yourself. Often it is appropriate to say nothing, and it is seldom helpful to give unsolicited advice—your friend knows best what s/he needs to do in his or her particular situation.

Timing each person's turn is usually effective in insuring that each of you has approximately equal listening time. If the person listening does the timing, the speaker is freer to focus more attention on his or her thoughts and feelings.

Evaluation:

How did it feel to you as the listener?
As the speaker?
Did you friend's attention help you think more clearly?
How was it for your friend?
What would have made you a better listener?
What would have made your friend a better listener?
How was it helpful to your relationship?

One problem to be aware of as we take turns listening to each other is that sometimes what we say intensely restimulates our friends' painful feelings. When this occurs they will no longer be able to give us their attention, and their listening will be helpful to neither them nor us. Often this happens when we use the opportunity to take out our hurt or angry feelings on them. Rather than building a constructive relationship, such use of listening can only decrease the amount of trust and support two people have for one another. The following is an example of a misuse of the listening process:

SPEAKER: I can't stand you when you act like that. You're just being a stupid oaf. . . . Yuk . . . I don't know what I ever saw in you in the first place. . . .

LISTENER *(clearly upset)*: Well you're no prize yourself, with your uppity attitude and. . . .

We have no right to expect anybody to listen to that kind of abuse and not develop feelings in response. We thus must be careful when exchanging listening time with our partners not to dramatize or take out our feelings on them. This defeats the main purpose of our listening, which is to help each of us take full charge of our lives, our relationships, and the world.

Listening is too vital a tool of human relations for us to allow it to be unused or misused. It will improve almost any relationship in which it is employed, from the home to the workplace to the street corner. It is one of the best means human beings have of combating the effects of years of cumulative distress. It is not complicated and does not require degrees or credentials. It is simply listening, something that everyone of us has the innate ability to do.

six
Improve Your Communication

Excuse me, but I think you have a banana in your ear.
I'm sorry, I can't hear you very well. What did you say?
I said, you've got a banana in your ear.
I can't hear you. What did you say?
I said you've got a banana in your ear, dammit!
I can't hear you, I have a banana in my ear.

Ah, the joys of communication. One partner says something and means something else, and the other partner hears a third thing and responds accordingly. Have you ever heard a conversation such as the following?

EMILY: Is dinner ready yet?

RALPH: No, and stop bugging me about it. I'm working as fast as I can.

EMILY: Well, it's not fast enough.

RALPH: Do it yourself then *(stomps out of the kitchen)*.

Or perhaps the following:

> What do you want to do tonight?
> Oh, I don't know. What about you?
> How about a movie?
> I don't really feel like a movie.
> How about going to visit Marcie? That's always fun.
> Nah, I don't feel like that either.
> Say, what about going dancing? Jack and Billie are going, and we could join them.
> Well . . . I don't know. . . .
> You never want to do anything. You're always like this . . . stick-in-the-mud!
> Oh, leave me alone.

Why is it perfectly normal conversations can start with simple questions or comments and end with vicious invectives? What begins as sharing or asking for information sometimes ends up as volleys of personal attack.

Good communication is necessary for relationships to function well, whether they are casual, business, or intimate. The result of good communication is that we correctly understand each other, which enables us to think clearly about what makes the most sense for us to say or do. Interactions such as the above, however, have the effect of muddling our thinking and our relationships. We end up feeling angry, hurt, and misunderstood.

To investigate some of the problems in communication and to help us develop some tools for dealing with these problems, it is useful to think about communication in terms of its two complementary aspects. The first involves the *sending* of information, and the second, the *receiving* of it. When either the sending or the receiving is done inaccurately, the relationship suffers.

PROBLEMS AS SENDERS

Because our rigid patterns of behavior and our feelings cloud our thinking processes, often we either do not say what we think or say it in such a way that the other person cannot accept or understand it. Instead of responding appropriately to the current situation, we play out old recordings. Consider the following example. Margy had just finished breakfast and was late and in a rush to leave for school; she was upset because she had an exam in just a few minutes. Don, the person with whom she was intimate, was in the middle of cooking breakfast and was tending the stove.

DON.: Would it be helpful if I gathered your books together for you?

MARGY: No, thanks, I'll have to do that myself . . . (*rushes around the room, picking up books and papers to take with her*). You can go out and warm up the car for me and take it out of the garage, though.

DON (*in a relaxed tone of voice*): I don't want to do that, because I'm in the middle of cooking an egg.

MARGY (*furiously*): Ooh, you make me *so* mad! Can't you tell I'm in a hurry? Get out of my way . . . (*continues rushing around the room, and on her way slams a couple of doors*).

DON: Well, good luck on your test.

MARGY (*walking out the front door*): Go to hell.

Don had said nothing to warrant the treatment he received here. Later, when Margy was talking about this incident, she agreed that her feelings had nothing to do with him. Her anxiety and tension at the time interfered with her ability to think and act rationally. Outside of her feelings and her patterns, she had no desire to yell at Don. The messages that she was sending him, however, were almost completely shaped by these emotions.

This interaction is a little unusual; typically when we respond irrationally to our partners we at least in part are restimulated by one of their rigid patterns. They may be yelling at us, continually talking in a low, depressed voice, forgetting again to take out the garbage, or overeating. We respond with hurt, angry, fearful, or embarrassed feelings, which then prevent us from communicating sensibly. This dynamic is well illustrated in the following short conversation:

SAM: Last night when Paul was here you were a real drag. You didn't say a thing all evening. You just sat there for hours. I started wondering if you were still alive. Several times I tried to bring you into the discussion, but you didn't bite once. It really bugged me.

JANET: Oh, leave me alone. If you don't like the way I am, that's tough. I don't have to please you all the time.

SAM: Yeah, well don't worry about it, because you're not, not by a long means. It would have been better if you hadn't been there at all.

Sam is very upset over a particular way Janet acted the previous evening. Whenever she is in a social group, her feelings and behavior from the past are replayed, and she withdraws, becoming quiet and shy. No matter how irrational Janet's behavior may be, however, it does not make Sam's treatment of her in this conversation any more sensible. Upbraiding Janet will not take away the hurt that caused her behavior, nor will it help her to act differently in the future. In fact, this interaction will serve as another invalidation on which Janet will need to discharge before she will be completely free of this behavior pattern. Although Sam genuinely would like Janet to be rid of the pattern, his own restimulated behavior actually reinforces it. The source of his restimulation came out in a counseling session.

COUNSELOR: What happened with you when Janet was not contributing very much to the conversation?

SAM: I got furious . . . actually, I was embarrassed. . . . It felt like she didn't like Paul, and it just made me uncomfortable . . . like he wouldn't come over any more or something. . . . I mean, we have a hard enough time making friends anyhow.

COUNSELOR: What does it feel like not having many friends?

SAM: Pretty alone.

COUNSELOR: Would you try saying something?

SAM: Okay.

COUNSELOR: Ask Janet for her help.

SAM *(laughs)*: . . . I can't do that.

COUNSELOR: Yes you can. Try it.

SAM: Janet, will you help me make friends . . . *(laughs)*. . . . She won't do it.

COUNSELOR: Keep asking her.

SAM: Please help me. I need your help . . . *(starts crying)*.

We can see from this that Sam was responding to Janet's behavior because of his own fears and hurts about not having friends. Because he has not discharged these emotions, she becomes the target on which to take out his feelings.

This need to discharge, rather than "dump" our feelings onto someone else, is the single most important factor interfering with our ability to send information clearly and precisely. Painful feelings prevent us from communicating in the most sensible and appropriate manner.

Based on the above discussion, we can now discern three different levels in the sending of information. The first level, what we may call the *code*, consists of the actual message sent. For example, this message would include Sam's saying to Janet, "You're a pain to be around, do you know that?" The second level, the *meaning*, involves what the sender is really thinking and feeling. The underlying meaning in Sam's message is something like "When we're in a group and you withdraw and say nothing, I feel hurt and angry." In other words, he is communicating that it bothers him when she behaves in a certain way. Although in the code he may be blaming Janet, as if it were her fault he is angry, what is actually happening is that his painful feelings are restimulated by her behavior.

The third level is the *source of restimulation.* Janet does *A*, Sam feels *B*—but why? What are the recordings that are being replayed whenever Janet does *A*? In this instance Janet's behavior brought out Sam's own fears about not having friends and feeling lonely.

We can now look at the conversation between Sam and Janet schematically:

	Code	*Meaning*	*Source of Restimulation*
SAM:	You're a drag. You didn't say a thing all night long.	I get angry when you don't talk, and I have to do it all.	I don't believe that people like me, and I'm afraid of being alone. I'm afraid I won't have any friends.
JANET:	Oh, leave me alone. If you don't like the way I am, that's tough.	I feel hurt and angry when you say that.	I feel unloved and put down, and am reminded of the countless times I was put down by my mother.

The feelings of anger which Sam and Janet are taking out on one another are not their primary feelings. Instead, they are secondary responses based on their inability to discharge the primary feelings of grief and fear. Dramatizing their anger at each other prevents them from actively supporting each other in the most needed areas.

Sam could be Janet's biggest ally in helping her push through the feelings and patterns blocking her from being her normal, zestful self in social groups. First, he could help her discharge the painful feelings, and thereby help to free her from the patterns. Second he could ask her what support would be helpful to her.

To give Janet this kind of support Sam may need to discharge his own restimulated feelings so he can think more clearly. In the midst of his feelings, the focus of his attention is not on her but on himself, on how bad *he* is feeling. His lashing out at her is the acting out of his own patterned response.

Thus, the best thing to do when we are hurt, angry, embarrassed, or fearful in response to the actions of others is (1) discharge our own feelings, and not take them out on anyone else, and (2) think about what support the other person needs. If Sam were doing both these things, their interaction might be as follows:

SAM: I noticed that you didn't seem to be your normal, talkative self last night. What was going on?

JANET: Oh, I don't know. I guess I was tired. I just didn't feel like talking.

SAM: You had a hard day yesterday.

JANET: I guess so.

SAM: I'd like to give you support to feel more relaxed when we have people over. I think you're a lot of fun to be with, and I bet you'd like to be that way with other people, too.

JANET: I don't know, I just can't think of anything to say in groups.

SAM: It feels a little scary.

JANET: Yeah, I guess it does.

SAM: What's scary about it for you?

JANET: I don't know. I guess I'm afraid that they'll think I'm stupid.

SAM: Why would they ever think that?

JANET: I don't know. *(laughs)* I know I'm not, but it sure feels that way sometimes.

SAM: Well, what can you do next time we're in a group, and what can I do to help?

JANET: Well, I think it might help if you gave me some attention before people came over, so that I could deal with some of the scary feelings beforehand. Also, if I'm withdrawn during the get-together, you could just remind me by saying "Hi" or something.

SAM: Great.

Of course such a conversation is not always going to go this smoothly. Sometimes the other person will become angry at us no matter how carefully and lovingly we try to show our support. Later in this chapter we will discuss a communication skill to use when this response occurs.

When we are not able to step outside our feelings and think about our friends and partners, the next best thing is for us to be sure not to load our feelings on them or blame them for our feeling bad. One good way to do this is to relate our communication code to our meaning. Dr. Thomas Gordon[1] has used the term "I-message" to describe the kind of message in which the sender tells the receiver how s/he feels when the receiver acts in a certain way.

> I feel upset when we go out together to visit friends and you hardly talk to them, because then I have to do the talking for both of us.
>
> I feel angry when you don't do the dishes when you say you're going to, because it means I have to work around your mess in order to fix my breakfast.
>
> I'm worried about losing my job.
>
> I get discouraged when we talk and talk and can't seem to reach agreement, because it feels as if we'll never get anywhere.

In these statements the sender is taking most of the responsibility for his or her own feelings, as well as explaining why s/he is feeling this way. There is still the slight implication

[1] Thomas Gordon, *Parent Effectiveness Training* (New York: David McKay Co., Inc., 1975).

that "I'm feeling this way only because you are doing such and such," but it does avoid much of the heavy invalidation inherent in such statements as "You're a real drag."

The latter kind of statement is what Gordon calls "You-message," and it is characteristically a variation on the theme of "You are bad":

You're so messy.

You're a baby.

You dummy.

You've been acting awful all night.

You're acting just like a spoiled brat.

Stop that, or I'm leaving.

You shouldn't talk that way to him.

All these messages involve invalidation: some attack, some criticize, some shame, some threaten, and some lecture. They all have the effect, however, of telling people that they are worthless or inadequate. This not only makes them feel bad but also makes it less safe for them to discharge. As a result they are more likely to dramatize their feelings at us or somebody else. What we call fights are usually volleys of You-messages being thrown back and forth.

You-messages also deter positive changes, because people will be operating from hurt feelings. We can be coerced into being quiet or whatever by threat, but it will help neither our personal development nor our relationships with others. When fear and embarrassment motivate behavior, we can expect it to be rigidly patterned instead of freshly creative.

In contrast, I-messages own and take responsibility for our feelings and put less on our friends and partners. They are less likely to feel attacked, and thus will be better able to hear the information we are sharing. Compare these two statements:

1. You're always leaving the front door open. Won't you ever learn?

2. It really bothers me when you leave the front door open because it costs a lot of money to heat the house.

Almost any person will respond more positively to the second statement than to the first, which is of course very reasonable; in the first we are treated as an enemy, and in the second as a friend. When I-messages are used instead of You-messages, we tend not to get as restimulated.

EXERCISE 13   USING I-MESSAGES

Purpose: To make it easier for your partner or friend to hear your concern when you are having hurt or angry feelings.

Task: Next time you have hurt or angry feelings over something your partner or friend has done, use an I-message; that is, acknowledge your feelings directly. An example of such a message is, "I feel frustrated trying to talk with you when you interrupt me, because it feels like you're not listening to what I say."

Do your best to avoid invalidating your friend by distorting your I-message, as discussed in the text. If your friend responds defensively to your statement, you may then use active listening (discussed in the following pages) if it seems appropriate. Repeat the use of I-messages and active listening until your friend understands what you are saying. Then the two of you can talk about a solution.

Evaluation:

How did your I-messages work to help you be understood?
If they were ineffective, why were they?
What was difficult about the exercise for you?
What will you do differently next time?

Exercise 13 allows us to practice using I-messages when we experience painful feelings about something a friend or partner does. It is simple to do—just talk about how you feel instead of blaming, ridiculing, or in any other way invalidating him or her. If s/he has hurtful feelings restimulated despite your best efforts, it is then often appropriate to be the best listener you can be. (A skill called "active listening" will be discussed in the next section.)

There are some problems with I-messages that should be discussed here. The first is what Gordon has described as disguised You-messages, statements that masquerade as I-messages but are really invalidations. An example occurred in a class I taught, in which students were asked to use I-messages if an appropriate situation arose. Many people reported great success. Henry, who had total failure, shared his experience with the class. He and his younger brother Mike (aged twenty-one) got along very poorly, and always seemed to be picking at each other. On this occasion Henry used the following I-message:

> I feel bugged when you always act so juvenile. I wish you'd grow up. I'm tired of your stuck up, know-it-all attitude.

Needless to say, Mike did not respond too positively to this supposed I-message, and most people in the class immediately saw why: Diguised as an invalidating You-message. Henry tells Mike, "You're juvenile," "you're a baby," and "you're stuck up," all under the pretense of telling Mike how he feels. Such supposed I-messages will not work; the recipient will be able to tell or feel whether s/he is being disparaged, and will respond accordingly. We must be careful really to take responsibility for our own feelings, and not blame them on our friends and partners. In this example, Henry's pattern of taking out his feelings through anger prevented him from sending effective I-messages.

A second problem is that by implication I-messages still tend to make others responsible for our feelings. As such, I-messages are manipulative, and can be used to coerce others to do our bidding. The natural correlate of "When you do X, I feel Y" is that you should stop doing X because it makes me feel bad. When we say to our friends that "When you slam the door, I get a little frightened," essentially we are telling them not to slam the door. This is a perfectly reasonable request, but sometimes what we ask our friends to do is not sensible but based on our own rigid patterns. For example, if we say to someone, "When you cry, it makes me feel bad because I don't like to see you hurting"—implying that the other person should stop crying—we will be contributing to his or her becoming more distressed and rigidly patterned. We thus cannot use I-messages blindly; we must think about what we say, how we say it, and the effect it will have on the other person and the whole situation.

A safeguard against the misuse of I-messages is to include a clause explaining why we feel the way we do: "When you do X, I feel Y, because Z." This "because" clause tends to minimize the implication of others' responsibility for our feelings. When they can see that the "because" is reasonable, that their behavior has direct adverse effects, they usually will act in a responsible way. If the explanation we give for our feelings is not reasonable, then they may choose not to alter their behavior. "Because it costs a lot of money to heat the house" is a quite sensible reason to be upset about an open door. Most of us would try to be more careful about closing the door as a result of this statement. If the person had been upset about the open door "because someone might see in," we might be less inclined to accede to their request; maybe we have better reasons for wanting it open than they have for wanting it closed, in which case it makes sense to negotiate with them about it. Adding the "because" gives the receiver more information on which to base her or his behavior.

In I-messages it usually is not advisable to use the word "angry" to describe our feelings. Frequently there are feelings of grief or fear underlying the anger, and I-messages are more effective if these deeper feelings are presented. Because most of our parents have taken out their angry feelings on us, having somebody tell us, "I'm angry at you," tends to be restimulative, no matter what the reason. Even substituting the word "upset" for "angry" can make the I-message easier to hear and be accepted.

PROBLEMS AS RECEIVERS

As discussed in the previous chapter, aware listening is a crucial aspect of good interaction between people. Receiving communication is not always easy, however, because people do not always communicate clearly and directly. Often their communication is laden with feelings, and frequently these feelings are taken out on us. Receiving the information, then, is doubly difficult: people are not sending very well, and our own feelings, restimulated by their invalidation, interfere with accurate reception and interpretation.

Also, we often fail to communicate our understanding in such a way as to encourage people to talk, discharge, and solve their own problems. Sitting next to someone and staring blankly at them with a glazed-over look is the most rudimentary form of listening, and while it is better than nothing, it will yield only limited results. Even listening with aware attention is sometimes not enough, particularly if people have patterns of shyness and reticence.

Dr. Thomas Gordon has coined the term "active listening" to describe a way of receiving information. It involves feeding back to the sender what we hear as the meaning underlying the code. In essence we decode the message we receive and send back to the other person what we have decoded.

Usually it makes sense to send the message back in a statement rather than as a question.

DOROTHY: Isn't that dryer ever going to finish?

GEORGE: You're pretty anxious to leave.

DOROTHY: I sure am. I'm supposed to meet Ed in fifteen minutes.

GEORGE: You're afraid you're going to be late.

DOROTHY: I sure am. Last time we went out I was late, and we ended up missing the beginning of a movie. He was real angry.

GEORGE: You're afraid if you're late he'll be angry with you again tonight.

DOROTHY: That's right.

Or

ROGER *(coming into the house)*: Hi. Where's the newspaper? Dammit, why can't I ever find it in this house? Nothing's ever where it should be.

KEN: You're a little upset today.

ROGER: Yeah, I am upset! I had a miserable day at school, and I feel rotten.

KEN: Got a bad grade on a test today?

ROGER: No, not that. My experiment in lab just blew up today, and three weeks of work went down the drain.

KEN: You're angry about that.

ROGER: Damn right. I've put a lot of work into that experiment, and I'm really bugged that it blew up on me. I let the flask get too hot, and it broke. Everything, all over the floor. I spent an hour just cleaning it up.

KEN: That's really discouraging for you.

ROGER: Yeah. Now I have to start over.

KEN: You have a lot more work cut out for you now.

ROGER: Yeah. .

Or

DANNY: I never want to see you again.

SUE: You're really angry at me.

DANNY: I'm furious at you. Go to hell.

SUE: You feel I was unfair to you by what I did.

DANNY: You sure were. You had no right to do that.

SUE: You feel I wasn't very considerate when I did that.

DANNY: That's right.

In each of these interchanges, the person listening has fed back to the sender what s/he has heard the sender really say.

> In active listening, then, the receiver tries to understand what it is the sender is feeling or what his message means. Then he puts his understanding into his own words (code) and feeds it back for the sender's verification. The receiver *does not* send a message of his own—such as an evaluation, opinion, advice, logic, analysis, or question. He feeds back *only what he feels the sender's message meant*—nothing more, nothing less.[2]

Active listening lets the sender know that s/he is being understood, and has a quality of acceptance which allows and encourages the sender to continue communicating. Not only is the receiver saying "I understand," but s/he is also saying that it is okay to be feeling that way, that "You are okay." Active listening thus meets most of the criteria for good listening discussed in Chapter 5 and is a valuable tool for facilitating thinking and discharge on the part of the sender.

Active listening also avoids the mutual restimulation so common to intimate relationships. One person says something nasty to the other, and s/he responds by saying something nasty back, and so on. Simply feeding back to our

---

[2]Thomas Gordon, *Parent Effectiveness Training* (New York: David McKay Co., Inc., 1975), p. 53. Reprinted by permission of the publishers.

partners what we are hearing them say puts an immediate end to the destructive dynamic of "let's see who can hurt the other the most." Danny and Sue's conversation shows how this dynamic can be short-circuited. For another example we can return to the case of Sam and Janet, in which he was upset over her lack of participation when a friend was present. Let us look at what might have happened if Janet had used active listening when Sam got angry at her:

SAM: Last night when Paul was here you were a real drag. You didn't say a thing all evening. You just sat there for hours. I started wondering if you were still alive. Several times I tried to bring you into the discussion, but you didn't bite once. It really infuriated me.

JANET: You really wanted me to participate more.

SAM: Yeah, I wanted you to talk and carry your share of the ball. Paul is your friend, too.

JANET: You're angry that I wasn't more friendly to him.

SAM: Yes. How can anyone enjoy being with us when you're like that?

JANET: You're afraid that Paul won't want to spend time with us any more.

SAM: Yes, I'm afraid that we won't be able to make any friends at all, with anyone.

JANET: That feels pretty scary.

SAM: It does.

JANET (*no longer active listening*): I was a little withdrawn last night. I think sometimes I need your help to be more energetic and attentive.

SAM: I guess so. . . . What can I do?

By letting Sam know that she understood his meaning and by not responding from her own patterns and feelings, Janet was able to defuse the encounter and actually turn it into a useful interchange.

It is clear from these examples that we must listen for both feelings and content in people's communication to us. We can only let people know we understand them if in fact we *do* understand them—which means paying attention to the feelings that are underlying the code of the message. If we incorrectly interpret the message or miss its main meaning, our active listening may not be very helpful. Consider the following:

A: My boss is a stupid idiot!

B: You think your boss isn't very intelligent *(misses A's angry feelings)*.

A: No, I just can't stand him. I wish he'd drop dead.

B: You'd like him to have a heart attack.

A: Oh, come off it . . . *(A walks away, still angry)*.

By completely missing the point of the sender's message, the receiver came in for some of the sender's angry feelings. If the listener had correctly understood and fed back the speaker's message, the speaker would have felt supported rather than misunderstood, and would have been encouraged to continue telling what happened and how s/he felt.

All of us have the ability to "read" other people's feelings from what they say and how they say it. Tone of voice, facial expression, and posture provide clues to what people are feeling, as do the codes themselves. The main reason we have difficulty reading feelings is that our own feelings and patterns interfere with our perception and cognitive processes. People who were treated insensitively while young tend to develop rigid patterns of insensitivity themselves, for example. It is not that they are incapable of understanding other people's feelings; rather, their ability to do so has been inhibited by how they were hurt and invalidated. When such people have the opportunity to talk about and discharge their own hurts, they in fact do become more sensitive and understanding toward others.

One common mistake people make in active listening is to

parrot the code instead of feeding back the underlying meaning. For example:

A: Boy, am I angry at him!
B: You're really angry at him.
A: I'd like to knock his block off.
B: You'd like to knock his block off.
A: What are you doing? Are you making fun of me?
B: You think I'm making fun of you.
A: You'd better stop it.
B: You want me to stop it.
A: *(Long and elaborate curses.)*

The person sending the message correctly feels misunderstood and poorly listened to. Active listening is effective only if we make an effort really to understand what people are saying, and if our caring is communicated in our responses.

Active listening is a skill, to be used when it will be helpful. It is not a replacement for thinking, and it is not applicable to all situations. If we are asked, "What time is it?" it is not appropriate to reply, "You want to know what time it is." Tell that person the time! We must think all the time about how we respond to people, and no shortcut can replace our thinking. Active listening is an excellent tool, which can be used well or poorly.

Exercise 14 involves active listening in an appropriate situation. Simply feed back to the person the meaning underlying the code s/he is communicating. Continue to do so as long as it seems to be productive. Also, pay attention to the effect of your active listening. With practice, your listening abilities will improve greatly.

Initially, active listening often feels uncomfortable to use. One tendency is to want to feed back the information as a question rather than as a statement, which does not draw out

```
┌─────────────────────────────────────────────────────┐
│                                                     │
│         EXERCISE 14   ACTIVE LISTENING              │
│                                                     │
│   Purpose: To help you build a better relationship  │
│   by developing more effective listening skills.    │
│                                                     │
│   Task: Try using active listening with your        │
│   partner or friend at a time when s/he is feeling  │
│   hurt or angry. Simply feed back your              │
│   understanding of the message your friend          │
│   is communicating to you. It is usually helpful to │
│   respond with a statement rather than a question   │
│   ("You're really angry at him," "You really        │
│   wanted that raise," and so on). Continue          │
│   listening well until your friend's feelings are   │
│   released or s/he takes charge of the problem at   │
│   hand.                                             │
│                                                     │
│   Evaluation:                                       │
│                                                     │
│   Was active listening helpful? Why or why not?     │
│   What was hard about it for you?                   │
│   Were you able to avoid coloring your listening    │
│   with your own thoughts and feelings?              │
│   How could you have listened better?               │
│   What will help you listen better next time?       │
│                                                     │
└─────────────────────────────────────────────────────┘
```

the other person as well. For example, instead of getting this response with questions:

A: I sure hope I get that job.
B: Are you worried that you might not get it?
A: I guess so, a little.
B: Are you feeling scared?
A: Well, not exactly.

statements elicit the following:

A: I sure hope I get that job.
B: You're worried that you might not get it.

A: Yes. There were lots of applicants, and I'm sure some had better credentials or connections or something.

B: It's pretty scary thinking that you might not be able to find a job.

A: It really is.

Active listening can be an enormously effective communication skill. When I have asked people in my classes to practice it, they have reported much success. One woman got her shy girlfriend to talk about herself for the first time. Another woman helped her husband deal with a difficult problem he was having at work. One man used active listening to establish better communication with his boss; another, to help his daughter deal with problems she was having with her homework. In each of these situations, active listening enabled the sender to talk about what was really happening and to think more clearly about her or his problem.

Another application of active listening is in conjunction with I-messages. Often people will respond to I-messages from their own restimulated feelings. If we can then use active listening in our response to them, we can help them deal with their feelings and at the same time establish a firm basis for further communication. After they feel less defensive or upset, we can repeat the I-message; eventually through this process we should be able to be heard. Consider the following conversation:

JODY: Patricia, would you please lower your radio? When it's so loud, I can't concentrate, and I have an exam tomorrow.

PATRICIA: Oh, you never like my music. You'd like this place to be like a morgue.

JODY: You think it's unfair of me to ask you to lower the radio.

PATRICIA: I do. You always want it quiet in the house. What about me? Don't I have any rights?

JODY: You think you should be able to have the radio on louder more of the time.

PATRICIA: That's right. I do.

JODY: That seems reasonable to me. I do have an exam tomorrow, though, and I lose my concentration when the radio is so loud. How about lowering it tonight, and tomorrow we can talk about what we can do in the future so that we both feel okay. All right?

PATRICIA: Okay.

By using active listening, Jody was able to both hear Patricia's concern and get Patricia to hear her own. This result did not itself solve the problem, but it did lay the groundwork for a good solution later—which would not have happened had Jody responded to Patricia's You-message out of her own feelings.

For further examples of active listening and a more detailed discussion, read *Parent Effectiveness Training*, by Thomas Gordon. Although his discussion deals specifically with parent-child relationships, it relates well to all forms of human interaction.

STATING WANTS AND NEEDS

Our feelings and rigid behavior patterns interfere with our stating directly what we want or need in many different kinds of situations. It often is hard to say exactly what we would like to see happen, or to say what we really need. This lack of assertiveness is of course rooted in each of our individual experiences and relates to painful emotion we incurred while in some way asserting ourselves. Maybe as infants we cried when we were hungry but were not fed, or maybe we were punished for speaking out of turn in school. In either case, we developed patterns that affect our ability to communicate.

One way to combat these patterns is to make a conscious effort to say precisely what we want and need, and to encourage others to do the same. This step avoids the manipulative behavior arising from our patterns and facilitates open communication and problem-solving. Rather than trying to get other people to fill our wants and needs by making them feel bad or pressuring them, we can build more solid relationships by treating our friends and partners with the same respect with which we would like to be treated. This method involves openness and trust. If they choose to meet our wants, great. If they do not, then we can think about modifying our wants or getting them met in some other way.

Exercise 15 is designed to help each of us state our wants and needs clearly and openly. Be sure to avoid the common mistake of using the word "need" when you really mean "want." (For example, say "I want us to be friends," rather than "I need us to be friends.") Using "need" instead of "want" tends to be manipulative, because it implies that we will suffer some harmful consequence if our "need" is not fulfilled.

EXERCISE 15   STATING YOUR WANTS AND NEEDS

Purpose: To help you avoid manipulative situations by stating your wants and needs directly.

Task: Next time you are in a situation in which your getting what you want is dependent on your partner's agreement or cooperation, try stating your wants clearly rather than attempting to manipulate your partner.

Evaluation:

What effect did stating your wants and needs directly have on the interaction?
How did your partner respond to your directness?
What will you do differently next time?
What was hard for you about being straightforward in stating what you wanted?

As with all the exercises in this book, Exercise 15 is not a cure-all to the problems that abound in intimate relationships. The way to make love relationships work well is to discharge the feelings that interfere with our thinking, our feelings of love, and our best functioning, and to act on our clear thinking. All the exercises and tools in the world will not make much difference if we do not think about what we are doing. Concerning communication, the most important thing we can do is to let other people know that we love and care about them, and that they are safe to be themselves with us. If we can do this, then the communication skills presented in this chapter will be easy to learn and practice.

seven
Feelings, And What to Do With Them

The other night, dear, as I lay sleeping,
I dreamed I held you in my arms,
When I awoke, dear, I was mistaken,
So I lay down my head and cried.

From the folksong,
"You Are My Sunshine"

It is clear that *how feelings are dealt with is crucial to how well relationships function.* This chapter is devoted to developing an understanding of the role of feelings in human behavior and the important part discharge plays in freeing us from the effects of emotional and physical distress.

Because they are widespread throughout our culture, false assumptions about feelings have been inculcated in all of us. Some of these myths have been mentioned previously but bear repeating here. They all affect how we think about feelings and what we do when we are confronted with them.

1. *We can feel love for or be emotionally intimate with only one other person.* Discussed extensively in Chapters 1 and 2,

this myth is based on the false assumption that feelings of love and intimacy are things to be hoarded and guarded and cannot be shared with more than one person. Thus we face many problems when we are confronted with the reality of loving more than one person. We are then in the curious position of feeling guilty because we feel too much love.

2. *Crying is bad.* This assumption results in the belief that crying should be stopped whenever and wherever it is found, an attitude harmful to both the person maintaining it and the person invalidated for crying.

3. *Crying means falling apart.* The myth is that people who cry cannot cope and must be in a state of extreme duress. Crying is also seen as an indication of incompetence, and is often ridiculed. This belief is based on a misunderstanding of the role of crying and contributes to our cultural invalidation of it.

4. *People cannot think when they cry.* It is assumed that people think and function better when they "pull themselves together" and hold in their feelings. Experience has shown that crying has just the opposite effect.

5. *Crying is childish.* This myth is best epitomized perhaps by the ultimate put-down, "Crybaby!" The assumption is that young people cry and adults do not, and that therefore it is immature to cry. Not only does this belief invalidate young people, but it also deters us from a very human activity.

6. *Being afraid is bad.* Feeling scared is supposedly a sign of weakness, and therefore is ridiculed. People who are afraid are often goaded into acting tough. The effect of this myth is that we feel guilty for feeling afraid.

7. *Trembling involves weakness and incompetence.* The same myths surrounding fear also encompass the act of trembling or shaking, "Scaredy-cat" and "chicken" are two of the disparaging phrases used in childhood; we may no longer use the words as adults, but the attitude remains.

8. *Acting angry is a sign of strength and toughness.* The myth is that to be powerful and important persons we must be tough, angry, and hard. Generally we respect anger (mostly in men)

when we see it, and allow people to take out their angry feelings on us or others.

9. *Men don't cry.* Part of the sexism inherent in our culture, it is assumed to be improper for men ever to cry. Men are supposed to be strong and stoical, to "take it like a man." A crying man contradicts all our stereotypes about what a man should be and how he should act. This aspect of men's conditioning is tremendously hurtful to all people—men, women, and children.

10. *Yawning means we are tired.* We assume that people yawn when they are tired or bored. This is in fact not necessarily true, as will be discussed later.

11. "If it feels good, do it." This attitude, which has gained prominence in recent years, implies that feelings are a good guide for behavior; but it can and often does lead to much irrational and harmful action adversely affecting other human beings.

12. *Rational behavior ignores feelings.* It is often assumed that rational behavior and thinking are "cold and unfeeling," that people must either act on the basis of their feelings or ignore them. The possibility that we can take feelings into account and still act on our thinking is not considered.

These false assumptions about feelings affect almost all aspects of our lives, particularly our interactions with the people with whom we are close. It is with us that our intimate friends are most likely to share their feelings. How we respond makes a difference not only in their relationship with us but also in their own sense of themselves and their ability to function well in the world.

THE TRUTH ABOUT FEELINGS

Having feelings is a natural part of being human. Feelings are found in every human society and are experienced by all human beings of all ages. Although it is sometimes difficult to pinpoint them, feelings have definite physiological bases. How we label feelings may differ from person to person or from culture to culture, but their existence is universal.

We can divide emotions into positive feelings, those that feel good or pleasurable, and negative feelings, those that feel bad or uncomfortable. Positive and negative feelings are not complementary, although their presence or absence is related to the fulfillment of real human needs. In general, positive feelings result from needs being met, and negative ones from needs not being met or some hurt being inflicted in the past or present. For the sake of clarity, let us begin our discussion with the infant, a human being who has little past experience.

When infants' needs for food, water, love, attention, and so on are met, they feel good. They are alert, attentive, happy, and full of curiosity—the natural state of human beings when their needs are fulfilled and physical or emotional distress is absent.

When their needs are not met, or when some form of physical or emotional hurt is inflicted on them, infants feel bad. They cannot tell us in words what they are feeling, but they immediately release the feelings by what we are calling discharge. When they are scared or hurt, they cry. When they are angry, they rage, flailing their arms and legs in a tantrum. When they are undergoing some sort of minor physical distress, they yawn and stretch.

The acts of crying, raging, yawning, stretching, sweating, trembling, laughing, and sometimes talking, and changes of body temperature are the methods of physical discharge. They are physiological processes, and are observable phenomena. They are not learned, being innate behavioral traits common to all human beings. They are furthermore the mechanisms by which human beings heal themselves from physical and emotional hurts. If the cause of the distress is removed and the infant is allowed and encouraged to release his or her feelings, s/he will completely recover from the emotional effects of the hurt. In addition, the body's healing from physical problems will proceed with speed and efficiency.

For example, I was recently among several adults who were playing with a three-month-old infant. One of the adults started laughing at the infant's facial expression, and he responded to the laughter by crying. Whether he felt embarrassed, scared, or grieved we could not tell, but it was clear by his response that he was feeling bad. Rather than trying to stop his crying, we gave him our attention, touched him, and allowed him to continue. After about five minutes he stopped, and after gazing around the room at us and playing with somebody's finger, he acted as if the incident had not occurred: The healing process was complete.

Another example involves a time I stayed with a five-year-old girl, Rachel, while her mother went out for an afternoon. She really did not want her mother to go, and when her mother left, she went up to her room and slammed the door behind her. Because I knew Rachel well and knew she felt fairly safe with me, I went up to her room and opened the door. She immediately started screaming and pounding the bed with her arms and legs, yelling at me to get out and leave her alone. I stayed with her, and she continued screaming and crying. After about fifteen minutes she stopped, and with my assistance brought her attention away from the painful feelings and back to the present. Suddenly it was as if nothing had happened—she was active and alert, with no trace of bad feelings left over.

Discharge is innately a spontaneous process. When an infant or a young child experiences emotional or physical distress, s/he will immediately begin to discharge. Unless it is interrupted by some external force, it will continue until recovery is complete. If you have the good fortune to know an infant or toddler, you can observe directly this phenomenon yourself. When s/he starts crying, simply allow him or her to continue to cry until s/he appears to have finished. Often hugging him or her will facilitate the discharge, but give whatever support you can to help the infant continue to cry (except hitting or yelling). Pay attention to what happens, and watch how quickly and totally s/he emerges from the distress.

Of course, if the cause of the distress continues, we cannot expect discharge to result in the cessation of painful emotion. If an infant is hungry, having him or her cry about it will not completely relieve the feeling unless s/he is also fed. We thus cannot assume blindly or without thinking that discharge is all that is needed. We also must look for the cause of the painful feelings, and stop it if appropriate.

With each kind of painful emotion there is associated a particular mode of discharge. That is, the form of discharge is inexorably related to the kind of hurt, and it will spontaneously occur when the hurt is experienced unless it is inhibited in the present or was so in the past. The modes of discharge are related to painful emotion in the following table:[1]

Kind of Painful Emotion	*Mode of Discharge*
Zest (absence of painful emotion)	Happy relaxation, turning of attention away from experience of hurt
Boredom	Laughter, animated talking, reluctant talking
Light Angers	Laughter, warm perspiration
Heavy Angers	Angry noises, violent movements, warm perspiration
Light Fears (embarrassments)	Laughter, cold perspiration
Heavy Fears	Trembling, shivering, cold perspiration, active kidneys
Griefs	Tears, sobbing
Physical Pains and Tensions	Yawns, stretching, scratching

[1] From *Fundamentals of Co-Counseling Manual* (Seattle: Rational Island Publishers, 1962), p. 7.

Each mode of discharge is an observable, physical phenomenon. In a sense the discharge has more of an objective reality than the painful emotion; it is certainly more identifiable and easier to label. What we call "anxiety"or "depression" is simply one or more of the above painful feelings that have not been released.

The fundamental mistake made in most cultures concerning discharge is that the hurt itself (the painful emotion) has been equated with the healing process (the discharge). It is assumed therefore that if we stop someone from crying, s/he will stop grieving or feeling sad; if we stop someone from raging, s/he will stop feeling angry; if we stop someone from trembling, s/he will no longer be scared. This basic misconception has resulted in our trying to stop the discharge of those around us, because we wanted them to stop hurting. How many times have we heard people say, "There, there, don't cry, it will be all right"? Or maybe it was done more harshly: "If you don't stop crying, I'll really give you something to cry about!" Of course, stopping the discharge does not stop the hurt.

Our parents, siblings, teachers, and friends laughed at, cajoled, and punished us into stopping our discharge because they were operating out of their own restimulated behavior patterns. For example: Maria is the mother of Roberta, a delightful six-year-old girl. Sometimes when Roberta cries, Maria gets angry at her, and other times she comforts her, but she almost always tries to stop the crying.

MARIA: I don't like to see her cry. I want her to be happy. I was unhappy myself as a child. We were very poor, and had very little money. We all had to work and scrape to get by. It was hard, and I felt bad a lot. I want it to be different for Roberta; I want her to be happy.

COUNSELOR: What does her crying remind you of? First thought.

MARIA: That's funny, I haven't thought about this one for a long time. I just remembered a time when my father hit

Tony for some reason. I can't remember why right now. Anyway, he was hitting Tony, and Tony was screaming. I started screaming at Dad to stop. I think he yelled something at me, I can't remember what.

COUNSELOR: Yes you can. What might he have said?

MARIA: Maybe something like, "Shut up or you'll get it too."

COUNSELOR: A little bit scary for you.

MARIA: It sure was . . . *(laughs)*. I was scared to death. I really thought he was hurting Tony.

COUNSELOR: What would you like to have said to him right then? What's your first thought.

MARIA: Stop hitting him.

COUNSELOR: Tell him again, as if your telling him will make him stop.

MARIA *(more assertively and louder)*: Stop hurting him! Stop it! *(Starts crying.)*

Roberta's crying restimulated Maria's own distress recordings, so that she could not think rationally about what was appropriate for Roberta. Because a component of our distress recordings is that our discharge was inhibited, it is common for us to inhibit the discharge of others.

Distress recordings resulting from the inhibition of discharge affect not only what we do in the present but also *how we feel*. A large proportion of the painful emotion we feel in our everyday adult lives is caused by restimulation, rather than by new hurts. The distinction here is crucial, because it affects how we deal with situations in real life. Restimulated feelings feel every bit as bad as those caused by current hurt, but they should affect our behavior differently.

For example, if we touch a hot pan and burn a finger, the cause of the pain is immediate. We may be reminded also of past hurts and have past feelings restimulated, but the major source of the painful feeling is a new hurt. One thing we will definitely want to do in this situation is to remove our finger from the source of the hurt, the hot pan. We will also want to discharge our painful feelings, and deal appropriately with the physical hurt.

If, in contrast, we go to a party at which we know very few people and feel depressed and left out, most of our bad feeling results from restimulation. There is little in the present situation that could be considered a new hurt. Similarly, if our partner forgets to wash the dishes or leaves the newspaper in the bathroom, it hardly can be called a new hurt. The painful emotion almost entirely is caused by undischarged distressful incidents from our past.

Thus, although it made sense to take our finger away from the pot to avoid feeling pain, it may not make sense to avoid parties just because they restimulate old, hurt feelings. We should continue to go to parties, discharge the restimulated painful feelings before or after, and do our best to avoid being controlled by those old recordings. This response might entail a concerted effort to make friends and talk to strangers, despite how bad it feels.

Restimulated feelings, like feelings directly resulting from new hurts, need to be discharged. If they are not, they add another layer of distress onto the original hurt, making the rigid behavior pattern more ingrained and encompassing— and thereby requiring more discharge. As they get older, people often seem to get more rigid: More and more layers of distress have been added and not discharged, resulting in stronger patterns.

In addition to physical injuries, other painful feelings in adults can be caused by new hurts—for example, hurts from oppression. These hurts are imposed on a group of individuals having something in common, and they provide another group with disproportionate advantages and privileges. Among the various kinds of oppression are sexism, racism, anti-Semitism, and the discrimination against homosexuals and the working class. The hurts and invalidation inflicted on people oppressed in these ways are ongoing, and are thus new hurts. (They also restimulate old hurts.) Blacks, for example, were not only treated as inferior while growing up but continue to experience subtle and not so subtle dehumanization on a daily basis. It is not just that old hurts are being recalled; the new ones are very real indeed.

Let us reiterate some of the major points we have presented so far. Our awareness of them is crucial to our understanding the origin of feelings and their role in human behavior.

1. Painful feelings in infants result from their human needs not being met, emotional or physical hurts being inflicted upon them, or some physical dysfunction.
2. When the natural healing process of discharge is inhibited, painful feelings are tied to the distressful experience itself, resulting in a distress recording.
3. Painful feelings in adults, except those related to oppression, death of a loved one, physical injury, or the aging process, involve the restimulation of old distress recordings and are mostly not new hurts in and of themselves.
4. Feelings from both new and old hurts need to be discharged. If they are not, distress recordings will result in increased operation of rigid behavior patterns.

Not discharging has other adverse effects. Our thinking becomes frozen in the areas in which we have been hurt and have not discharged. For example, many of us frequently were treated unfairly as children when we did something that displeased our parents. Some of us were physically abused, some were sent to our rooms for the slightest reason, some were threatened, and some were ridiculed. When we did not release the feelings attached to this kind of treatment, distress recordings developed. Now it is difficult for us to think well about how to relate to young people when we ourselves are upset with their behavior. Often what we "think" we should do is precisely what was done to us. If we were hit, we hit them; if we were yelled at, we scream at them. Sometimes we may respond by doing the exact opposite of what was done to us; because we were treated so harshly, we may allow our children to do whatever they like. In either case, the ways we were hurt affect our thinking.

Lack of discharge also leads to emotional numbing and insensitivity. We become less in touch with our positive and negative feelings, to the point where it sometimes seems as though we cannot feel anything. Not being in touch with feelings does not mean they are not there, however. To the contrary, emotional numbing is the consequence of having "shut off" feelings in the past because it was not safe to release them. When distress recordings are restimulated in the present, we will again shut off the feelings. This cycle of distress, restimulation, and shut-off will diminish with adequate discharge.

Insensitivity to others is directly related to the inhibition of discharge. As our thinking is impaired, so are our powers of perception; as we become more distressed, we tend to focus more attention on our own hurt and have less attention for others' feelings. Lack of attention is often noticeable with new hurts; someone who has just broken an arm or lost a job will not be very sensitive to others until s/he gets rid of some of her or his negative feelings. If we do not discharge and distress continues to accumulate, the amount of attention we have for others continues to decrease.

Moreover, the inhibition of discharge often leads to physical distress. There are many physical ailments known to be related to "stress" and "tension," for example, colitis, ulcers, headaches, arthritis, asthma, and heart disease. The exact physiological relationship between the discharge process and these ailments is not yet known, although there is evidence that physical symptoms caused by tension tend to disappear when enough discharge has occurred. Further, recovery from other ailments tends to be faster when emotional discharge is facilitated. Inhibiting discharge seems to result in people being ill longer and more frequently.

The process of emotional discharge is not a gimmick. It is

not a technique recently discovered, nor is it a fad which will disappear with the passing years. It is rather the natural human response to painful emotion.

CONTROL PATTERNS

None of us ever willingly stopped discharging. From being goaded, laughed at, threatened, and physically punished, we developed specific behaviors that interfere with the discharge process. These *control patterns* block our discharge even when there is no one trying to stop it. Like other patterns, these operate in the present whenever they are restimulated.

I have a good friend named Albert, who is six years old. Whenever Albert is upset, he covers his eyes with his hands. If someone pries his hands off his eyes, he immediately starts crying. If that person lets go of Albert's hands, he immediately places them over his eyes again and stops crying. Pull his hands away, and he begins crying again. This behavior began when Albert was quite young. He realized that his crying was not acceptable, and that he needed to find a way to make himself stop in order to avoid being punished or ridiculed. Covering and rubbing his eyes served this purpose. Now Albert does not even need to be told to stop; when the feelings arise in him, he automatically covers his eyes. This behavior constitutes a control pattern.

Whenever Charles, aged thirty, feels bothered or upset, he starts to pace around the room. His pacing is a sure sign that he feels distressed and needs to discharge. Because he has more controls than Albert, just sitting him down is not enough to bring discharge. It is, however, a necessary precondition.

Other readily observable and common control patterns are

biting one's lip, darting one's eyes around the room, blowing one's nose, looking down, changing the subject, and so forth. Every person's control patterns are of course unique, based on his or her own unique experiences. All of them must be interrupted for discharge to occur.

One other very common control pattern involves the use of drugs. All drugs affecting the central nervous system inhibit the discharge process and/or the process of reevaluation of past events, which occurs spontaneously with discharge. The effect of caffeine, nicotine, alcohol, marijuana, barbiturates, heroin, and other narcotics is to inhibit discharge. How many people do we know who come home from a hard day at work and immediately have a couple of drinks? Or people who feel too nervous without a cigarette? Or people whose feelings keep them awake at night, so they take some sleeping pills? Not only are these control patterns physically harmful, but by inhibiting discharge, they also contribute to the development of more rigid behavior patterns.

The inhibition of discharge is an individual phenomenon which relates to each of our personal experiences. However, different kinds of discharge seems to be more inhibited in one sex than in the other. Crying is much more socially unacceptable for men than for women, and men have generally been punished more than women for crying. As a result, it is usually harder for men to regain their ability to cry. In contrast, women have been consistently punished more than men for getting angry. Thus it is often quite difficult for women to get in touch with and discharge their feelings of anger and rage.

This differential inhibition of discharge in men and women is directly related to sexism and the differing roles of men and women in our society. Men are forced into competitive and aggressive roles, and can function in these roles only as long as their feelings are held in or taken out on others. Similarly, women have been conditioned to be accommodating and to put other people's concerns and welfare above their own. If women were in touch with and discharged their anger, they would not endure being second-class citizens. Thus the blocking of discharge plays a major role in how our society functions.

A WORD ABOUT ANGER

In Chapter 1 we talked about the difference between discharge and dramatization. Discharge is the physical process of getting rid of painful emotion, whereas dramatization involves acting out the painful feelings instead and is itself a behavior pattern. As such, dramatization has the same effect as other control patterns—to keep us from discharging the painful emotion we are experiencing. Dramatizations must be interrupted for discharge to occur.

Concerning anger, we must be especially careful to distinguish between dramatization and discharge. In infants and young children the discharge of anger is immediate and spontaneous. The person kicks out in all directions, the voice becomes high-pitched, movements are violent, skin temperature rises, and the person sweats profusely. There is no calculation or premeditation in the anger; it is quick and self-justified. Next time you see anger in an infant, observe it closely and do not try to stop it. The infant is doing just what s/he needs to do.

With older children and adults, the feeling of anger and the associated behavior tends to be quite different. First, it seems that anger is usually a secondary response to a situation. In counseling sessions it often quickly becomes apparent that feelings of grief and fear underlie the anger, and the anger soon gives way to these other feelings. That is, the anger seems to be a patterned response to the feelings of grief and fear.

Second, adults seldom discharge anger in the same way as young children under five or six. The violent flailing of limbs and the spontaneity of sound and movement usually are absent from adult responses to anger. Instead, adults verbally hurt other people, physically hurt them, or make loud noises designed to let them know how angry they are. None of these responses are real discharge; instead they replay old distress recordings and are based on restimulation. Therefore, this behavior does not free people from behavior patterns based on old hurts. If it did, door slammers and other violent people would be much more rational than they are.

In many of the counseling sessions presented in this book, it will be noticed that angry words and motions are often used to get to the deeper feelings related to crying and trembling. In the right situation, pounding a pillow or screaming angry words can lead to discharge or may be accompanied by discharge in the forms of trembling and perspiring. Even in these cases, we have to think about whether we are using anger to "get at" the other person or to make him or her feel bad or guilty. This reaction of course is mostly likely to occur if the person listening to our discharge is very close to us.

FACILITATING DISCHARGE

The relationship between discharge and new hurts is easily understandable. We are hurt, we feel bad, we cry about it, and it's gone. It has been discovered in addition, however, that by discharging in the present we can recover from the effects of *past* hurts. With adequate discharge rigid behavior patterns disappear, and *reevaluation* spontaneously occurs. The distress recording formed at the time of the hurt dissolves, old information is interpreted correctly, and the connection between the painful emotion and the details of the incident are erased.

Discharge seems to occur when there is a *balance of attention* between the feeling of distress and the present, unpainful reality, and when no control patterns are blocking it. If people focus entirely on how bad they felt in the past, often they will be sunk in the distress and unable to discharge it. Similarly, if they try to focus their attention completely away from the distress, they will not be able to release their painful feelings. What works is to divide one's attention between the hurt itself and information or material contradicting it.

For example, Ken has been married to Robin for many years, and she recently decided to end their marriage. A few days after she told Ken she wanted a divorce, Ken talked to me about how he was feeling:

KEN: You know, Michael, I'm nothing without her. She's the only important thing in my life. Without her I'm nothing.

ME: It feels like that, but it's not true. You are a good person.

KEN *(starts crying)*: If you only knew the rotten things I've done. . . . She's what makes the things I do important . . . *(stops crying)*.

ME: You're important all by yourself. You are a good person.

KEN: That's garbage . . . *(starts crying again)* . . . I'm no good, she's the only thing that makes me okay. . . . All the things I've done . . . *(stops crying)*.

ME: You've only done those things because you were hurting yourself.

KEN: Maybe, but. . . .

ME: Ken, you *are* good.

(Ken starts crying again.)

When Ken was sunk into his own grief, he was not discharging. My firmly telling him that he was good brought his attention out of his distress enough so that he could discharge some of those feelings. Each time he focused all his attention on his pain, he stopped crying, and each time I reminded him that he was okay he started again. When his attention was balanced between how bad he was feeling and my support, the discharge came spontaneously.

In other situations, people must have their attention drawn back to the hurt in order for them to discharge. It is often useful, for example, to have people tell the story of distressful incidents over and over again. As they go over it, they again get in touch with the painful feelings they experienced at the time, and are able to discharge them. In this case we help them attain a balance of attention by focusing on the hurt, because they are already feeling safe and secure in the present.

There are no rules for facilitating discharge. Generally, the more that people have discharged themselves, the better able they are to be effective counselors or facilitators of discharge. Their own feelings tend to interfere less and their attitude toward discharge will be more relaxed, making it easier for people to discharge in their presence.

> What the [person] has needed all along is the warm understanding regard of another friendly human who will not get upset by his distresses while he allows himself to feel, express and discharge the stored-up upsets and be free of them. All the familiar tricks of analyzing, or suggesting, tend to get in the way of the [person] and prevent this thorough discharge and re-evaluation which can follow.[2]

The most important thing we can do to help another person discharge is to give him or her our complete attention. Our attention establishes a balance of attention in that person because it contradicts the conditions of the original hurt—s/he was not receiving good attention or being thought about when the hurt occurred. Giving our complete attention means looking at the person, being interested in what s/he is saying, thinking about him or her, and appearing relaxed. It also means not talking too much ourselves or shifting the focus onto ourselves or some other subject.

There are some techniques we can use to help people discharge their feelings. Of course, these techniques only work if they are used when the situation is appropriate and if the listener has good attention.

---

[2] Harvey Jackins, *The Human Situation* (Seattle: Rational Island Publishers, 1973), pp. 29–30.

1. Have people tell their life story. People will invariably talk about some of the painful things that have happened to them. When they reach distressing parts, they will in some way let us know—by laughing, coughing, blinking their eyes, or fidgeting nervously. We can then help them focus on these particular areas.

2. Touch them. Touching and hugging often contradict the isolation that accompanied the original hurtful experiences. The safety provided by the physical contact frequently allows the discharge to occur.

3. Have them tell a painful incident over and over again. If a good balance of attention is maintained and control patterns are circumvented, as the story is repeated more and more discharge will be obtained.

4. Firmly contradict or interrupt the pattern. If people are verbalizing or acting out a distress recording, often discharge will occur if we contradict the pattern and point out the unpainful reality. (See the previous example: "Without her I'm nothing." "That's not true. You're a good person.")

5. Have them contradict the pattern themselves. If the distress recording says that they are stupid, try having them say, "I'm smart." This positive contradiction of the pattern often brings copious discharge, as well as reminding them of what is real outside the painful feelings.

6. Have them repeat a phrase that obviously involves their feelings. For example, if a woman is relating an incident and tears start to well up in her eyes when she says, "And then he told me to get lost," we might ask her, "What did he say to you?" Making her repeat the phrase "Get lost!" may produce many tears, in which case it makes sense for us to stay with this phrase for a while.

7. Ask the question, "What's your first thought?" This technique has been used extensively in the counseling sessions included in this book. In conjunction with other questions, it provides uncensored clues into what is really happening. (For example: "What would you like to say to him—what is your first thought?")

8. Verbally encourage them to discharge. Simply saying "Go ahead" or "Stay with it" is often enough to start people laughing or crying or doing whatever they need to do. Of course, this technique will work only if people are on the verge of discharge.

9. Use active listening. Sometimes feeding back to people the meaning behind what they are saying will immediately bring them to laughter or tears.

10. Interrupt control patterns. Stopping a foot from tapping, insisting that eye contact be maintained, and so on will greatly facilitate discharge. Sometimes we can ask people to stop doing the control pattern; other times we will have to physically prevent them from doing it; and other times it is effective to mimic the pattern ourselves.

11. Copy or mimic the pattern. Sometimes it helps people get outside the pattern enough to discharge the painful feelings if we act out the pattern in front of them. For example, if a man is saying in a depressed tone of voice that "Nobody likes me," it might be effective to use the same tone or even a more depressed tone and say, "Yeah, nobody likes me either." This technique may produce laughter or crying. Of course we must be careful to avoid any hint of ridicule in our mimicry.

With all these techniques, thought and awareness are necessary. None of them works by itself, and none of them is appropriate for every situation. When the proper conditions are established, discharge will occur spontaneously. None of us ever has to "try" to cry. We can, however, stop our control patterns from operating and balance our attention between the painful emotion and the unpainful reality outside the feelings. When this balance occurs, the crying, laughing, or whatever will come naturally.

The physical mechanism of discharge is the only thing I know of that has the potential to completely free us of the effects of past distress, the rigid patterns of behavior with which we are all saddled. Attempts to circumvent the discharge process can modify behavior patterns but not eliminate them. We have to feel again how bad it felt back then, only this time we must release the feelings.

However, we do not have the right and in fact cannot force people to cry or tremble or otherwise release their feelings. If people are feeling pressured they will not feel safe, and discharge will not be forthcoming anyway. What we can do is let other people know that discharge is okay and good, and invite them to discharge in our presence. This attitude of invitation rather than pressure will help other people feel secure and loved, establishing the necessary preconditions for discharge.

Another way to encourage discharge in others is to model the process ourselves. Modeling is particularly effective with young people in whom discharge is not so inhibited as in adults. By laughing and crying and yawning and trembling, and at the same time maintaining an attitude that it is okay to do so, we will contradict at least some of the negative conditioning people have internalized concerning these mechanisms of emotional release.

In Exercise 16, we are encouraged to facilitate discharge in another person by giving him or her our aware attention when s/he is feeling bad.

The most important thing to remember in this exercise is to maintain a relaxed attitude toward discharge, no matter how bad the person may be feeling. We must be interested and concerned, not showing signs of worry and upset that will interfere with the other person's discharge. It is appropriate while listening to others to swallow our own feelings temporarily, and then afterward to take the time ourselves to discharge the painful feelings.

Above all, we must remember that discharge is the natural healing process to recover from distress, no more and no less. By its use we can regain our ability to use our functioning intelligence to guide our actions instead of old, rigid patterns of behavior.

EXERCISE 16   ENCOURAGING DISCHARGE

Purpose: To help a friend use the natural process of emotional discharge to recover from the effects of painful experiences.

Task: When a friend who feels fairly safe with you is feeling distressed or upset, give your loving attention and help him or her focus on what is hurting. If your friend's attention is correctly balanced between the hurt and the safety provided by you, discharge will occur. Often the best approach is just to ask what happened, and have him or her tell the story over and over again. Do not let yourself look worried or upset because they are experiencing physical or emotional pain, because this will decrease the feeling of safety. Maintain an attitude of relaxed and delighted support. If discharge does not occur, do not be disappointed—for people who have not cried or trembled in years, beginning to do so may take awhile.

Evaluation:

What happened?

How did it feel to you?

What did you do well?

What will you do better next time?

Feelings are not a good guide for action. Sensible behavior may feel good, and it may not. Sometimes completely irrational behavior—such as murder, rape, and the use of narcotics—"feels good." Sometimes rational behavior feels awful, as in kicking a drug habit or relearning how to be assertive.

Feelings are meant to be felt. If they are good feelings, enjoy them. If they are painful feelings, discharge them. In neither case should they determine our behavior.

The only productive guide to action is thinking, which means evaluating all the information, including feelings. All human beings would function in this way all the time were it not for the distress recordings formed because discharge was inhibited. Fortunately, we can use the discharge process to free our ability to think.

eight
On Fighting And Conflict

HE: By the way, Jack's coming over tonight.

SHE: What, again? What do you see in him?

HE: He's my friend. What of it?

SHE: I can't stand him. He gives me the creeps.

HE: Well, I think your friends are pretty crummy myself. When Polly comes over she makes me sick, she's so stuck up. So you can just shut up about my friends.

SHE: No I won't. You always bring these people home I can't stand. It's my house, too, and I have a say in who comes to visit.

HE: Listen, as long as I'm bringing in most of the money around here, I'm going to bring home whomever I like.

SHE: As if you're the only one who does any work. What do you think I do all day, just sit around? I work harder than you do. You've told me how you mostly loaf on the job, so don't give me any of that garbage about how hard you work.

HE: You're always complaining. You never like anything. If you don't like the way things are, you can just shove it.

This is my house, and I'll do what I like. Stop being a lazy, good-for-nothing complainer.

SHE: You are a pig! *(Starts crying.)*

(He stomps out the door, slamming it behind him.)

Such ugly encounters occur in almost all love relationships at some point or other. Their frequency of course varies from relationship to relationship, depending on people's feelings about themselves, how they handle their feelings, their behavior patterns, what is happening in their lives, and their cultural patterns affecting conflict. Even the most "genteel" people have fights; they may be enacted differently, but they are fights nevertheless.

Why do we fight? Is fighting an inevitable aspect of intimate relationships? Many of us would say yes, that that is just the way people are; but fights are almost always regretted afterward, when we are no longer caught up in hurt and angry feelings.

People turn an interaction into a fight by dramatizing their feelings at one another. It is not just that people are feeling bad, but that they direct their feelings at their loved ones rather than discharging them. Often the origin of the painful feelings is unrelated to the other person. We have all been in situations where it seemed as if another person was just itching for a fight. What was actually happening was that s/he was feeling bad and was not discharging the feelings. Our interaction served as a catalyst for releasing their feelings— right at us!

What occurs in fights is that one person feels bad and dramatizes his or her feelings at the other person. The other person is then reminded of past painful incidents, and his or her own painful feelings and distress recordings are restimulated. Instead of discharging these feelings (it seldom feels safe to do so under the circumstances), s/he dramatizes back at the other person. This behavior continues with both persons feeling bad and playing their distress recordings at each other. If the situation really gets out of hand, people go so far as to say the most hurtful things they can think of, and they may even hurt their partner or friend physically. None of this behavior is based on clear thinking or functioning human intelligence.

However, fights are not all bad, and through them much useful information often comes to the surface. People say what is bothering them, how they are hurting, and what they are needing. They often see what rigid patterns their partners have and how they are affected by them. In the argument at the beginning of this chapter, for example, the woman was telling the man that he had a pattern of thinking only about himself: "You always bring these people home. . . . It's my house, too, and I have a say in who comes to visit." She was also telling him how she felt in response to this pattern. Getting this information out in the open frequently helps relationships function more effectively.

During a fight, however, it is difficult to hear the information being shared. First, it is often communicated as invalidation, the message being that "You are bad because you have this pattern." Second, the level of painful emotion felt by both people is usually so high that the information probably will not be received and interpreted correctly. It is not unusual for people to forget what was said and remember mainly the feelings. Third, because messages are so laden with hurt and angry feelings, much awareness and attention are required to decode what is being said—attention lacking in the middle of a fight.

Destructive fighting is not necessary. The restimulative element in fights is the product of distress recordings and can be avoided. If either one of the persons involved is thinking freshly and clearly, the necessary discussion and resolution of conflicts still can occur without invective or invalidation. The key is not to respond out of our own distress recordings but instead to use all the skills at our disposal to deal constructively with the issues at hand. Everyone can do it, and only one person needs to act rationally to avoid destructive fights.

WHAT TO DO ABOUT CONFLICTS

No two people have identical interests and concerns. Within every relationship there exist real, identifiable differences between the persons involved, ranging from different times of rising in the morning to different cultural, ethnic, religious, or class backgrounds. Some form of conflict is nearly inevitable, and is certainly healthy. If people want different things, and want things of each other, it is natural to assume that at some points their desires will conflict—Jill wants to go boating with Judy, but Judy wants to stay home and read. People's activities and short- and long-term goals will not necessarily coincide just because they love each other. One of the joys of being with other people, in fact, is hearing a different perspective, learning how they perceive and interpret their reality. The difference between their understanding and our own is one of the main goads to our own thinking.

It does not make much sense to want or expect people we love to have the same likes as we do. Such a desire is unrealistic and can only lead to disappointment and frustration. The only times I have seen two people who seemed never to disagree were relationships in which one of them had strong submissive patterns and completely subordinated his or her own interests to those of the partner. This is not a rational solution to conflict.

Conflicts do not arise merely because people want different things. They are also affected and influenced by the feelings and distress recordings of both people and whatever extenuating circumstances exist.

One of the first steps in dealing well with conflicts is to develop an understanding about what really is happening. A superficial glance at the dialogue beginning this chapter might produce the "insight" that these two people just do not like each other. However, to diagnose the problem we must look at many different levels and aspects of it: the actual behavior, the issues and values inherent in the conflict, the feelings and the relevant rigid behavior patterns, the sources of restimulation affecting each person, the ways in which the conflict is affected by advantages and privileges conferred on one of the people at the expense of the other, and elements of the situation that will facilitate a satisfactory resolution. Omitting any one of these factors will interfere with our ability to achieve solutions beneficial to both parties.

Let us look at these different levels and aspects one at a time, and see in what ways they help us arrive at solutions. Together they form the initial portion of a problem-solving procedure effective for resolving all kinds of conflicts. To better illustrate our discussion we can use one specific example of a conflict. Barry and Vanessa have been living together for several years and have no children. Recently, Vanessa has left her job and gone back to school, working toward a bachelor's degree in sociology. Barry has a low-paying job in a factory, with which he is quite unhappy. A conflict that has been affecting their relationship will be discussed in the context of our procedure for resolving conflicts, a procedure based on a complete diagnosis of the conflict at hand.

A MODEL FOR RESOLVING CONFLICTS

I. The Conflict

1. *What is the basic conflict?* Barry wants to quit his job and move to another city in a different part of the country, and Vanessa does not want to move; however, they both want to continue living together.

2. *What are the issues surrounding the conflict?* Between Barry and Vanessa, some of the issues are: (a) How decisions affecting the relationship are made, (b) how they earn enough money to live comfortably, (c) how to deal with Barry's discontent with his job, (d) how important their relationship is to each of them with regard to their respective careers, and

(e) should Vanessa continue to give in to Barry's desires to move? Most of these issues are not discussed directly, but are instead talked around and hinted at.

3. *What is the history of the conflict?* The history of Barry and Vanessa's conflict goes back several years, when they moved to the area in which they are now living. Barry had strongly pushed for the move, having an old army buddy in the vicinity. Vanessa did not want to leave her family and agreed to the move only after months of persuasion. She initially had a hard time getting used to the new city and was resentful about the move for some time. Two months ago Barry again broached the subject of their moving, this time across the country. Vanessa has again strongly objected, which is the state of the conflict now.

4. *What are the personal causes of the conflict?* What is happening in both persons' lives to affect the conflict? Barry's wish to move is related to his dissatisfaction with his work. He has an unrewarding job, receiving little emotional satisfaction to compensate for his low pay. He also does not have many friends in the area, and seems to have a hard time making them. In general, Barry likes to move around; he seldom forms strong attachments to places in which he lives.

Vanessa, after two difficult years here, has finally gotten herself into a relatively satisfying situation. She is going to school, working part-time, and enjoying the challenge of college. Upon going back to school she has made a number of new friends, particularly other women who themselves returned to college after an absence of several years. She does not want to give this lifestyle up to move to another area. Also, she never has liked to move. In the past it has taken her a long time to make friends, and she does not want to go through that experience again, particularly when things are going so well for her.

5. *What aspects of the conflict relate to larger social problems in the society?* How is the conflict directly or indirectly caused by patterns of irrationality widespread throughout the culture? Barry's feelings about work, common among low-paid fac-

tory workers, can be seen as part of the oppression of
working-class people in this country. It is no wonder that he
does not like his job; it is inherently alienating under the
present economic system.

Another feature of their conflict relates to sexism. It is a
pattern throughout our culture that women move with their
husbands and that men have more power in making decisions of importance. If Vanessa asserts her desire to stay, she
will be going against a powerful cultural pattern as well as
Barry's wishes.

II. The People

1. *What are the human qualities of the people involved which will
help resolve the conflict?* Barry and Vanessa love and care about
each other, and this caring can be mobilized to help them
resolve their conflict. Vanessa is quite understanding, which
should help her listen more effectively to Barry's concerns;
Barry has a sense of justice and fairness, which will make it
easier for him to see Vanessa's side of the conflict; and they
both have a good sense of humor, which will help them make
the conflict less serious and heavy.

2. *What happens between the people in the interaction?* How
do they respond in the conflict? Barry is the one who brings
up the issue in many different ways. He continually tells
Vanessa that he wants to move and disparages her desire to
stay. He also emphasizes that he is earning most of the
money, that in effect Vanessa is going to school at his expense. Vanessa generally responds with silence, withdrawing
from the situation and trying to avoid dealing with it. When
Barry brings up the subject, their conversation usually ends
with Barry getting angry and Vanessa feeling bad.

3. *What feelings arise when the conflict comes to the surface?*
Some of these were just mentioned. Barry feels frustrated
and angry when he talks about moving. With each bad experience at work, he becomes more insistent. When he talks
to Vanessa about moving, his voice is hard and rigid, and he

quickly gets angry when she does not agree. He feels unsupported by her, and many of his hurt and angry feelings about work and not having friends come up at this time.

Vanessa's primary emotion when Barry brings up the subject is fear. She is fearful of moving and is intimidated by Barry's aggressive tone. She finds his anger frightening and feels powerless to confront it.

4. *What rigid behavior patterns relate to the conflict and interfere with its resolution?* A number of patterns play a large role in this conflict. Vanessa has a hard time getting to know others, because she usually becomes quiet when meeting people. Her fear about moving is based on past, painful experiences. The conflict is affected by her pattern of not asserting herself around men, in this case Barry; the pattern is enacted by her withdrawal from the situation whenever Barry wants to talk about moving.

First, partly because of his working-class background, Barry has a false image of himself as stupid. This distress recording limits his ability to think about all the options open to him. Second, when he experiences painful feelings, he responds by leaving the situation—which has resulted in his moving frequently and walking out of arguments before they can be resolved. Third, in response to Vanessa's reluctance to go along with him, he dramatizes anger at her. This dramatization is an enactment of a pattern that goes back to his early childhood. Fourth, Barry has internalized part of a cultural sexist pattern: He implicitly assumes that Vanessa will move because he wants to.

It is easy to see how much these patterns interfere with the resolution of the conflict. In fact, without any of these patterns there might not be any conflict.

5. *What are the sources of the restimulation affecting the conflict?* Understanding what happened in the past will help us understand why the distress recordings operate in the present. This is particularly important with respect to patterns due to oppression—the way women have been invalidated, how non-whites have been disparaged, and so on. Two sets

of oppressive patterns are operating here. Vanessa and Barry come from working-class backgrounds and carry distress telling them that they are not intelligent. Vanessa also has patterns related to how she was treated as a girl. Her thinking was consistently ridiculed, and she was expected to be cute and accommodating.

6. *What behavior by each person particularly restimulates the other?* For example, Vanessa is instantly reminded of hurtful encounters with her father whenever Barry's voice takes on a cold and angry tone or when he leaves and slams the door. Vanessa's refusal to talk to him and tell him what she really thinks immediately infuriates Barry. There are, of course, other things that restimulate each of them, which would be useful for them to think about and try to avoid in their interactions.

These six points will provide most of the information necessary for finding appropriate solutions to conflicts. In looking for solutions we must consider patterns and feelings but not let ourselves be ruled by them. What we want are solutions that are best for the people, not for the distress recordings.

III. Ideal Solutions

1. *What would be the best solution for one of the persons?* This question is not asking what would make the person *feel* good. What we want instead is to meet this person's real human needs and free his or her behavior from the effect of past distress. In other words, what will help this person grow and develop as a human being?

For Barry, the ideal solution would not be perpetuating the pattern of running away from dissatisfaction. We might propose instead that he train for a more fulfilling job and develop the interpersonal skills to make friends and acquaintances. We might also change his way of dealing with conflict, so that he and Vanessa could give real support to each other.

2. *What would be the best solution for the other person?* For Vanessa, the best solution might be to stay where they live

now and to continue her education, which is challenging and provides much satisfaction and some training. We also might wish that she developed more confidence in herself and became more assertive in stating her wants and needs.

IV. Choosing a Course of Action

1. *Brainstorm all the possible solutions you can think of,* no matter how fantastic or unimaginable they may seem. Brainstorming means bringing out all the possibilities, without evaluating them or criticizing them in any way. The purpose of this technique is to give our creativity a chance to work without impeding it with fear of rebuke. Some of the possible solutions for Barry and Vanessa are (a) Vanessa stays and Barry goes to a new city; (b) they both go, Barry finds a new job, and Vanessa starts college in a new place; (c) they both stay, and nothing is changed; (d) they stay, and Barry looks for a new job; (e) they stay, and Vanessa quits school to support Barry while he gets training for a better job; (f) they make an agreement to stay until Vanessa graduates; (g) they both move, and if Vanessa does not like it she will move back.

2. *Evaluate each solution.* What is good about it? What is bad about it? Is it workable? Based on the earlier, in-depth analysis of the conflict, Barry and Vanessa considered each of the possible solutions, immediately rejecting some and retaining others.

3. *Choose one.* Barry and Vanessa chose to investigate the possible solution of her continuing school and his looking for a new, more satisfying job.

V. Thinking about the Solution

1. *What will allow it to work?* The solution Barry and Vanessa chose seems to meet most of their needs, and the major issues of concern are dealt with. The fact that both Barry and Vanessa agreed to the solution will certainly make the chance of its success much greater. Also, going through this whole

process has made it easier for both of them to talk about what is happening.

2. *What might interfere with its success?* It was clear to both Barry and Vanessa that what would interfere with the solution would be their behavior patterns and feelings. Unless Barry gets active support, both to look for a job and to deal with the feelings that come up, his distress recordings will continue to affect his relations with Vanessa. For Vanessa, her fear and timidity may keep her from speaking out and asserting herself in the way that would be most helpful to both of them. Also, Barry might not be able to find a better job, and he still might not have any friends—which would nullify the value of this solution.

3. *What can be done to minimize these counterproductive factors?* Vanessa and Barry can stay in close touch with each other about how they feel, devoting some time each week specifically for this purpose. Vanessa can continue to give Barry support for finding another job and can help him deal with his feelings about work. Barry can do his best to listen well and to encourage Vanessa to think out loud and assert herself.

4. *What are the steps needed to implement the solution?* The first step was to help Barry think about what kind of work he was qualified for and would like to do. He set some goals for himself and talked about the kind of support from Vanessa that would be most helpful. Weekly times were also established to check on how things are going and to provide additional support.

VI. Implementing the Solution

This step involves following through on those above.

VII. Evaluating the Solution

1. *How are things going?* What is going well? What is going poorly? What needs to be improved? The process of evaluation must be ongoing. Depending on the situation, it may be

useful to reevaluate every week or two. We cannot afford to sit back and let things go as they may, because the reactive pull of distress recordings will tend to keep both people from thinking and acting according to the agreed-upon solution. Vanessa and Barry kept track of what was happening, particularly with Barry's search for a new job.

2. *What are the appropriate next steps?* What does it make sense to do next? And after that? Continuing to think about next steps is an essential aspect of the problem-solving process. Without it, the conflict will stagnate at another place, until painful feelings again erupt into unthinking behavior.

Barry eventually did find a job that was more satisfying. Everything did not end happily ever after, however, and the behavior patterns that affected this conflict continue to interfere with their relationship. These patterns will be diminished only through the thorough discharge of the painful emotion connected to the incidents from which they originally developed. Nevertheless, the use of problem-solving procedures such as this can greatly mitigate the influence of these patterns, and can help us use our creative intelligence to resolve our conflicts.

Exercise 17 presents this procedure, which will be of value for almost any interpersonal conflict. We may not come up with solutions that feel good or give both people everything they want, but we can use our thinking to arrive at the best possible solution to the problem at hand.

EXERCISE 17   THE INTERPERSONAL CONFLICT-RESOLVING PROCEDURE

Purpose: To help you diagnose conflicts at many different levels, and to initiate the process of finding solutions.

Task: Answer the following questions:

I.   The Conflict

1. What is the basic conflict?

2. What are the issues surrounding the conflict?

3. What is the history of the conflict?

4. What are the personal causes of the conflict? What is happening in both persons' lives to affect the conflict?

5. What aspects of the conflict relate to larger social problems in the society?

II. The People

1. What are the human qualities of the people involved which will help resolve the conflict?

2. What happens between the people in their interactions? How do they respond in the conflict?

3. What feelings arise when the conflict comes to the surface?

4. What rigid behavior patterns relate to the conflict and interfere with its resolution?

5. What are the sources of the restimulation affecting the conflict?

6. What behavior by each person particularly restimulates the other?

III. Ideal Solutions

1. What would be the best solution for one of the persons?

2. What would be the best solution for the other person?

IV. Choosing a Course of Action

1. Brainstorm all the possible solutions you can think of, no matter how fantastic or unimaginable they may seem.

2. Evaluate each solution.

3. Choose one.

V. Thinking About the Solution

1. What will allow it to work?

2. What might interfere with its success?

> 3. What can be done to minimize these counter-productive factors?
>
> 4. What are the steps needed to implement the solution?
>
> VI. Implementing the Solution
>
> VII. Evaluating the Solution
> 1. What is going well?
> 2. What is going poorly?
> 3. What needs to be improved?
> 4. What are the appropriate next steps?

THE FIVE DIMENSIONS OF EFFECTIVE PROBLEM-SOLVING

We can take another approach to resolving interpersonal conflicts by looking at some of the dimensions of the problem-solving process. Different aspects of the process, these dimensions all play a part in the resolution of the conflict (or lack thereof), whether or not we realize it. How much we take each of these aspects[1] into account will greatly affect how well we resolve our conflicts.

1. *Goals.* We must be able to set appropriate and realistic goals and work effectively toward achieving them. This dimension involves thinking about what we want from the situation and determining how to achieve it, as well as carrying out our plans.

2. *Values.* We need to understand our own and other people's values in the conflict. On what values are our goals based? How do our values and those of the other person(s)

---

[1]These dimensions are elucidated in the context of professional competence in Audrey C. Cohen, "The Founding of a New Profession—The Human Service Professional (unpublished, 1974).

differ, and how does this difference affect our conflict? How do we deal with value differences? Understanding the values implicit in our actions and those of our partners will help us to understand why the conflict is happening and how it can be resolved.

Values are based on the beliefs we hold, and they affect how we both think and behave. Our values come from church, state, parents, and schools, and most of them are not consciously held. It is vital to look at the source and decide for ourselves whether or not in truth a value is one we want to hold. Wearing clean jeans, for instance, is a value that parents impart to their children all the time. Where did this value come from? How sensible is it? Is it worth the resulting problems in the relationship to impose that value on the child? Working through these questions will greatly affect how conflicts are resolved.

3. *Self and others.* This dimension involves understanding what is really happening in our life and that of the other person in the conflict. What are the feelings and patterns affecting the conflict? What is restimulating each person's distress recordings, and how can it be avoided? What do we and the other person need to grow as human beings, and how can we be encouraged to use our intelligence to resolve the conflict?

4. *Systems.* Looking at our relationship as a functioning system operating in the context of a larger social and economic system, how do we view the conflict? How central is it to the ongoing relationship? How is it the consequence of inequality or injustice in the larger social and economic system? Many conflicts in love relationships, for example, are clearly affected by such factors as unemployment, sexism, the role of the family as the place to unload distressful feelings, and so on. Understanding conflicts in terms of the systems in which they are manifest is crucial to our knowing their real causes. We also must know the historical context of the conflict and its relation to the growth and development of the relationship.

5. *Skills*. This dimension involves the application of appropriate skills to the conflict at hand, that is, skills to diagnose the problem, interpersonal skills to communicate clearly and effectively, skills to help us come up with creative solutions, and skills to help us carry them out. Our ability to deal with feelings and facilitate discharge is also an important aspect here. These skills allow us to put into practice the understanding developed in the previous dimensions to achieve our goals and purposes.

These five aspects of the problem-solving process are all interrelated. If we do not have appropriate goals or cannot carry them out, our awareness of the conflict's causes is not going to help us. If we are good at developing goals and strategies, but these are based on values developed as a result of past hurts, we may do more harm than good by achieving our ends. If we know exactly what we want to do and why we are doing it, but do not have the necessary skills to bring it about, we also will fail to achieve a viable resolution. We must be competent in all five dimensions.

Exercise 18 is included here to apply these dimensions to our own particular conflict. This is another tool with which we can look at our conflict and think about what we can do to bring it to a successful resolution. Some of the material in this exercise duplicates that of Exercise 17, but it has additional value in this context; as we function well in each of these aspects, so we can deal well with problems in relationships.

EXERCISE 18   EXAMINING THE DIMENSIONS OF THE PROBLEM-SOLVING PROCESS

Purpose: To apply these five dimensions to resolving conflicts.

Task: Thinking about a conflict you have, answer the questions relating to each of the following five dimensions.

1. *Goals*

What are your goals in the situation?

Are these goals realistic and appropriate?

Can you develop strategies to achieve them?

Can you carry out these strategies to their successful completion?

2. *Values*

On what values are your goals based?

Where did you get these values?

On a scale of one to ten, how important are these values to you?

What are the other person's values in the situation?

How do your values differ?

Would you risk a friendship over your values?

To what extent are each of your values based on clear thinking? On old distress recordings?

How can you deal most effectively with the conflict in values?

3. *Self and Others*

Do you understand your own motivation? Your wants and needs?

Do you understand what is happening in the other person's life?

What distress recordings and feelings come up for you in the conflict?

What recordings and feelings come up for your friend?

What is happening in your lives to cause or aggravate the conflict?

What behaviors or circumstances are restimulating each of you?

What can be done to reduce the amount of restimulation?

What are you really needing in the situation?

What is your friend really needing?

4. *Systems*

How does your relationship function in terms of each of your lives?

How does the conflict relate to the whole of your relationship?

Is the basis of the conflict rooted in the very nature of your relationship?

How is the conflict related to injustice or inequality in the larger social system of the whole society?

5. *Skills*

What skills can you use to diagnose the problem?

What communication skills can you use to talk to each other more clearly and directly?

Can you discharge your feelings and help your friend discharge his or hers?

What other skills are applicable to this situation to help it become resolved?

Evaluation:

In what dimensions do you have the most competence?

In what dimensions do you most need to increase your ability and awareness?

How was this exercise helpful to you?

How did it help you think about or resolve your conflict?

One of the dimensions in which many of us have a definite lack is that of skills. For most of us, the models we have from childhood are none too promising, and subsequently we have been taught little about how to relate to people in the midst of conflict. With this in mind let us turn to some skills and techniques applicable to many conflicts.

TEN SKILLS AND TECHNIQUES
TO APPLY IN CONFLICTS

Some of these skills involve specific things to do; others are suggestions for facilitating the problem-solving process. As with every method presented in this book, these techniques and ideas are merely tools to be utilized when we think they may be helpful. They themselves provide no solutions, but their use will make solutions easier to achieve.

1. Use active listening. As discussed earlier, this technique improves communication and circumvents the dynamic of each person trying to "get" the other.

2. Use I-messages. Instead of taking out feelings on or invalidating the other person, claim responsibility for your own feelings. The less the other person feels attacked, the more s/he will be able to think clearly.

3. Be specific. When something is bothering you, do not unnecessarily generalize. Human beings relate much more easily to concrete facts and statements than they do to abstractions. This technique also works when people make general criticizing statements about us or others. Asking them to be more specific will help us to understand their meaning and help them to clarify their thoughts.

4. Specify points of agreement and disagreement. Try to ascertain where you agree and where you disagree. This technique has several benefits. First, it changes the situation from an adversary one to one of cooperation. Second, it helps to clarify what the similarities and differences between the two people really are. Third, it serves to narrow the area of disagreement, so that the relevant issues and concerns can be effectively worked on.

5. Watch for fouls or low blows. We all know there are things we can say to our partners that will immediately re-stimulate their bad feelings, often by calling them names or treating them as though they were their rigid patterns. For

example, people who find it hard to make friends will probably feel hurt and angry if referred to as "unlikeable" or "unsociable." We, of course, only say these things while dramatizing our own feelings, but this does not alter the destructive effect of the abuse. It effectively puts an end to the possibility of rationally discussing the issue at hand, at least for the present.

One device for dealing with fouls is to have a mutual understanding of the concept and to call "foul" whenever such an invalidation is verbalized. This technique can help both people keep the conversation on the immediate concern, instead of descending into name-calling.

Words like "always" and "never" ("You always leave the toilet seat up!") also have the effect of raising the ante and escalating the fight. These words also can be treated as fouls, and it makes sense to avoid using them.

6. Exchange listening time. Take turns listening to each other, and use the time to think out loud. When listening, do not interrupt, and consider it a time when you are lucky to have the opportunity to hear what your friend is really thinking. When it is your turn to talk, be sure not to use the time to dramatize or in any way invalidate your friend—this is an unfair and destructive use of his or her attention. If both persons use this opportunity responsibly, the underlying issues in the conflict will become clearer, and both will be able to think about what they need in the situation.

7. Try reversing roles. Take a few minutes and each play the other person. Continue the discussion or argument as if you were s/he and s/he were you. Try not to exaggerate the other's position, or use the role-playing to ridicule or invalidate. The effect of reverse role-playing is that each person has the opportunity to see and understand the other's feelings about and views of the situation. An added benefit is that you can see how the other person perceives you by the way that s/he is enacting your role. Exercise 19 provides an opportunity for reverse role-playing.

8. Go scream into or pound a pillow. If you are so angry that you want to say the meanest and nastiest thing to your friend that you can think of, or you want to beat him or her up, go scream into a pillow at the top of your lungs or beat the pillow to death. Although this technique may not feel as temporarily satisfying as screaming at or hitting your friend, it will help rid you of some of your surface feelings. Thus, you will be able to think more clearly, and your friend will not be physically hurt or more restimulated emotionally.

9. Exchange discharge time. This technique is often difficult when an interaction is heated, but its benefits can be immeasurable. It is similar to taking turns to think out loud, but instead you take turns to discharge. One person pays attention to the other for a specified period of time, and then the roles switch. Use the time to laugh or cry or shake, or if you are angry scream into or pound a pillow. This technique can completely change the character of a fight—people again can start to see each other as feeling, caring human beings, and not as wicked enemies. Also, each person will be able to

think more clearly once some of the feelings are discharged.

People must be very aware in this situation not to dramatize their feelings at the other person. It is very tempting to use the time to disparage your friend: "You rotten, no-good idiot. I hate you, and I wish you were dead. You are the most unfair person I've ever met," and so on. Saying these things in this context will only hinder a real resolution of the issues. Sometimes it is helpful to make and wear a sign saying, "Remember that I love you." This sign can make it easier to remember that our partners really are our friends,

---

EXERCISE 20 EXCHANGING DISCHARGE TIME DURING FIGHTS

Purpose: To provide partners the opportunity to release their anger, hurt, and frustration in the middle of fights.

Task: In the middle of a fight, take five minutes each in turn to release some of the feelings that have built up during the encounter. Do not use your time to get back at your partner. If you feel like screaming mean things, growl at your partner or scream into a pillow so that the words are unintelligible. Sometimes pounding a pillow also is effective. Let the feelings out, but do not take them out on your friend. You can demand and expect the same from your partner during his or her discharge time.

Evaluation:

Did exchanging discharge time help you deal with your feelings in the fight?

Did it help your partner?

What effect did it have on resolving your conflict?

Were you and your partner successful in not taking out your feelings on each other during the discharge time?

What will you do better next time?

despite our immediate feelings. Exercise 20 will help you put this tool into practice.

10. Talk and make agreements during times of low conflict. One of the unfortunate aspects of most conflicts is that they are often discussed only under conditions of much stress. Because there are so many painful feelings surrounding the conflict, people do not want to bring it up when they are feeling good. It thus mostly comes up when people are already feeling hurt or angry, when there is little attention to thinking about the conflict constructively or creatively. This problem can be avoided to some extent if the subject is brought up when people are feeling good and warm toward each other. Under these conditions they are much more likely to achieve positive resolutions.

As was stated above, all these tools and techniques cannot replace thinking. Their use can nevertheless make the difference between a conflict going on for days and days or being resolved in an hour or so.

Rigid behavior patterns are the main deterrents to viable solutions, and some behaviors will defeat any attempt to achieve rational solutions to conflicts. The two behaviors I would like to discuss are (1) when one person will not discuss the conflict, and (2) when physical violence is threatened or used.

WHEN S/HE WON'T DISCUSS THE CONFLICT

Obviously, it is difficult to talk to someone about something when s/he refuses to talk about it. Nevertheless, it is common for people to avoid facing conflicts. Some people withdraw and refrain from saying anything; others immediately change the subject; others walk out in the middle of discussions; and when both people want to avoid the conflict, it may not be brought up at all.

Sometimes it is rational to put off dealing with a conflict. If we are tired or want to watch a particular television show or have to go to work in five minutes, it may make sense to say, "Let's talk about it later." Usually, however, conflict is avoided not because of reason but because of fear. Most of us have painful memories and distress recordings caused by our mistreatment or someone else's in antagonistic encounters. The fact is, however, that conflicts must be dealt with; avoiding them seldom makes them go away. If we are going to resolve conflicts to the benefit of both people, usually both must take part in the resolution—which means both must talk about it. The behavior patterns resulting in avoidance must be interrupted in some way.

It does not do much good to become angry with people when they avoid the conflict. Our anger will only make them more afraid and intimidated, and will not help them to think clearly. Admittedly, it is frustrating to have people walk out on us when we are attempting to resolve a problem; but acting on our feelings of frustration by yelling or invalidating them will not help. Without our own restimulation, we would lovingly stop the pattern (in the other person) from operating. Despite our feelings of frustration and anger, it is always possible to communicate our caring; it only feels otherwise because of our painful emotions. Of course, *how* we stop the pattern depends on the person and the situation.

Sometimes mimicking the avoidance pattern effectively interrupts it. On one occasion, for example, I was talking to another person when he said, "This is stupid, I'm leaving." He then proceeded to leave the room and put on his coat, preparing to leave the house. I immediately followed him, and started grumbling, "That Michael [meaning me] . . . he really bugs me some time. I'd like to feed him to crocodiles or grind him to little bits and feed him to chipmunks." My friend started to laugh, and his blind rush to escape from the situation was over. The mimicking had just the right tone to enable him to step outside his pattern and start discharging some of his feelings. Soon we were dealing again with the problem.

Active listening can also be very effective when people

avoid talking about conflicts. When it is used well in this kind of situation, it is very difficult for the patterns of avoidance to continue to operate. An interaction might be as follows:

A: I don't want to talk about it.

B: It makes you uncomfortable to think about my going back to school.

A: Listen, I just don't want to talk about it! Do you hear me?

B: I hear you. You don't like this being brought up.

A: That's right, I don't.

B: You don't even want to consider the idea of my going back to school.

A: That's right.

B: It's pretty scary to you.

A: Yeah. Listen, can we talk about this some other time? This will spoil my whole day.

B: It is really important to me that we talk about it. If we don't talk about it now, then let's set up a time to talk about it later. Okay?

A: Well, we might as well talk about it now.

The persistence of *B* in this interaction prevented *A* from avoiding the issue. When it was clear to *A* that s/he would not be permitted to continue the avoidance, s/he agreed to face the conflict. Notice that *B* did not once invalidate the other person for having the avoidance pattern. The whole interaction was handled with care and love.

When we interrupt patterns, we can expect discharge or dramatization to occur. We should not be surprised if people's feelings of hurt and anger come to the surface when we stop their patterns from operating. After all, these feelings were the cause of the patterns in the first place. When these feelings do come up, we can use our best listening skills to help our friends deal with and discharge them. We will be able to help them to the extent that we can avoid acting from our own distress recordings.

One other suggestion for dealing with patterns of avoidance is to think about what to do before the interaction actually occurs. This preparation can take two forms. One is to work out a prior agreement with the other person that you will both stay with the discussion until together you have reached a solution or have at least decided upon the appropriate next step. Thus, both people are allies against the rigid pattern. The other is to think ahead of time about what to do if the pattern starts to operate—if the person leaves, stops talking, changes the subject, and so on. Role-playing with another friend may be very helpful in this regard. Have your friend play your partner, and try interrupting his or her avoidance patterns in different ways. From this technique you may discover what might work and what might not. By being prepared, we can help prevent ourselves from being frozen when and if the other person does leave, withdraw, or change the subject.

WHEN PHYSICAL VIOLENCE IS THREATENED OR USED

Responding to a conflict with threats or acts of physical violence is also a rigid behavior pattern, based on old distress recordings. People who assault others were themselves assaulted. This is not an excuse for people to be violent, but it does enable us to see that violent people are not bad people—they are people afflicted with bad patterns.

We were all victims when distress recordings formed. When restimulated, however, we sometimes act as victimizers. What seems to happen is that as adults or older children, when we are distressed we have someone else on whom to take out our feelings. We then do so in the same way feelings were taken out on us—through physical abuse. Take, for instance, a husband who was beaten as a child. Say he has a rotten job, with low pay, menial work, and an unpleasant boss. He is constantly restimulated, but he cannot let go of his feelings at the source of his restimulation, the oppressive work environment, his boss, and so on. He can, however, go home and take out his feelings on people who cannot or do not fight back, his wife and children. He then beats them in the same way he was beaten.

Men and women have both had violence inflicted upon them as children. Because of a number of factors, however, men abuse women much more frequently than women physically hurt men. Men are bigger, they often have economic power over women, and they have been conditioned to be more aggressive and violent. Women also act abusively, but seldom toward men. More frequently children are their victims.

Violent behavior must not be allowed to occur. It reenacts old distress recordings and inflicts new hurts upon the victim. It is the responsibility of all of us to interrupt violent behavior wherever we see it. In fact, observing violence and doing nothing about it reinforces our own patterns of powerlessness in the face of abusive behavior.

If we are not intimidated (that is, restimulated) ourselves, there are many things we can do when violence is threatened or about to be enacted. Sometimes it helps to mimic the pattern; once I saw a person in such a situation start lightly hitting himself in the stomach, saying "Take that, and that, and that," as he pretended to hurt himself. This act immediately pulled the other person outside his pattern, and the threat of violance ended. Sometimes it helps to use active listening to get to the feelings behind the pattern, and sometimes it is effective to just say "Stop it!" In most cases, however, the elimination of violent behavior should be a nonnegotiable demand.

There is a widespread myth that if people get hurt, they must have done something to deserve it. *This belief is never true.* It is never the victim's fault for getting hurt. Sometimes the victim's patterns help restimulate the attacker's patterns, but even in this case the locus of responsibility remains with the attacker. This myth is one of the things that allows violence to go unchecked in our society.

One thing we should consider when someone is about to physically abuse us is the option of walking out. We can just leave. It does not make sense to stay when our bodies are at stake. When the other person is that restimulated, s/he cannot be reasoned with at that time. Wait until later to talk about the problem, when physical danger is not imminent.

I am not saying that it is never appropriate to use physical force. It may be quite rational to physically keep someone from hurting another person, for example. What I am saying is that violence as a patterned response to painful emotion produces harmful results and should be avoided. Using threat or intimidation to get what we want in relationships can yield only temporary satisfaction. Unless two human beings decide of their own free wills based on their own thinking that they want to behave in a certain way, the behavior will be neither constructive nor worthwhile.

WHEN TO GIVE IN

Conflicts do happen. People have different wants and needs, and it often happens that both people in a relationship cannot get exactly what they want. One or both persons must compromise or give in on something. If we reject coercion as a means for determining who gives in where, on what basis do we decide what we are willing to give up, and when we should not give in? These questions, of course, can only be answered by each person individually, based on his or her best thinking. Unfortunately, the rigid patterns and distress recordings inflicted upon men and women—in particular, those involving accommodation and assertiveness—frequently influence these decisions.

Women generally have been socialized to take on support roles in this society. Even when they work full-time, they still cook and take care of their children and try to take care of the emotional needs of their partners. One of the ways that women were conditioned to take on these roles was that they were punished for asserting themselves and putting themselves first. For example, at the dinner table maybe Daddy always received preferential treatment, or perhaps Daddy and the boys were always served first. Probably the girl(s) were scolded for trying to go first until they "learned their manners." This kind of incident had to occur over and over again hundreds of times in both subtle and gross forms for women to take on the patterns of accommodation that let them accept second-class status. When women are controlled by these patterns, they tend to be willing to give up a lot when conflicts arise.

Men, in contrast, have been conditioned to be tough, unemotional, assertive, and aggressive, and have been trained to put themselves first and not think about other people. This conditioning was done by inflicting physical abuse or humiliating them when they attempted to discharge or show warmth and tenderness toward others, resulting in emotional numbing. When these patterns are operating, men are much less likely to compromise or to give in than they would otherwise be.

Patterns of accommodation and assertiveness do not conform necessarily to sex roles. Many boys were also punished for speaking out and asserting themselves, and as adults, have much fear about saying what they think. There are women who escaped some of the oppressive conditioning and can assert themselves clearly and strongly; and there are also women who have some of the patterns typically found in men. In any case, these patterns interfere with the ability to think about when to give in and when not to.

What often happens in relationships between men and women is that their patterns of accommodation and assertiveness interlock. That is, the patterns function well together—the man puts the man first, the woman puts the man first—so that their relationship seems to be serene. This state of affairs can continue only as long as the woman operates from this oppressed basis. It is ironic that what we call conflict only appears when the woman starts emerging from under these conditions; otherwise things are "fine."

Exercise 21 is a questionnaire designed to help you think about your own behavior in terms of assertiveness and accommodation. Use this exercise to expand your own awareness about how you relate to your partner and how s/he relates to you.

**EXERCISE 21   QUESTIONNAIRE ABOUT
ACCOMMODATION AND ASSERTIVENESS**

Purpose: To help you become aware of the extent to which your behavior is accommodating or assertive.

Task: Answer the following questions "yes" or "no":

1. When you and your partner have a disagreement about what to do or where to go, do you usually get your way?

   _____

2. Do you often put the needs of others before your own?

   _____

3. Are you the one who usually initiates sexual activity?

   _____

4. Is it hard for you to say "no" when asked to do things?

   _____

5. Do you usually have the last word in arguments?

   _____

6. Do you often agree to have sex in order to please your partner?

   _____

7. Is it relatively easy for you to state what your opinions are, and why?

   _____

8. Are you good at taking care of other people's emotional needs?

   _____

9. Did you initiate your relationship with your partner?

10. Do you often agree or say nothing rather than get into a conflict?

Give yourself one point for every "no" on the odd-numbered questions and one point for every "yes" on the even-numbered questions. The higher your score, the more you tend to be accommodating; the lower your score, the more you tend to be assertive.

We must step out of patterns of assertiveness and accommodation in order to determine intelligently when it makes sense to give in. One thing we can do is to take the time to listen to each other think about what each wants, and encourage each other to think about both people. Indeed, just being aware of the pitfalls of the patterns will make a difference.

Another thing we can do to shake the patterns up a bit is to temporarily switch roles of accommodation and assertion. This role-playing may reveal the depth of the pattern, bring much laughter, and help both people see what it is like being outside their own pattern. Exercise 22 provides a few more details for making this switch.

**EXERCISE 22   REVERSING ROLES OF
ACCOMMODATION AND ASSERTIVENESS**

Purpose: To help us break through rigid patterns of assertiveness and accommodation by temporarily adopting the opposite behavior.

Task: This exercise can be done either individually or in couples, for an evening, or a whole day.

If you are usually assertive, try:

1. putting your partner's needs and wants above your own
2. being very understanding
3. spending lots of time listening
4. letting your partner decide where to go or what you do together

If you are usually assertive, try:

1. putting yourself first
2. firmly stating what you think
3. deciding what you want to do, then insisting that it happen
4. saying "no" loudly and firmly when you are asked to do something that you do not wish to do
5. doing no more than your fair share

Evaluation:

What happened?

What did you learn about yourself?

About your partner?

What was most difficult for you about the reversal?

What was easy?

What were the positive things about the opposite role?

What were the negative things about the opposite role?

What insights did you gain that will affect your behavior and your relationships from now on?

It is not that being accommodating or assertive is wrong or necessarily interferes with the resolution of conflicts. In fact, to function creatively and flexibly we need to be accommodating some times and strongly assertive at others. What interferes with our ability to solve our problems and relate well to other people is the rigidity around these behaviors, the way we respond with one or the other of them without thinking. It is my goal in this book to help each of us free ourselves from these patterns.

nine
If You Are Thinking About Leaving

These boots are made for walkin'
And that's just what they'll do.
One of these days, these boots are gonna
Walk all over you.

From "These Boots Are Made
for Walkin',"
by Lee Hazlewood[1]

"Til death do us part" is no longer an accurate motto for marital or love relationships. The percentage of marriages and intimate relationships ending in divorce or separation increases every year. In fact, for many people it seems as if the phenomenon of lifelong marriage has been replaced by serial monogamy: Wendy and Phil split up after several months; two months later, Wendy and Greg become partners, and remain so for about three years; after this relationship ends, Wendy is single for several months, and then becomes coupled with Simon; this relationship lasts for seven months; and so on.

In the absence of painful emotion, people would continue to love and care about one another, whether or not they decided to stay together as a couple. Staying together would be based on not just the feeling of love but also an evaluation of the benefits and disadvantages of being together as a couple. Unfortunately, painful emotion plays a large part in determining what happens to a relationship.

There are many reasons why intimate relationships end. First, people frequently become coupled for the wrong reasons. As discussed in the first chapter, people take partners to avoid being alone, to try to fill (unfillable) frozen needs for love and affection, to have sex, and to be taken care of. Some of us also became coupled because we were inculcated with the myth that we are not whole unless we are "one" with another person. With these motivations, it is no wonder so many intimate relationships fail to last. It is difficult to feel satisfied with a relationship when there is no way it can fulfill the "needs" for which we entered it. It is not uncommon to find people moving from one partnership to another in search of the love they did not get from their mothers or fathers. They can never find it, because the old distress recordings about not being loved continue to replay no matter how much the people are actually loved by their present partners.

Second, when people do not discharge their painful feelings, they tend to become more rigid with time. Their behavior becomes less and less flexible and creative, and their ability to build a mutually supportive relationship diminishes. People stop seeing each other as separate individuals, relating to one another without thinking. When this behavior continues for a long time, it may not take much to turn the emotional and psychological separation into a physical one as well.

Third, relationships end because people become dissatisfied with their lives, and instead of discharging their painful feelings they act them out by leaving. Maybe they don't like things about their partner; maybe they have miserable jobs, or maybe they don't have any job at all. When people are hurting a lot and do not release the painful feelings, it is understandable that these feelings are taken out on the relationship. "I just couldn't take it anymore" is a common phrase accompanying the abandonment of relationships for this reason.

Fourth, the goals of one or both of the persons change. It may be that the relationship is no longer suited to the current reality, and therefore needs to be altered. For example, if both people have careers that are important to them and these careers take them to different parts of the country, it may be necessary to live apart. This decision may be mutually agreed to and rationally made.

It may also happen that one person's goals or wants change, and the other person's patterns interfere with his or her ability to support that partner. For example, a woman may decide that she wants a career of her own after staying at home raising children, and her husband strongly objects. She may have to leave the relationship to get what she wants for herself if her husband continues to interfere with her growth and development.

Fifth, often people just do not have the skills for dealing with conflicts. They do not know how to communicate well, and their feelings and behavior patterns prevent them from using their intelligence to solve their interpersonal problems. The problems thus continue to grow until they seem insurmountable, and the relationship finally ends.

TO STAY OR GO

Staying in an ongoing relationship is not necessarily the best thing to do; neither is leaving. To arrive at the most appropriate behavior we must look at the actual circumstances of the particular relationship. To demonstrate, let us look at some examples in which leaving is rational and some in which it is not.

1. Leaving is rational: Jack continually invalidates Jane, telling her in many different ways that she is stupid and cannot do anything well. He wants her to stay at home and take care of their house, and insists that because he makes all the money he has the right to say how it is spent. Jane feels as if she has no say in her own life and affairs. She has tried to talk to Jack about it on many occasions, but he refuses. He will not go to any kind of counseling, because he does not see that anything is wrong. Jane decides that the best way to get out of this rut is temporarily to separate, which will give her the chance to figure out what she wants for herself.

2. Leaving is irrational: Peggy and Anne have been a couple for three years and have lately been having some rocky times. Peggy has started to make new friends through her work, which makes Anne feel threatened. Anne's initial reactions to Peggy's relations with other people were feelings of hurt, anger, and fear. Peggy continues to be loving toward Anne, and has made it clear that she wants to continue their partnership. In this case, it makes sense for Anne to deal with her feelings within the context of the relationship rather than by leaving it, as her feelings dictate.

3. Leaving is rational: Matt and Julia have been living together for eighteen years, and both feel as if they are a little constrained by always being half a couple. They were both in their early twenties when they married, and neither of them had the opportunity really to experience a single life. Their only child is now seventeen and about to enter college. Matt and Julia decide to live separately for an indefinite period of time, but to keep in touch.

4. Leaving is irrational: William and Ruth are both in their late thirties and have three children. Parenting keeps Ruth busy most of the time, and William financially supports the whole family as an electrician. Over the last few years, William has been feeling more and more as if he is growing old, and that his life has lost its excitement and challenge. He fantasizes about starting over again, without the "burdens" of a family. He never shares these feelings with Ruth, because

he "doesn't want to upset her." So, one day William just leaves, with only the slightest explanation and without any willingness to discuss his action. Ruth is thus left with the responsibility of raising the children herself and dealing with all problems of being a single parent. She must also work through her feelings about being abandoned by her partner of many years with almost no sign of caring. Further, the children also have to deal with their abandonment.

Whether or not leaving itself is rational, the way in which people do it frequently does not make much sense. When one partner initiates the separation and the other person opposes it, the latter almost always feels betrayed and abandoned. For both people, the sense of love and caring seems to be absent from their interaction; instead there are feelings of grief, fear, resentment, and guilt. This is unfortunate, because whatever feelings are on the surface, the real human caring is still there at some level. It is not necessary for relationships to end in such a painful and alienating fashion, and when it does, both people lose a lot. None of us should have to lose touch totally with another person about whom we cared deeply and with whom we shared a large part of ourselves and our lives.

Let us take an in-depth look at one particular relationship and analyze why it ended. In this case study we can observe the interrelationship of several different causes and factors contributing to the demise, and we can also see how the feelings of love were covered over by the painful feelings experienced over a long period of time. Throughout this example we can consider these questions: Why did the relationship end? Was the cessation of intimacy beneficial to either person? To both people? Would it have made more sense to continue the relationship? What would have had to happen to make the relationship healthy and worthwhile? Would it have been worth the effort?

Vicky and Lee first met each other in their third year of college at a fairly large eastern university. He was majoring in accounting, and she in sociology. They began dating on a regular basis, and soon stopped going out with others. They liked each other a lot, and as the year progressed spent more and more time together. After seeing each other for about six months, Vicky started letting Lee know that she wanted to get married. At first Lee was not in favor of the idea, and he responded to it with avoidance. As their relationship continued into their senior year, Vicky talked more and more about marriage. Although he clearly loved her, Lee was still quite reluctant to get married. He really did not feel like "settling down," and he was secretly envious of his friends who were not coupled with one person. As graduation approached, however, Vicky made it clear that she wanted to get married or break off the relationship. Lee was offered a job in an accounting firm in another part of the country, and he was a little afraid to go there by himself and encounter a potentially lonely situation. He therefore agreed to marry Vicky, although he still had some doubts.

Upon moving to the new area, Vicky could find work only as a secretary. After working for a large corporation for a couple of years, she got a job as an administrative assistant in a small law firm.

Lee, working as an accountant, took courses at night so that he could pass the actuarial exams and move up in the company in both position and salary. Soon he was earning a good income. When it was no longer financially necessary for her to work full-time, Vicky took a part-time secretarial job.

During the first few years of their marriage some things started happening that began to affect how Vicky and Lee related to each other. For Vicky, getting married did not bring her the happiness she had implicitly expected. Although her own insecurities apparently had disappeared during the first few months of their marriage, they soon came back and interfered with her positive sense of herself. The old feelings telling her that she was not okay began playing again, as strongly as before.

Vicky also was not satisfied with what she was doing with

her time. She only became a secretary because she could find no other work, and typing other people's letters and memos gave her little satisfaction. As time went by she became more and more frustrated, and changing jobs did not help. Even when she started working only part-time, she still did not know what she wanted. She was bored and unhappy, and felt that she had no one to blame but herself.

As she was feeling worse about herself, Vicky became increasingly dependent on Lee for satisfying her emotional needs and wants. It became more important to her that she have his approval, and at the same time she was jealous about his job and his success. She started acting irritable around him more frequently, and became annoyed whenever he started talking about his successes or problems at work.

For Lee, things started changing also. While at college he and Vicky were essentially equals, both pursuing their respective academic goals. Since their marriage and their move, however, he was definitely the "more important" of the two in the relationship. They had moved for his job, he made much more money than Vicky did, and he was taking more responsibility in the firm in which he worked. His sense of identity came much more from his work than it did from his marriage. As he saw how dissatisfied Vicky was with her work and how difficult it was for her to find worthwhile things to do, he started looking down at her. This feeling was compounded when Vicky took out her feelings of dissatisfaction on him or exhibited her feelings of dependence on him.

Lee also had a number of tensions and frustrations that developed around his job. He worked in a highly competitive environment and much of the time was anxious and tense. There was no outlet for these feelings at the office, so usually he focused them on his relationship with Vicky. He became more bothered by the relationship, and at the same time, more bored with it. He lost touch with his positive feelings toward Vicky, beginning to see her only as a burden and a bundle of distress. He gradually withdrew from Vicky emotionally, without really being aware of it himself.

Vicky sensed his withdrawal, which only exacerbated her own fears and negative feelings about herself. As she became more afraid and less self-confident, she acted more angrily toward Lee; he then withdrew from her even more. This cycle—subtle at first, but then becoming more manifest— eventually became the dominant aspect in their relationship.

As this dynamic developed, it was never talked about directly by Lee and Vicky. They sometimes hinted around it, but they both felt too embarrassed and scared to bring it up. When it was finally discussed, it was done so in the form of vitriolic attacks on one another:

VICKY: You're really stuck up. All you ever want to do is talk about work.

LEE: Well, you never want to talk about anything. You don't do anything, you just sit around and feel sorry about yourself.

VICKY: So what? You don't care anyhow.
(And so on.)

In the meantime, Lee started fantasizing about having sexual relations with other women. He eventually did start a sexual relationship with a woman at work, which gave him some of the emotional closeness he was no longer getting at home and also countered some of his feelings of boredom and frustration. He did not tell Vicky about his relationship, because he felt guilty and also because he was afraid of what might happen if he did tell her. His rationale was that he did not want her to be any more upset than she already was. When she did find out about it, she felt more betrayed by his hiding it from her than she did by his having the relationship.

After five years of marriage, Lee decided to leave. He felt "fed up" and "just wanted to get out." He and Vicky had been fighting a lot, and neither of them was enjoying being together any more. Nevertheless, when Lee told Vicky that he was leaving, she was stunned and extremely upset. She did not want the relationship to end. She pleaded with him to stay and try to work it out, but Lee maintained that his decision was final. One of the most hurtful aspects of Lee's action was that it was almost totally unexpected by Vicky. She knew things were not going well, but she had had no idea that he was thinking about separation. Out of the blue her marriage was over, and there was nothing she could do about it.

Vicky and Lee did separate, and were divorced about a year later. The separation was much harder on Vicky than Lee. He was quite upset, but the routine and involvement of work helped him ease the transition from marriage to a single life. Further, because there was another woman with whom he was close, he did not have to deal with much loneliness. He did experience much grief and guilt over the ending of his marriage, however.

Because Vicky did not have a job or another lover to depend on, the separation was much more difficult for her. She felt she was to blame for the end of the relationship, which further confirmed her sense of herself as "good for nothing." She had some friends who gave her support, but mostly she felt rejected and abandoned. It took her about a year before she recovered from the experience sufficiently to date other men, and she retained a distrust of men for quite awhile thereafter.

We can look at what happened between Lee and Vicky on different levels. On one level, the demise of their relationship largely was caused by sexism. There are at least seven different features of their relationship that can be related to sexist patterns rampant throughout our society: (1) Women are seldom encouraged to study mathematics or business. Hence Lee obtained a usable degree, whereas Vicky's degree in sociology was of little help in getting a good job. (2) Job discrimination on the basis of sex also played a role. Because of his training and because he was a man, Lee had more job possibilities than Vicky did, and he received a salary almost double that of hers. The only kind of work she was able to find was that of a secretary, for which a college degree is not even necessary. (3) Vicky and Lee moved to where his new job was located. In this new place neither of them knew any-one, but he had security and support from his job. (4) Be-cause of the kind of jobs they each had and how they were raised to think about marriage, Vicky had much more stake in the relationship than did Lee. Much of his positive self-image was tied up in his work, and he was less dependent on their relationship for his emotional needs. For Vicky, it felt as though her marriage was all she had. (5) Men are much more likely to act out their painful feelings through sex than are women, because of the patterns and feelings men and women respectively have accumulated about sex in this cul-ture. Thus it is not surprising that Lee acted out his dissatis-faction with Vicky by establishing a sexual relationship with another woman. (6) The patterns of superiority and inferior-ity, which developed when Vicky essentially subserved her-self to Lee's interests and professional responsibilities, are common in male-female relationships. This subservience makes it difficult for women to feel good about themselves and regain the ability to take charge of their lives—which proved to be true for Vicky. (7) When Lee decided to leave, he presented a nonnegotiable position—he was leaving, and "That's final." This behavior conforms to the way men have been conditioned to be firm and assertive and not to back down or accommodate others. Vicky of course very much wanted to accommodate and to save the marriage.

On a personal level, each person's rigid patterns of be-havior were continually acted out. The painful emotion sur-rounding their relationship and the other parts of their lives was almost never discharged, and their negative feelings about each other continued to accumulate. Their patterns and fears prevented them from talking about what was hap-pening; and instead of discharging their feelings and think-ing clearly about what to do, they acted according to old distress recordings. When each of them was having prob-lems, the other was never outside his or her own distress enough to think about what kind of support the other really needed. As this patterned interaction continued, their feelings of love receded deeper and deeper beneath the surface.

Could this relationship have been turned into a supportive and productive one? Certainly. The only barriers to establishing the kind of relationship they each deserved were their painful feelings and rigid patterns, both of which would disappear with sufficient discharge. Of course, the earlier the rigid patterns were interrupted, the easier it would have been to make the marriage viable again.

Should the relationship have continued? Probably not as it was going, but the way it ended was not sensible either. Lee's unilateral decision to leave was extremely hurtful to Vicky, reinforcing her own negative feelings and distress recordings. The way he left was neither caring nor thoughtful, and was a further reenactment of his distress recordings resulting from sexism.

However, it would not necessarily have been more rational to continue the marriage. It may have taken an enormous amount of time, energy, and commitment to work through all the feelings and patterns, which may not have been sensible while still living together.

In my experience working with many people, I have found it definitely worthwhile to work through the feelings and patterns that prevent a relationship from functioning well, even if the intimate relationship is not going to continue. First, this resolution allows ex-partners to remain lifelong friends after the intimacy is over, and enables them to continue to support each other in whatever ways are most appropriate. Second, working through the patterns and feelings around past relationships will help us to act more rationally in future relationships; we will be able to think better about how to relate to our partners.

If a decision to leave a relationship is going to be rational, it had better be based on our clear thinking rather than painful emotion. We will have to take many factors into account: what effect our leaving will have on our partners and our children (if there are any); what the financial implications of a separation will be; what will be gained by our leaving, either for us or for the other person; what will be lost; what feelings and rigid patterns are affecting our decision; and so on. If you are thinking about leaving your relationship, a list of some of the relevant questions is included in Exercise 23.

EXERCISE 23   DOES LEAVING MAKE SENSE?

Purpose: To help you think about whether ending your present relationship is a good idea or not.

Task: Answer the following as truthfully as possible:

1. What do you like about your partner?
2. Why do you want to leave?
3. What have you tried to help make the relationship work?
4. What can you try that you have not yet?
5. How is staying in the relationship hurting you or blocking your growth?
6. How is staying in the relationship hurting your partner or blocking his or her growth?
7. How is your relationship still supportive to each of you?
8. How much is sex playing a role in your decision to leave?
9. What effect will your leaving have on your partner?
10. If you were thinking about your partner's long-range best interests, what would you do?
11. What does s/he want?
12. Do you generally have a tendency to want to quit when things get difficult?
13. If you had a set of conditions that had to be met or else you would leave, what would they be?
14. If you do end the relationship, what will the financial, social, and emotional situation be like for each of you?
15. Are you still in touch with your feelings of love for your partner?
16. What effect will your leaving have on your children?

---

17. What are the major things in the way of your making the relationship everything you want and deserve it to be?

Evaluation:

What insights have you gained about the question of ending your present relationship?

It is common for us to make decisions about ending relationships by ourselves, without much input from others. At the same time, because we usually feel very upset or emotionally numb during this kind of crisis, we are not thinking well. A useful but seldom used procedure is to bring friends, people who know us well, into the decision-making process. They can help us think about and achieve clarity in our reasoning—the assumptions and values from which we are operating, their validity, our possible options, and the implications of our proposed actions. Our decisions can then be based on our best thinking, nurtured and facilitated by the best thinking of our friends. The Quakers have a tradition of using this kind of process, which they have appropriately called "clearness."

In Exercise 24 a procedure is presented to help people set up a "clearness" meeting for themselves about the question of ending a relationship. (This procedure will work for any decision, however.) It involves inviting some friends to a three-hour meeting focusing entirely on you and your wants, needs, and decisions in the area of concern—divorce or separation, for example. These friends are there, not to make decisions for you, but to ask questions and provide feedback so that your own decisions are well thought out. This help is particularly valuable when the area of decision-making is laden with as many feelings as is that of ending a love partnership.

Because things feel bad and seem difficult to correct is not a good enough reason to foresake a relationship. Often in

EXERCISE 24   HOLDING A
CLEARNESS MEETING*

Purpose: To help you make the best personal decisions possible, by utilizing the thinking, feedback, and support of your friends.

Task: The basic task of this exercise is to hold a three-hour meeting with several of your friends, focusing on you and a decision you wish to make. We can divide the procedure into three segments: preparation for the meeting, background questions for clearness, and the meeting itself.

I.   Preparation for the Clearness Meeting.

   A. Think and talk about the problem. Discuss the situation with friends, and think about it yourself. Try to clarify the important issues at stake, your options, and your goals. Some of the tools for re-solving conflicts presented in Chapter 8 will be use-ful here. Also, to the best of your ability separate your feelings from your thinking. If you can, dis-charge some of the feelings related to the problem, so that you can think more clearly.

   B. Choose the members of the clearness meeting. The meeting should include from three to seven people (in addition to yourself) for the most effective group process. Choose people whom you trust and know well, and who can think about the situation with some degree of objectivity. It is often useful to include people from different parts of your life— from work, play, church, and so on—to encourage you to develop the broadest perspective on the issue at hand. Be sure that everyone can stay for the whole meeting; otherwise, the process will be disrupted.

   C. Choose a facilitator. It is important to have one

---

*Much of this information comes from *Clearness—Processes for Supporting Individuals & Groups in Decision-Making*, by Peter Woodrow (Copyright © by Peter Woodrow, New Society Press, 4722 Baltimore Ave., Philadelphia, 1976).

person serve as facilitator for the meeting, to help it run smoothly and achieve its objectives. This role includes (1) obtaining the group's approval of the agenda; (2) moving the meeting from one item to the next, until the entire agenda is completed; (3) pointing out areas of agreement and resolution and those areas in which more thought and attention are required; (4) calling for breaks when necessary; (5) encouraging full participation of all members; (6) providing time for feelings to be expressed and discharged (where appropriate); and (7) helping the group reach decisions. The facilitator should be someone who does not have strong feelings about the subject being discussed, so that these feelings do not interfere with her or his role.

D. Meet with the facilitator. It is helpful to discuss the goal of the clearness meeting and how it can be most helpful. You and the facilitator can then make an agenda for the meeting, to best suit your needs. An example of such an agenda follows shortly.

E. Answer the background questions for clearness. Doing so beforehand will enable the meeting to flow more smoothly and cut down considerably on its length. It would be even better if the other members of the meeting had the questions and answers beforehand, to familiarize themselves with the problem and its various aspects.

II. Background Questions for Clearness

The answers to these questions provide some of the background information related to the problem and decision being discussed. When these answers are well thought out, reaching a decision is much easier. It is best if the answers are written down.

A. What is your personal history as it relates to the problem and decision?

B. What are your present commitments, both personal and other?

C. What are your present sources of learning, support, and affirmation?

D. What are your basic necessities in order to function well and creatively?

E. What are your long- and short-term goals, both personal and otherwise?

F. What are your dreams, and what do you perceive as keeping you back from reaching them?

G. What are the various options for the future you are considering?

H. What are the implications of your proposed action for those affected by it?

I. What are the positive and negative factors in each of the options you are considering?

In addition to these general questions, those in Exercise 23 are all relevant to the question of ending a love partnership.

III. The Meeting Itself

A. Suggested agenda:*

1. Gathering	(10 minutes)
2. Agenda review	(5 minutes)
3. Sharing memories of good times	(10 minutes)
4. Statement of questions for clearness and role of the clearness group	(5 minutes)
5. Check for personal biases	(5 minutes)
6. Sharing from the focus-person	(30 minutes maximum)
7. Questions of clarification	(10 minutes)
8. Break	(10 minutes)
9. Brainstorm of strengths of focus-person	(5 minutes)
10. Think time—silence	(5 to 10 minutes)

*Woodrow, *Clearness*, p. 12.

11. Brainstorm of questions/
concerns from   (5 minutes)
the group
12. Open time for discussion   (60 minutes)
13. Check on next steps for
focus-person and follow-   (10 minutes)
up roles of clearness group
14. Evaluation   (5 minutes)
15. Closing   (5 minutes)

B. Explanation of the agenda.

1. Gathering: The purpose of this time is to do something that brings the group together and is light and perhaps fun. For example, the people can share something positive that has happened recently in their lives.

2. Agenda review: After reviewing the agenda, everyone should approve it (or modify it accordingly). This step circumvents many problems that might otherwise arise later if people object to the procedure.

3. Sharing memories of good times with the focus person: The purpose of this short exercise is to direct the attention of the group to the person being focused on in a way that reaffirms each person's connection by recalling good or funny occasions from the past. Each person speaks briefly until everyone has had a chance to share.

4. Statement of questions for clearness and role of the clearness group: Here the focus-person states the problem s/he is dealing with and what s/he would like from the group. For example, s/he might say, "John and I have not been getting along for a long time, and I'm considering leaving him. From this meeting I would like feedback on this, and help thinking about what makes the most sense to do."

5. Check for personal biases: If members of the group have strong predispositions affecting their objectivity in the decision-making process, it is wise to have them stated openly at the beginning of the

meeting to help diminish their influence over the process. For example, if one of the group members wants John and Mary to stay together and says so openly, this bias can be taken into account throughout the meeting. This member can still function effectively in the group, but having this information about his or her bias will help everyone gain more objectivity.

6. Sharing from the focus-person: As briefly as possible, s/he should present information relevant to the problem, including the background information discussed above (if not disseminated before the meeting) and any other pertinent information. S/he should include a definition of the problem, a description of the options, and so on

7. Questions of clarification: These brief questions from the group members should clarify or fill gaps in the information presented. This is not the time to engage in discussion.

8. Break: Use your judgment about when to have a break, based on when people's attention begins to wander. Be sure to have someone call the group back together when the allotted time has expired.

9. Brainstorm of strengths of focus-person: Here members share things they appreciate about the focus-person. With no criticism or discussion, this step provides a good basis from which to discuss the question or problem being addressed.

10. Think time: A few minutes of silence is used to think about the person and his or her problem.

11. Brainstorm of questions or concerns from the group: It has been found helpful to put most of the questions and concerns of people on the table at once, so that everyone knows what the scope of the discussion will be. It also enables the focus-person to choose what directions will be most helpful to him or her, based on the kind of concerns that have been raised. It is useful to write these questions so that the group can see them throughout

the discussion, on either a blackboard or news-print, for example.

12. Open time for discussion: This part of the meeting is usually unstructured and is the time for direct feedback and discussion of the problem—say, whether or not to leave a relationship. Here members should focus on recognizing the good thinking of the focus-person and clearly challenge false assumptions and thinking that is clouded by feelings or misinformation. The focus-person may wish to have someone take notes of this discussion, as s/he may want to refer to it in the future.

13. Check on next steps for focus-person and follow-up roles of the clearness group: Following the discussion, the focus-person is given the opportunity to think out loud about what are his or her next steps in either the decision-making process or in executing a decision. One of the next steps for a woman considering separation, for example, may be to see a lawyer about legal problems. This is also the time to discuss what help members of the clearness group can give after the meeting. Staying with our example, one of the members might check with the woman to see how the conversation went with the lawyer.

14. Evaluation: The group should brainstorm what was positive about the meeting, what was negative, and how it could be improved. This step will help everyone continue to think about the process and will make future clearness meetings function more smoothly. Evaluative comments are presented without discussion.

15. Closing: The closing is something to end the meeting on a positive note. It might be everyone hugging each other or validating each other or singing a song together. Or it may just involve everyone shaking hands and smiling at each other.

such circumstances, staying and trying to make the partnership work helps us grow and develop much more than leaving does. Because leaving when the going gets rough is often a rigid pattern of behavior, repeated whenever distress recordings are restimulated, the patterns causing this relationship to end also cause the next one to end, and the one after that, and so on. Reenacting this behavior has harmful consequences for both us and our partners, none of whom deserve to be abandoned just because we were hurt in the past.

It is within our power to make any relationship work, given enough time, energy, commitment, and outside support. The outside support is crucial to help us step outside our patterns; we ourselves do not see them well and our partners are frequently too restimulated to support us to act outside them. If the outside support is unavailable, or if there is not enough time, energy, or commitment to work on the relationship, then it may make sense to leave.

The end of an intimate relationship is not the end of the world, despite the lyrics of our popular songs. We are all whole people by ourselves, and we do not "need" partners to be worthwhile human beings. While it makes sense to be in nurturing relationships, it is irrational to stay in relationships that are harmful or invalidating. Usually it is more rational to try to turn such relationships into validating ones, however, than to immediately abandon them and search elsewhere. If it seems to involve too much effort or attention to make the relationship healthy, then leaving may be the most appropriate alternative. Whatever we decide to do, our success will be largely dependent on our ability to think freshly and creatively and to communicate love and caring through our actions.

ten

Unequal Relationships– The Role Of Sexism

Hard is the fortune for all womankind,
We're always controlled and we're always confined.
And when we get married to end all our strife,
We're slaves to our husbands for the rest of our lives.

From an old folksong

We have all grown up with two conflicting images of heterosexual love relationships. One image is that of "equal partners in life," striving together hand in hand to grow in unity and harmony. Both partners do their best and contribute all they can to make their family healthy and happy.

The other image is closer to the reality of intimate relationships in this society, and is epitomized by the concept that "behind every successful man is a good wife." Here the husband goes out every day and takes charge of the world, and his wife washes his clothes, cleans his house, raises his children, satisfies his sexual and emotional needs, and entertains his friends. He earns the money and gets the status and privilege in the world; her status depends on him. If he is successful, then so is she—unless, of course, he leaves her, in which case she is seen as a failure. Both people can still be viewed as partners in a way, but not equal ones.

We can consider relationships unequal when one of the people has more power, status, and privilege than the other. This inequality can take the form of one person controlling how money is spent, having more power in making major and minor decisions affecting both persons, having his or her opinions valued more highly, having to do less "unpleasant" work, and so on. In the vast majority of male-female relationships, men do have these advantages and privileges over women, and the inequality is manifest throughout their intimate relationships.

The bases for this inequality are the culturally reinforced distress recordings instilled in men and women. Males and females have been systematically hurt in different ways and have developed different kinds of behavior patterns accordingly. This concept has been discussed previously in the context of men's assertiveness and women's accommodation patterns. Because of these patterns, men tend to get their way and to have more power in relationships.

What makes these patterns so pervasive is that they are constantly reinforced by all our institutions. Men make more money than women generally, and have more access to positions of responsibility; their thinking is more respected, and they are rewarded for being assertive and creative. Women, in contrast, have had their thinking, creativity, and assertiveness thwarted in the home, in school, in church, in work, and in politics. This reinforcement of distress recordings makes emerging from them that much more difficult.

Both men and women have been hurt by being conditioned into sex roles. It has been harmful to men to have their discharge inhibited and to have their sensitivity to other human beings blunted. By being forced to act aggressively and competitively, men have lost the ability to respond flexibly and appropriately to many kinds of situations. It has been hurtful to women to have had their natural assertiveness blocked and to have been forced to take on patterns invalidating themselves and putting others' needs above their own.

The effect of the instillation of these respective distress recordings on men and women has not been equal, however. Men gain real advantages and privileges *at the expense of women*—which is why we can say that sexism patterns result in the real, observable oppression of women in our society.

It is too simplistic just to say that sexism is something that men inflict on women. Men serve as the agents of oppression, but it is not productive to view them as the enemy or as the cause of sexism. Men only hurt women because distress recordings were inflicted upon them by their parents, peers, and the whole cultural and social system. We only have to look at boys aged one to ten to see how sexist attitudes and behaviors are formed. If a boy does not act tough and aggressive or does not treat girls as weak and inferior, he is ridiculed and ostracized by his friends. This behavior can be observed on any street, school bus, or playground. To fully understand sexism we must see that the distress recordings are the enemy, not the male who was hurt over and over again and who acquired sexist behavior patterns as a result.

Nevertheless, the hurt of sexism imposed on women is both real and ongoing. Women face situations daily in which they are treated as sex objects, their ideas are ignored, and they are assumed to be servants of others. I would like to quote at length from a talk given by Kathy Miller to a group of men on how sexism has affected women.[1]

Sexism is a culturally enforced distress pattern. That implies a couple of things. One is that as with all patterns it is not the fault of the victims, it is not something that the particular individual asked for, either the man or the woman. It also means that in moving out of it there is more pressure for the pattern to remain in existence than with a pattern that is not culturally reinforced. It is more difficult for women to give it up, to move out of it. It is also more difficult for men to give it up as contrasted with a

[1]Kathy Miller, "A Woman Talks to Men About Sexism," *Re-Evaluation Counseling Sisters*, No. 3 (Seattle: Rational Island Publishers, 1977), pp. 25–27.

distress pattern which has not had that kind of continual and ongoing reinforcement. . . .

There are some incorrect, continually reinforced, assumptions that go along with sexism. One of the central assumptions is that a woman essentially forever remains a child. This is a part of the basic way sexism functions. From this it follows that she is seen as property, does not have control and possession of her own body, is not seen as a thinker. The position that she has been relegated to in the economy assumes she does not need to be paid for what she does. . . .

It is important to remember that sexism is a day-to-day reality. Women have to deal with sexism, with the oppression that comes from sexism every day. It doesn't let up. It's not something that comes and goes.

One thing that has been difficult is that part of the operation of sexism is to convince women that they're not oppressed. There are a lot of women who still don't *see* the role that they play as being oppressed. They don't understand the position they're in or why they're there. This is part of the culturally reinforced distress pattern and part of being seen as a child. For almost all people there is a pull to be taken care of. Because we didn't have our needs met as children there is a pull to be taken care of now. It feels like a certain amount of safety to have a role as someone who will be taken care of. It means sacrificing a lot, however, to stay in that position.

It is important in thinking about moving against sexism and moving out of it—away from it—to realize that women have been victims and that has made them afraid to move from where they are. They have to move out of the pattern of being a victim and that is not an easy thing to do. A lot of times men get impatient with women because they don't move fast enough, they don't just go ahead and step out and do things, because they don't take charge, because they're scared of trying new things. It is important to realize that it's not just a matter of giving space for someone to go ahead and do something that they've not been allowed to do, but that there needs to be active support to do it. You can't just step back and expect someone to do something that they've been pushed away from before. There has to be active support toward doing it. . . .

It's important to remember that almost all women have been physically abused by men. That is a reality. This affects the way they function. We know about restimulation. We know that all a new situation has to do is look enough like, smell enough like, seem enough like an old situation to be restimulative. The very presence of a man is restimulative and brings up a lot of fear in most women. It may not be a restimulation of anything that the individual person has done, but the roles which men and women have been in in society are such that there is an automatic triggering of fear.

That fear has continual reinforcement from reality. There is a reason why it's scary for women to walk on the streets. The danger of being physically abused, sexually assaulted, or molested is at this time in our culture a reality. One of the day-to-day realities is that women have to make decisions where they go, when they go, what time of day it is, whether it is too dark to leave, making sure to leave before it's dark, with that danger in mind. A lot of energy goes into thinking about self-preservation. It is a reality for us, it is not just something we can slough off lightly. . . .

I think it's important to keep in mind what's happened to women because of the oppression. Think of how women view themselves—how we view ourselves. Women are not as a rule validated for their thinking. Again, this is part of staying the child, not being seen as competent, intelligent, capable human beings.

This invalidation happened to all of us as children. One reality, however, is that it happened and continues to happen to women as adults in a much stronger way than it does with men, so that women grow up not trusting their ability to think. We lose our ability to put into words the thoughts and ideas that we have—it becomes difficult, either verbally or in writing, to explain why we know what we know, or why or how we understand things.

The ability to use language gets lost because we lose that command of our ability to think. We don't trust our ability to think and we don't trust other women's ability to think. We buy into the image of non-thinking. The other thing that happens is because we can't express ourselves well anymore—then we women begin to assume we're wrong and that someone who can explain it must be right, which isn't necessarily true.

Ms. Miller has expressed well the nature of women's oppression, the effect that sexism has on women's self-images, their behavior, and their ability to think and express themselves. The following lists a few ways in which the patterns of oppression are reinforced by everyday experiences.

1. When women are whistled at by men, and examined and evaluated in terms of the shape and size of their bodies.
2. When men's gazes rivet on various parts of women's bodies, the act of which is both embarrassing and dehumanizing. In classes I have done role reversals of this behavior, in which men pretended to be women walking down the street, and women pretended to be men staring at them. When the women (playing men) threw out sexist remarks (such as, "Wow, what a dish!") and stared at the men's breasts and genitals, the men began to realize how degrading it felt to be judged like cattle. They felt embarrassed to have their bodies appraised, and powerless to stop it.
3. When women's thinking and opinions are deemed less important than those of men. This disparagement happens when conversation between women is referred to demeaningly as "girls' talk." Another common example occurs in mixed groups in which the conversation is almost entirely dominated by men. Often a woman will interject a comment or opinion that can potentially change the course of the conversation, but instead it continues where it left off when the last man spoke.
4. When women are told that their concerns are unimportant or less valuable than men's. When women who are home all day or who work in menial jobs, for instance, try to express their concerns to their husbands, they are laughed at as having "minor problems" compared to what the men have to face each day.
5. When women receiving attention depends on how close they

come to fulfilling a cultural standard of "beauty." The implication is that how she looks is more important than who she is and what she thinks. This attitude is hurtful to all women, not only those who do not fit the cultural standard. For "beautiful" women labor under the doubt that "they only like me because of how I look."

6. When women's friendliness to men continually is taken to mean sexual advance. This attitude places women into very constricted roles and ignores their potential to relate in many different human ways.

7. When women are treated as though their bodies do not belong to them. From the time women are small they are continually touched without their permission. Women are patted on the behind by their bosses, grabbed at by their children, and required to have sex with their husbands whenever the men so desire.

8. When women stepping out of the passive role are treated with ridicule and invalidation. Such women are often seen as "aggressive" and "hostile," and the patterns of men and sometimes other women operate to put the person back into her "proper" role. I know a woman who is a television director, and she was discussing what it was like for her on the job. The crew working under her was all male, and they would simply not cooperate with her if she talked to them in the same straightforward manner male directors used. They were working at a much slower pace with her, even though she and the male directors occupied the same position in the company and had the same amount of authority. She candidly stated that when deadlines were near the only way she could get them to do their work was to turn on "feminine" behavior— she pleaded with and cajoled them, and in effect acted "helpless." To this act the men responded, out of their own patterns of taking care of women.

These are just some of the kinds of incidents that reinforce the oppressive patterns of sexism in both men and women. Unfortunately, like other institutions in our society, intimate relationships also tend to reinforce these patterns. When men talk and women listen, when men make the important decisions in the relationship, when women's thinking is ridiculed or ignored, when women are physically beaten or sexually abused, or when women are in any way treated like children, more distress is added onto a heavily inlaid recording that keeps women from taking charge of their lives.

If either men or women did not already have their respective patterns of oppressor and victim, the inequality in intimate relationships could not exist. If women had not been so oppressed throughout their lives in the ways previously indicated and had not developed the patterns they did, they would not put up with any invalidation or inequality. If they had not been hurt they would never accept being treated as anything less than a whole person. Rather than bringing the man his coffee every morning, she might insist that he get it for her some of the time. Rather than having sex whenever he wanted it, she might insist that they make love only when *she* wanted it also. One of the things making it difficult for women to stand up to sexism is that one aspect of their distress recording says "It's my fault," "There's nothing I can do," "I deserve it," "There's something wrong with me for wanting more," and so on. These were some of the thoughts and feelings that accompanied earlier hurts and became recorded along with the hurts themselves.

Of course, if men did not have sexist patterns and recordings, they would not act oppressively toward women. It makes great sense to have as partners women who feel good about themselves and who think and express themselves well and who take charge of their lives. All desire to have women be anything less than this is entirely the result of distress. As men discharge their own feelings about having taken on the oppressor patterns, they realize this fact more and more.

Fortunately, no patterns are insurmountable. With sufficient discharge, all rigid behavior patterns will diminish and eventually disappear. However, when the patterns are consistently reinforced by the environment (as is the case with sexism, racism, the oppression of homosexuals, and so on), it will be much more difficult to emerge from under the distress. In these cases we must both discharge our painful feelings about the hurt, and at the same time, work to eliminate the oppression from the environment. No matter how much women cry and tremble and rage about how they were hurt in the past, they will still suffer the effects of sexism if they are beaten and invalidated in the present. The discharge will help, but the ongoing oppression must stop also.

Despite how it may seem on the surface, eliminating sexism in relationships will benefit men as well as women. It will enable men to recover those aspects of their humanness that are covered over by the distress recordings resulting from their sexist conditioning. These aspects include being able to express loving; knowing how to think about, nurture, and support others; being gentle and tender; cooperating with other people; being able to listen well to others and be sensitive to their feelings; knowing how to touch nonsexually and without discomfort; accommodating other people when appropriate; being more open and accepting about feelings; and regaining the ability to cry. In these areas men have a lot to learn from women, in whom these qualities have not been so inhibited and suppressed. As men emerge from their roles as oppressors, they will lose some of the privileges they derive from sexism; but these losses are more than recompensed by gaining women as real allies in relationships and the world, and recovering basic human qualities. Men become no less strong, capable, intelligent, or assertive by giving up their sexist patterns; rather, these attributes become supplemented with the qualities of loving, listening, and accommodating.

RESPONSES OF MEN TO SEXISM

When men are confronted with the issue of sexism, either in themselves or in the wider society, several responses are common. One of them is that men feel "threatened"; that is, they feel a little afraid. Part of the reason for this fear is that the patterns of sexism—that men are better than women, that women need to be taken care of, and so on—have been deeply ingrained into men from their early childhood. It feels very much as if these patterns are "just the way we are," and that it is impossible to be any different. In the face of these feelings, thinking about the possibility of change is scary—what am I going to lose, and what will take its place?

Another response is guilt. Guilt in this case involves the sense that men are to blame for sexism, that it is men's fault for exhibiting sexist behavior. The result of guilt is that men feel bad about themselves and disparage themselves and other men: "We're bad for being sexist," the recording says. Of course, it is not true. Men have been sexist only because they were hurt themselves. Men have every reason to feel and discharge their grief over how women have been hurt and how their behavior has contributed to this hurt. Men also have the responsibility from the present onward to work against sexism wherever it is found. It is useless and counterproductive, however, for men to wallow in guilt or blame themselves for their sexist conditioning. Feeling guilty makes it hard for them to get in touch with and discharge the grief they really feel, and it also interferes with their ability to be effective allies for women. Men are okay. Men also have acted as agents of women's oppression, and this behavior must stop. The best allies women have are men who feel good about themselves, are strong and assertive, and use their talents and skills in the service of liberating women from the effects of sexism and other forms of oppression.

A third response is essentially to replay their oppressor recordings, to come back with such things as "That's right, a woman's place is in the home"; "Women *are* less capable than men"; and so on. In this response, men recite what they heard while growing up and reenact rigid behavior patterns developed during distressful experiences. When it happens, the sexist patterns must be interrupted, both to prevent the reinforcement of women's oppression and to help men free their thinking and behavior from the control of these patterns. Sometimes active listening effectively interrupts sexist remarks—"You're feeling attacked now"—and sometimes a firmer interruption is required—"It is hurtful to women when you say things like that, so please stop." In any case, no human being willingly operates from a rigid pattern. When it is interrupted and the feelings associated with it thoroughly discharged, the person will experience great relief.

The fourth common response "Wait a minute, women aren't the only people who feel bad and are afraid to assert themselves. I've been hurt too. In fact, my mother did some pretty mean things to me." In other words, men often respond by saying that they are hurt by sexism, too, and that sometimes women oppress men. It is true that men have been hurt by sexism. In the ways previously mentioned, we have had our humanness blunted in the process of being conditioned to be tough, competitive, aggressive people. We have also been oppressed as children (by our parents, both male and female), as wage earners (by our employers), as members of minorities (if relevant), and so on. These forms of oppression are just as hurtful as sexism. But women are not agents of oppression for adult men. It is true that in many relationships women heap abuse upon men as much as it is heaped upon them, but there is nowhere the kind of systematic reinforcement for the invalidation of men as there is of women. The plain fact is that sexism functions to provide men with benefits and privileges denied to women. The means by which women are denied them vary from legal, economic, educational, and moral restraints to emotional manipulation and threats of physical violence. No, men are not oppressed by women in terms of sexism.

SOCIETAL CAUSES OF SEXISM

Sexism is perpetuated by people with patterns of oppressor and victim who hurt young people in the same ways that they themselves were hurt, thereby instilling similar patterns.

Sexism has deep historical roots, going back at least to the origin of agriculture over fourteen thousand years ago. It is not within the scope of this book to discuss in depth the causes of sexism, but we can say that functionally it is related to how society is organized and how wealth is obtained and distributed. Sexism did not arise with capitalism nor will it necessarily end with its decline, but the oppression of women could not have continued under capitalism unless the economic system in some way benefited from it. In fact the role of women and the nature of the family have changed significantly under capitalism, indicating that how sexism operates is very much related to how production is organized and goods distributed.

Could our present economic system function if women were not oppressed? As it now stands, women do an enormous amount of unpaid work in the home, cleaning, cooking, washing, and childcare. If women were not oppressed, this work would be more valued and they would be paid for their labor. After all, custodians, childcare workers, and teachers all are paid—shouldn't housewives, who do the same work, also receive remuneration? But if women were paid for housework, from where would the money come? From the wages of men? From the profits of employers? Owners of businesses and male workers make as much money as they do because women receive so little for their labor.

The oppression of women also results in their having the lowest paid and most menial jobs in our society. If women were not so oppressed and conditioned to expect so little, there is no way they would accept being at the bottom layer of the economic hierarchy. Having a group conditioned to take these jobs enables the exploitative system to function with a minimum of disturbance: People who do not expect any more will not complain.

Having women in an inferior economic and social position also gives male workers a group to look down on and feel superior to—which has several effects. One, it gives men a false sense of satisfaction ("I'm better off than she is") and makes them more "content." Two, it provides men with a place to vent the feelings built up at the workplace—they take them out on their woman friends. Three, it keeps men and women apart and at war with each other, thereby taking the focus away from the fact that both of them are hurt by a system in which a small, wealthy group benefits from the labor of and at the expense of all working people.

Making our economic system more rational will go a long way toward combating sexism, but alone it is probably not sufficient to eliminate it. We also must launch a frontal assault on the rigid patterns men and women operate out of; and we must receive the support we need to emerge from these patterns.

INEQUALITY IN SAME-SEX RELATIONSHIPS

Male-female relationships are not the only ones to be affected by patterns resulting from sexist socialization. Relationships between men and between women also suffer from the effects of sexism. Whether or not the same-sex relationships include sex, the people involved still have to deal with their patterns of accommodation and assertiveness, timidity and aggression, and so on. If the relationship is between two men, for instance, both may have patterns of aggressiveness which interfere with their interaction. Similarly, two women may have patterns of accommodation. Although the typical element common to heterosexual relationships of one person being assertive and the other being accommodating may be absent from same-sex relationships, the patterns resulting from sexism still affect how the persons relate to one another. A man who has patterns making it difficult for him to accommodate will probably have trouble doing so with men as well as with women.

Because the relationship involves two men or two women does not automatically mean that it will be one of harmony and equality. People were still hurt, and still act out of patterns based on those hurts. These rigid patterns do affect how decisions are made and who has more or less power within the relationship.

Exercise 25 will help each of us examine the degree of equality in our intimate relationships. This exercise is relevant to both heterosexual and same-sex partnerships or friendships, with some of the questions being less relevant for less intimate relationships. (For example, if people are not sharing money it may not be appropriate to ask who decides how the money is spent.)

EXERCISE 25   HOW EQUAL IS YOUR RELATIONSHIP?

Purpose: To help you examine the dynamics of power in your relationship.

Task: Answer these questions:
How is money earned and distributed?
Who tends to decide where money is spent (for example, on a vacation or a car)?
Does either one of you use or threaten to use physical force on the other?
Does one of you tend to decide where or when you go out for entertainment together?
Does one of you usually win arguments and have the final say?
Is one of you frequently intimidated by the other?

Evaluation:

What can you do to make your relationship more equal?
What can your partner do?

Whatever the nature of the relationship, we can use the exercise to investigate the dynamics of power in our interactions, and we can use our understanding to make the relationship more productive for both parties.

COMBATING SEXISM IN RELATIONSHIPS

We have established that sexism helps neither men nor women develop their human potential. Thus it is in the interest of both sexes to eliminate sexism and all its adverse effects on behavior. Eliminating sexism will make relationships more equal and beneficial to both people, whether or not sex is involved and whether or not the relationship is heterosexual. Freedom from the constraints imposed by sex roles and rigid sexist patterns will improve enormously our ability to think and respond flexibly to those we love and care about.

Sexism cannot be eliminated quickly or easily, but there are many concrete steps that can be taken to eliminate its effects on intimate relationships.

1. We must step out of our conditioned sex roles. We must no longer expect women to respond to men's needs, take major responsibility for raising children, do the cooking and cleaning, and so on. Women will be oppressed as long as they do unpaid labor and are put in roles that effectively place other people's needs above their own. This is not to say that women will no longer do any cooking, but it is saying that women will not cook just because they were socialized into that role. To help people become more aware of how sex roles affect their relationships, a sex-role reversal is presented in Exercise 26. In this exercise the partners in a relationship are invited temporarily to exchange roles for a specified period of time.

2. Men must discharge their feelings associated with their patterns of sexism. They can scan their memories of things they heard about women and ways women were treated while they were growing up. (It is best not to do this around women; it is not helpful for them to hear sexist remarks and attitudes, even in this context.) Discharging the feelings about these memories will help loosen the stranglehold they have on our behavior. More importantly, men must cease

deprecating and invalidating behavior toward women. This
behavior includes staring at women's bodies, labeling women
as incompetent or unintelligent, making nasty cracks about
women, and assuming that women naturally will handle the
childcare and cleaning. It also includes such subtle things as
always being the one to pay in restaurants, being the one to
drive when the two of you get into a car, and being "nicer" to
women than to men. These acts reinforce patterns of sexism,
and both men and women are better off if they no longer
occur.

   3. Women need to discharge their painful emotion over
how they have been treated, and then move on to take charge
of their lives. Crying, raging, laughing, and trembling about

what happened from childhood to the present will help women to step outside the feelings and patterns of hopelessness and powerlessness to be strong and assertive. The reality is that women are intelligent, competent, creative, and powerful. The only things keeping women from acting this way all the time are rigid patterns and old feelings, which are reinforced by the oppressive environment.

It is often helpful also for women to take positive directions out of the feelings of hopelessness, powerlessness, and inadequacy. That is, women can think about what they want to do to take charge of their lives, and set goals to do so. This step may bring up many feelings because it goes against all the oppressive conditioning to ignore one's own needs and pay attention to other people. If these feelings are released, they will not block the positive actions necessary for taking control of one's life.

4. Men need to think about women. They must think about what support will help women they love grow and become fuller human beings, and they need to follow through by providing the necessary support. One aspect usually will be listening well to them. As Kathy Miller mentioned earlier in this chapter, men must be careful about how they support women; because of their respective patterns, it is easy for men to "take over" for women under the guise of support. ("Come on, you want to call about that job. Here's the phone. Do you want me to dial it for you? What's wrong, don't you want to call? You said you did. . . .") The benefits of men really thinking about and nurturing women are tremendous, however. It helps women to move out of their patterns and their constricting roles, and at the same time, helps men develop their ability to care about, nurture, and pay attention to others.

Along the same line, it is also very important that men start to think about other men—how to demonstrate their caring, how to help other men develop their abilities to be fuller people, and so on. Men focusing their attention and love just on women is another aspect of sexism in our society.

5. Women need to consciously think about their own wants and needs. What would they do if they were to put themselves first? Of course it does not always make sense to put oneself first, but addressing this question will help women counter the patterns of accommodation, which operate to put other people's concerns above their own. It certainly is important to think about other people, but it is about time that women have the opportunity to think about themselves and to act in their own interests.

6. Both men and women need to think together and separately about sexism in their relationships. How is sexism being reinforced? How is it being confronted and interrupted? In what areas are we doing well? By addressing these questions directly, both partners can work together to eliminate sexism's effects.

One cautionary note is that when men and women discuss sexism together, often women will say that a particular behavior is sexist and men will deny it. When this conflict happens, it is particularly important that men listen to what it feels like to women when the behavior occurs. Men may not think that what they are doing is oppressive, but if women experience it as such, men should give great weight to this feeling. If men continue to say that "You're wrong, it is perfectly okay that I did that; you're just being irritable," or some such thing, this in itself is oppressive and invalidating to the woman involved. Despite all the recordings and however it may feel, men can trust women's thinking in this area, as well as in all others.

7. Sexism must be stopped in the world as well as in intimate partnerships, for we never can be completely free of sexism as long as we are confronted with it every time we turn on the television, walk down the street, apply for a job, or go into a restaurant. It will take a lot of work to cleanse our society of sexism, but it is a necessary task if we are totally to emerge from our rigid patterns of behavior. We can work to put women in positions of political power, we can fight for equal pay for equal work, we can push for job-training pro-

grams for women, and we can combat sexism in education. Also, we can stop sexist remarks, sexist jokes, and all forms of violence inflicted upon women.

8. Both women and men need to look to members of the same sex for support, attention, and ideas. It is particularly useful for women to find out that each is not the only one experiencing the oppression of sexism. It contradicts the patterns of both men and women, however, for them to help other members of the same sex step out of roles and relate to everyone in a nonsexist manner.

9. Both sexes need to affirm themselves and each other as proud, competent men and women. "I'm proud to be a man" and "I'm proud to be a woman" are the directions in which men and women must go, respectively. This pride has nothing to do with arrogance or superiority but involves the total appreciation of ourselves as men and women. From positions of personal strength and confidence we can work together to eliminate sexism from our relationships and the world. In fact, the patterns of sexism in both men and women can be seen as a direct result of their feelings of inadequacy and insecurity. Patterns of sexism in men, for example, serve to cover up their low self-images and their sense of themselves as little boys. By seeing ourselves as strong, proud men who no longer need to be mothered or taken care of, we will be more able to help women and ourselves be effective comrades in the struggle for human liberation.

The phenomenon of sexism is a paper tiger: It is only powerful because we allow it to be so. There is no limit to what we could do if we refused to submit to the patterns of oppression that have been instilled in us by the whole social, cultural, and economic system. It is within our power to do exactly this, to say "No" to the oppression and to work for really human relationships.

eleven

What about Sex?

Doing, a filthy pleasure is, and short;
And done, we straight repent us of the sport:
Let us not then rush blindly on unto it,
Like lustful beasts, that only know to do it:

From "Petronius Arbiter," translated
from the Latin by Ben Johnson

Sex is one of the many things of which human beings are capable. It is an activity, like that of eating, walking, swimming, playing tennis, sleeping, and talking. The activity of sex is perhaps the most misunderstood and misused of all human endeavors. Think about these questions:

What is sex?
Is sexual activity inherently pleasurable?
What is the most sensible role of sex in relationships?
Should we have sex with only one person or with many people?
Should we have sex only with members of the opposite sex?
Is abortion rational?
Should young people be allowed or encouraged to experiment with sex?

Is pornography helpful or harmful?
Why does rape occur?
Why are men never raped by women?
Why do some people enjoy sex with animals, and why do others have to be beaten in order to have orgasms?
Why are feelings of jealousy so tied up with sexual behavior?
Why do some people feel a "need" for sex and not others?
Is masturbation unhealthy?

There is no consensus on the answers to many of these questions.

Sex is a part of almost all marriages and many other intimate relationships. It seems sensible that we as participants should know why we take part in sexual activity, what we get out of it, and what role it plays in our relationships. Unfortunately, we have all been inundated with misconceptions, incorrect assumptions, and irrational actions in the area of sex. No one growing up in this society can have escaped the effects of this irrationality. As a result, *almost everything we assume to be natural and inherent about sex is based entirely on distress recordings*. To understand this assertion we must look at the origin and development of sexual feelings and their relation to painful emotion.[1]

When we are born, our bodies are totally sensitized to what is happening around us. We see, hear, feel and smell it all. We are *sensual creatures*. The adults around us are relatively desensitized, and treat us as if we were like them. One of the first ways this happens is that our births are loud and bright and insensitive. And this is just the beginning. When the adults around us touch or caress us, they pick particular parts of our bodies. That is, they caress everything but our genitals, which they touch in the most perfunctory way while cleaning us. This is done hurriedly,

---

[1] Penny Jeannechild has contributed significantly to this chapter and has helped me clarify my thinking about sex. The following quotation is included with her permission (copyright pending).

with a good deal of embarrassment and sometimes fear generated towards us. Here we are feeling all warm and wonderful, sensations coursing through our bodies, oh, yummy, they are taking off my uncomfortable diaper, rubbing my tummy, she's smiling at me, rubbing my tummy, now ummm, that feels good, she's rubbing my penis, yum, it all feels so good, oh, why is she frowning at me, gee, she's being awful rough all of a sudden, just when my body was feeling so very nice all over. This is the first place children learn to associate pleasant physical feelings with distress. The distress radiating from adults around changing diapers comes from the feelings about excrement, of course, but I'm talking about the fear adults exhibit around genitals.

Baby boys get erections in response to the *total body feelings* they experience. This can be seen in infants from the time of birth. Also from birth, adults respond to erections with fear and embarrassment, and treat infants differently as a result. Often adults become tense, or call attention to the erection by calling out to other adults, who come and stare between the child's legs. So, what do you think is the message to the infant when the only time the genitals are touched is when they have to be, as opposed to the other body parts which get rubbed and caressed?

As the child gets older, less and less of his or her body gets touched, and the genitals stop getting touched altogether. With this cessation of touch comes messages about sex such as, "Don't touch yourself," "Mommy and Daddy go off and feel good together and leave me out," "It's not okay to be naked around people anymore," "I'm supposed to be a big girl/boy now and not snuggle up in laps," etc. So you have the groundwork for genital fixation. The genitals have been focused on first by being touched perfunctorily, roughly, and with embarrassment and fear, and then by not being touched at all. In addition, because of their biological function, they may have become a source of guilt, shame and embarrassment for the child. Those same parts of adults' bodies have usually been hidden all along from the child. What is the message here? Fear. Something is going on around the child that spells fear, fear, fear. And so those original good, sensual feelings begin to have fear attached to them. This association of fear with total body sensuality results in what we call sexual feelings.

As we get older, we continue to accumulate distress attached to bodily pleasure. We are further encumbered with a number of incorrect attitudes and ideas about the genital region in particular and sex in general. A typical nine-year-old boy or girl will have "learned," for example, that sex is dirty; sex is sinful; boys and girls are bad if they explore each other's genitals; girls must be afraid of strange men, who might do something bad to them; masturbation causes mental illness; it is bad for boys to "play with themselves"; sex before marriage is wrong, but men try to get women to have sex with them anyway; it is very bad for boys to play with the genitals of other boys, or for girls to mutually explore each other's genitals—this makes them "queer"; sexual activity is something very mysterious and secretive, which adults do only behind locked doors or when they think that everyone else is asleep; it is much worse for girls to have sex than it is for boys; and it is wrong for anyone to touch the genital areas of young people. We can add to this list information our nine-year-old has picked up on television and at the movie theatre, that "beautiful," "sexy" women get all the attention; that the more women men have sex with, the better; that sex and violence are often connected to one another.

Superimposed on all this supposed learning about sex are the feelings of fear and embarrassment that are communicated whenever the subject of sex and sexuality are discussed in the home, in school, or in the backyard or street. As young people we all undoubtedly wondered, what is this thing sex that people are so embarrassed about and afraid of? Unfortunately, even before we could formulate this thought clearly we were bombarded with invalidating messages and feelings about our bodies and our own sensuality.

Sex is not bad. The penis and clitoris and vagina are simply parts of the human body, like arms and legs and elbows. In the absence of distress, sexual activity is no better or worse than any other activity. It is appropriate sometimes and not at others, but it is neither the greatest good nor the worst evil.

Unfortunately, our nine-year-old person does not have a

fair chance to understand for her- or himself what sex is about: The very act of exploring is vigorously punished. What effect do you think this attitude has on young people? What effect do you think it had on us? We received and internalized all those messages about sex, and they have had a tremendous effect on what we think and how we function.

SEX AND BEHAVIOR PATTERNS

Distress recordings consist of everything that was happening at the time of a distressful incident—how we felt, how we perceived what other people felt, what the environment was like, and what actually occurred. When somehow we are reminded of this incident the recording replays, and we again experience the feelings and enact similar behavior. This response applies to sex as well as other areas connected to distress. When anything restimulates distressful incidents involving bodily pleasure, and particularly the genitals, sexual feelings are recalled. This restimulation is how men can have erections merely by gazing at pictures or reading books; their sexual feelings related to past, distressful experiences are restimulated and felt again. Ask the man what the picture reminds him of, and he will tell you exactly the source of the restimulation.

For example, Fred just recently met a woman named Maggy at his job and found himself immediately "attracted" to her; that is, he is sexually aroused when he sees her or thinks about her. He chose to address this reaction in a counseling session:

FRED: Whenever I see her, I just get turned on. I mean, I haven't even talked to her yet. I just found out her name a couple of days ago.

COUNSELOR: Who does she remind you of? What's your first thought?

FRED *(starts laughing)*: ... That can't be.... She reminds me of Amy, the girl I went steady with in high school.

COUNSELOR: What happened with Amy?

FRED: Nothing happened, literally ... *(continues laughing)*.... We kissed a lot, and necked, but we never got anywhere, if you know what I mean.

COUNSELOR: No, what do you mean?

FRED: You know ... *(keeps laughing)*.... Let's change the subject. ...

COUNSELOR: What did it feel like with Amy, kissing and necking and wanting to make love and everything?

FRED: Scary and yucky.... I wanted to have sex but she didn't, but we were both scared and didn't really know what we were doing. After going together she let me put my hand on her breast ... *(laughs)*. How ridiculous ... the constant struggle we had.... I think I always felt frustrated after we were out....

COUNSELOR: Can you remember a specific time?

FRED: Sure ... there was one time after a basketball game. We drove on out to the park and started kissing and, well, you know.

COUNSELOR: No, what?

FRED: I was putting my hand on her breast, and squeezing close to her and wanting to make love. But she didn't want to, and kept saying "No" to me. I just felt real bad....

The fear and embarrassment tied up with this incident from the past are restimulated when Fred sees or thinks about another woman who looks like his high school friend. These are the ingredients of most sexual feelings in adults—pleasurable sensations and a good deal of fear. These feelings become tied together into what we have come to think of as "sexual feelings." Each of us probably can connect many of our present "sexual feelings" to painful memories, times when our real need to be touched, stroked, caressed, and held became attached to the distressed response of some adult around us. Many of these memories may be occluded and difficult to remember, as they happened when we were very young.

It is as a result of the process of restimulation that people get "turned on" by pictures, objects, and situations that seemingly have no overt sexual content to them. A friend of mine, for example, for years masturbated to pictures of female underwear advertisements. Some people have sexual feelings when they are physically beaten; this response can be traced to experiences in their childhood when sexual feelings were associated with physical abuse.

For many of us, the act of being touched restimulates feelings of fear and embarrassment. This reaction is often directly connected to times in our childhood when we were experiencing the pleasure of touching or being touched, and an adult responded with discomfort. Perhaps the adult was a father, who did not quite know what to do with this six-year-old girl curled up in his lap, stroking his face and hair. Everything he had been taught about touch, sex, incest, females, and so on was restimulated by the gentle and caring touch of his daughter. He began to have feelings he was not sure what to do with, and what he communicated to his daughter were confusion and discomfort. She recorded the experience intact, with her and her father's pleasure connected to his feelings of fear and embarrassment. After several of these experiences the recording is ingrained: The pleasure and fear melt together to become one sensation—sexual feelings. As she grows older, the touch of a man in some way resembling her father will recall these feelings on an unconscious level. When we have sexual feelings, the painful emotions associated with past experiences in any way connected with sex are restimulated. If the people telling us about sex communicated their fear and embarrassment and we did not have the opportunity to discharge our feelings, then these feelings will be restimulated whenever we have sexual feelings. Because there is undischarged distress attached to almost every sexual experience we have ever had—including all the times we heard that sex is sinful, masturbation is bad, and so on—the amount of accumulated painful emotion in this area is quite large. It is no wonder, then, that some people grit their teeth while having sex, or do not want to do it, or want to do it without the slightest consideration of whether the other person wants to or not. Our thinking in the area of sex and sexuality is clouded by mounds of distress, which can only be removed by thoroughly discharging the painful emotion, reevaluating our past experiences, and paying close attention to our behavior in the present.

There is no such thing as a compulsive "sex drive." The feeling of "I gotta have it" is merely the replaying of an old distress recording. It is just like being in the grip of any other distress pattern—we feel no longer in control. Many of us have rigid patterns involving compulsive eating. When we feel nervous or anxious, it feels as if we have to eat, and we do so without thinking about it. What is sometimes called a sex drive is actually a rigid pattern of compulsive sex, which operates the same way as compulsive eating—when the pattern is somehow restimulated, it feels as if we have to have sex.

As with all rigid patterns, the compulsion for sex diminishes and eventually disappears when people discharge the painful emotions associated with the distressful incidents from our past with which pleasurable body feelings are associated. As the "need" for sex goes away, so does the treatment of other people as sex objects, as things to help us fill our "need." Men and women start seeing and relating to each other as valuable and interesting human beings in their own right.

Often when the relation between painful emotion and current sexual activity is discussed, people feel quite defensive and a little scared. "Does this mean that having sex is bad?" "But I *need* sex." "You're trying to take away the only pleasurable thing I do." When these feelings come up, I try to remind people of what they will gain by giving up the compulsion: They can again relate to people as people instead of as need-fulfillment objects; they can establish real, human-to-human contact instead of trying to manipulate each other; and finally, they will be more in charge of their sexual feelings and behavior—guided by their functioning intelligence instead of distress patterns from the past.

One way to start thinking about and working on our own sexual distress is to recall all our memories having anything to do with sex. The incidents that come to mind will be those in which sex or pleasurable body feelings are in some way associated with emotional or physical distress. What is your earliest memory in any way associated with sex? Your next memory? The next one? Going through these memories will help each of us uncover the nature of our restimulation, and by discharging the feelings associated with them we can free ourselves of their control. Exercise 27 presents an opportunity for this kind of scanning.

**EXERCISE 27   SCANNING MEMORIES ASSOCIATED
WITH SEX**

Purpose: To put you in touch with the distressful incidents from your past that are associated with sex, and to help you begin the process of getting rid of the painful feelings related to them.

Task: This exercise works best with two people, one of whom is giving her or his attention to the other. One person simply asks the other, "What is your earliest memory having anything to do with sex?" The second person then responds by telling the earliest memory that comes to mind, whether it seems to have anything to do with sex or not. The first person then asks, 'What is your next momory?" and the other person responds. This process continues until the person has gone through all her or his memories connected with sex, from the earliest to the present. If embarrassing or scary feelings come to the surface, feel free to laugh or cry or tremble or so on. This discharge is exactly what you need to free yourself from the effects of the experience.

Once all memories at all connected with sex have been recited, go over them again, adding ones you left out the first time. As you continue scanning your memories, you will notice that some of them start to stick out and seem more important. These are incidents to which much distress is attached and, therefore, need a lot of attention and discharge.

If doing this exercise with another person, one person should scan sexual memories for a specified length of time. Then the other can scan her or his memories for the same length of time. Thus, each person gets the benefit of the other's attention.

This exercise can also be done alone, by asking yourself the questions. After you think about and maybe write down the first memory, go on to the next one, and then the next one, and so on, up to the present.

Evaluation:

What did you learn through scanning these memories?

How are your present sexual attitudes and behaviors affected by these incidents in the past?

How did it feel to recall these incidents?

Were you able to discharge any of the uncomfortable feelings that arose?

Did you gain any other insights?

By way of example, I will share my earliest memories connected in any way with sex. The first was at the age of three, standing naked in a doctor's office, screaming at the top of my lungs. My mother and the doctor were standing in the room smiling and wondering what I was crying about. My next memory somehow connected with sex is from two years later, when I was riding tricycles with a girl. Somebody (I don't remember who) laughed at us and ridiculed me for having a "girlfriend." My next memory, from about the same time, involved being called a "sissy" for playing a game with another boy in which my name was Robin; I was told that "that's a girl's name."

None of these memories would seem to have anything to do with sex or sexual feelings. Yet they are not recalled if I am asked to scan my memory for incidents related to eating or to being ill. Somehow feelings about sex were attached to these distressful incidents, and they come to consciousness when painful events associated with sex are recalled. I have discovered that discharging the feelings related to these incidents has freed my thinking and behavior regarding sex, so that I can act sensibly instead of compulsively.

SEXUAL PROBLEMS OF MEN AND WOMEN

There are several common kinds of physical dysfunction which adversely affect sexual activity. For men these include premature ejaculation and impotence; for women, the inability to achieve orgasm and vaginismus, the involuntary muscular contraction of the outer third of the vagina, effectively blocking its entrance. All these problems typically have their roots in past, distressful experiences associated with the sexual act or pleasurable body feelings. The distressful experience may be something as blatant as a rape, or it may be as subtle as orthodox religious training equating sexual acts with the devil. Often researchers try to categorize the psychological causes of sexual dysfunction—religious orthodoxy, "paternal dominance," "maternal dominance," and so on. I see little point in so doing, because each person's experiences are unique. The most effective way to find out why people have a particular dysfunction is to help them trace their painful feelings back to their original distressful experiences and discharge those feelings.

One man I was counseling had a problem of premature ejaculation—as soon as his penis entered a woman's vagina, he involuntarily ejaculated. The following is a portion of his counseling session:

ERIC: It happens just about every time I have sex with a woman. I get really excited, and come really quickly.

COUNSELOR: When you get all excited like that, what does it remind you of? What's your first thought?

ERIC: The first time I made love . . . *(starts laughing)*.

COUNSELOR: What happened that time?

ERIC: Well, it was awful. I had known ~~Cindy~~ for a few weeks, and we were both attracted to each other. I really wanted to make love with someone—I had been trying a long time . . . *(laughs)*. Anyway, we got together a few times and got stoned, and were necking and everything. I was really excited. I remember thinking, "Wow, maybe it's finally going to happen. Maybe it will really happen" *(laughs)*.

COUNSELOR: What happened next?

ERIC: One of those times I remember coming in my pants. I think I was lying down hugging her, and I guess our bodies were rubbing together. I was so excited about making love, actually doing it, that I came right then and there . . . *(laughs)*. I was really embarrassed, it was awful . . . I was afraid I was going to do something wrong, and sure enough I did.

COUNSELOR: It was pretty scary.

ERIC: It sure was . . . I didn't know what I was doing? . . *(laughs)*. I remember wondering how I was supposed to get my penis into her vagina. I didn't know what to do. . . . It was awful . . . *(continues laughing)*. What happens now is that I worry about whether I'm going to ejaculate too soon, and when I worry about it I get more excited and ejaculate sooner. . . . I'm also afraid that the woman won't like me for coming too soon, and this also makes me lose control. It's awful . . . *(laughs)*.

COUNSELOR: Would you try saying something?

ERIC: Sure, what?

COUNSELOR: How about saying, "Umm, sex, nothing scary about that."

ERIC *(starts laughing loudly and continuously)*: . . . I can't say that! *(continues laughing.)*

COUNSELOR: Yes you can. "Umm, sex, nothing scary about that!"

ERIC: Umm, sex, nothing scary about that . . . *(bursts out laughing, and continues laughing and saying the phrase for quite awhile)*.

We can see that Eric's premature ejaculation is part of a distress recording attached to much fear and embarrassment. When he is in a sexual situation, his feelings of fear and embarrassment are brought to the surface, and the associated loss of ejaculatory control is also restimulated. This pattern is essentially no different from any other rigid behavior pattern. It is the result of a distress recording containing everything that happened at the time of an undischarged painful experience. Whenever the distress recording is in some way restimulated, the associated sexual and painful feelings are experienced and the patterned behavior reenacted. In Eric's case, the feelings about the original incident were compounded by repeated experiences of a similar nature, so that the pattern has become more ingrained with time, with more painful emotion attached to it. As he discharges the fear and embarrassment (evidenced by his laughing), he will become free of the pattern and regain his control over ejaculation—which is what happened.

No one else will have exactly the same experiences as Eric with the same effects. However, the mechanisms of physical dysfunction are the same. Premature ejaculation, impotence, inability to achieve orgasm, and vaginismus are all rigid behavior patterns, resulting from past, tension-filled experiences. We can use techniques in the present to help correct these dysfunctions, but the way to completely eliminate them is to get rid of the painful emotion to which they are attached.

SEX AND SEXISM

As we might expect, the area of sexual activity is greatly affected by patterns and hurts resulting from sexism. When the patterns of compulsive sex that many men have are acted out, usually it is at women's expense. What typically happens is that men "convince" women to have sex with them, through moral persuasion ("Why not?"), economic threat ("You owe it to me"), emotional pressure ("Don't you like me? Come on, I *need* you"), emotional threat ("Okay if you don't want to, but don't expect me to keep coming around"), or physical threat. The effect is that men impose their will upon women, who without this pressure often would not agree to have sex. Women accommodate men in this area for the same reasons that they accommodate in others—it is the result of the oppressive conditioning to which they have systematically been subjected.

> It is safe to say that most women have been raped. Not all of them necessarily by physical force, a lot by emotional force, by not knowing that she has the right to say "No," because of the assumption that it is not her body, that her role is to please. If you get any group of women talking, and you ask how many have ended up making love a number of times when they didn't want to, it's almost universal. There is a sense of obligation, a sense of duty, and a sense of complying with an implied physical force.[2]

In heterosexual relationships, men are consistently the initiators of sexual activity. Men are also usually the more active partner sexually, whereas women tend to be more passive and accommodating. Have you ever heard of a man faking orgasm so that his partner would not be upset? Of course not, but it is common for women to fake groans and grunts so that their male partners don't go away unhappy. Is this rational? I think not.

[2]Kathy Miller, "A Woman Talks to Men About Sexism," *Re-evaluation Counseling Sisters*, No. 3 (Seattle: Rational Island Publishers, 1977), p. 23.

What would it be like if sexual activity were not constrained by sex roles? What if men did not do all or almost all of the initiating? Our sexual activity would be much more human and intelligent and less patterned and unthinking. Stepping out of these role-related patterns will help us think about our sexual activity, thereby helping us and our partners achieve a more satisfying relationship in the long run.

In Exercise 28, it is suggested that you and your partner reverse your normal roles in sexual activity. If you are typically the initiator, let your partner do it. If you normally take a more active role, now take a more passive one. Much information about sex roles and patterns comes out through this exercise. For example, the other person might initiate sexual activity much less frequently; it may seem as if s/he never wants to have sex at all. This behavior may indicate

---

**EXERCISE 28   REVERSING ROLES
IN SEXUAL ACTIVITY**

Purpose: To help you appreciate sex more and to separate it from role-related behavior.

Task: Make an agreement with your partner to try reversing roles during sexual activity as an experiment. If you normally initiate sex, let your partner take the initiative. If you are normally the more passive partner, become the more active one.

Evaluation:

What happened?
How did it feel to you to play the opposite sexual role?
How did it feel to your partner?
How did the reversal affect your sexual arousal?
What was hard for each of you about being in the opposite role?
What have you learned by reversing roles in sexual activity?

how one-sided the sexual aspect of the relationship is, and many feelings may have to be worked through and discharged before a healthy sexual relationship satisfying both parties is achieved. But is it not worth the effort, to have sexual activity that both people enjoy rather than to have only one person calling the shots and the other going along against her will?

THE USES OF SEX IN RELATIONSHIPS

Sex serves a variety of purposes in relationships. First, it is used as a temporary substitute for real intimacy. Often when people are feeling lonely, they think more about having sex. Even within marriages, it is not uncommon for sexual activity to be the only time when the two people are intimate.

Second, sex is used to fulfill the real human need for physical closeness. Largely because of the amount of distress attached to sex in our culture, our distress patterns associate physical closeness with sex. It thus feels as if we need sex to obtain physical closeness; and, in actuality, for many people having sex is the only way they have a chance to hold and be held by another person.

Third, we use sex to fill the need for touching. Touching is a basic human need, and the connection between touching and sex throughout our culture is purely the result of distress. There is nothing inherently sexual about touching or being touched, but because of their patterned connection, we all carry much fear and embarrassment about touching other human beings. As a result we do not get enough touching, and sexual activity becomes the one area in which we know that it is okay to touch and touch and touch.

Fourth, sex is used as a replacement for love and attention. Throughout this book I have avoided using the term "make love" precisely because it implies a relationship between love and sex that does not exist in practice. Many tennis partners know and love each other more than do sexual partners. The act of meeting someone in a bar, getting drunk with him or her, and then going home and having sex together has nothing to do with love. The feelings of loneliness may be temporarily assuaged, but love was not obtained. Nevertheless, sex is used to try to find some of the love we did not get in the past, and some of the love we are not getting in the present.

Fifth, sex provides a safe place for discharge. Often people cry or tremble while having sex, because in their lives they have no other places where it feels safe to do so. Thus sex is used to enable people to release their tensions and frustrations, when otherwise they would just hold the feelings in or dramatize them.

All these things for which sex is used are human needs which must be filled for us to be happy and productive. We need intimacy and physical closeness; we need love, attention, and touching; and we certainly need to discharge our tensions. That sex is the main, and in some cases, the only avenue for meeting these needs, however, makes little sense. For one thing, it means that the only people who can meet these needs are people with whom we have sex. This attitude puts a heavy burden on sexual relationships. For another thing, it puts a tremendous focus on sexual activity, imbuing it with an importance that should not be attached to any activity, let alone one so laden with distress. It is no wonder that it is difficult for us to think about the role of sex in our relationships, and to act sensibly in this area.

We and our partners need to hug each other, touch each other, encourage each other to discharge, and express our love and caring in many different ways and at many different times. We do not have to restrict ourselves to touching or hugging only our partners, either. Why not hug other friends, both male and female? Why not cry in front of them? Why not tell them that we love them? The reasons we do not are our feelings of fear and embarrassment.

By freeing sexual activity from the burden of meeting all these needs, we can also devote more energy and attention to clearing up our distress around sexuality. In Exercise 29, it is suggested that you and your partner stop having sex for awhile and pay attention to what happens. This is a good opportunity to meet your needs in other ways, and at the same time to get in touch with some of the feelings and patterns associated with sex itself. When you do engage in sexual activity again, it will be with a new awareness and sensitivity and a better sense of what part sex plays in your relationship.

EXERCISE 29   INVESTIGATING THE ROLE OF SEX IN YOUR RELATIONSHIP

Purpose: To help you investigate the role of sex in your relationship, and to give you the opportunity to fill your needs for loving, touching, physical closeness, and attention in ways not involving sex.

Task: Make an agreement with your partner to abstain from sexual activity for an agreed upon period of time (for example a week, two weeks, or a month). Make it long enough so that it is noticeably different from your normal activity. Continue to sleep together and hug one another, and use the time that would have been spent engaged in sex to be emotionally and physically close to one another.

Evaluation:

How did you feel abstaining from sex?

How did your partner feel?

How did it affect your intimacy with each other?

What effect did it have on your whole relationship?

What do you think might happen to your relationship if you gave up sex entirely?

What other insights did you gain about the role of sex in your relationship?

What other ways were you able to express your loving and caring?

How did it feel to hold and touch each other without having sex?

RATIONAL SEX: HOW MIGHT IT LOOK?

We cannot know for sure what the area of sexual activity will look like in the absence of distress, but we can begin to speculate on it as we become less distressed through discharge. One of the most obvious changes is that sex will no longer be overemphasized. No longer will sex or sex appeal be used to sell everything from shaving cream to milk, from automobiles to furniture. Pornography will cease to exist, because its existence is entirely based on the restimulation of sexual feelings from past, painful experiences. Prostitution will also disappear, because men will no longer have patterned "needs" for sex.

Sex will be less of a preoccupation all around. Without sexual distress, women will not be molested by men in any way. "Kinky" sex—for example, sex with animals, sadomasochism, and so on—will also fade away, because like pornography, it is based on the restimulation of old hurts.

We will no longer talk about sex with embarrassment and shame, and the culture will be cleansed of the messages saying that sex is dirty and sinful. Young people will feel free to explore their bodies with each other, out of simple curiosity. From what I know of a few children who are being allowed to find out about sex in an undistressed way, once their curiosity is satisfied, their interest in sex recedes.

The decision to have sex or not will not be determined by our urges but by our intelligence, given all the relevant circumstances and information. This decision will include thinking about whether we wish to have children, whether the forms of contraception we are using are effective and not harmful or dangerous to either person, whether anyone else is going to be adversely affected, and what effect having sex has or will have on our relationship. Only if it makes sense in all respects will we have sex.

The sex act itself will probably be changed from the way it is typically performed today. It will involve people looking at each other, talking to each other about what feels good, and

EXERCISE 30   HAVING SEX AWARELY

Purpose: To help make sexual activity more aware and pleasurable and less controlled by the restimulation of past hurts.

Task: While thinking about or having sex, try some of the following suggestions:

1. Plan when you are going to have sex beforehand, to take some of the compulsiveness out of sexual activity.
2. Each of you take a few minutes to say what you would like to do to the other person and what you would like to have done to you. This step may be embarrassing, but you can always laugh or giggle!
3. Have sex with the lights on and eyes open. Try maintaining visual contact with each other, instead of retreating into a private space.
4. During sexual activity, talk about what you like and do not like. Give each other continual information and feedback about how you feel.
5. Take turns giving each other one-way attention. One of you lie back, let yourself be hugged, kissed, and caressed, and let the feelings come up. Feel free to laugh, cry, or tremble if it feels right to do so. Then switch roles, giving the other person the chance to be caressed.

Evaluation:

What happened?

What feelings came up for each of you?

What insights did you gain about sex for you and for your friend?

What did you learn that will improve your sexual activity in the future?

generally staying in close communication. Embarrassment and fear will be mostly absent from the interaction; and when these feelings do come up they will be discharged. Finally, because people will not be confined to particular roles, they will use their creativity and thinking to make the sexual activity as pleasurable as possible. Exercise 30 provides some suggestions of how these ideas can be put into practice in present relationships.

It will take a lot of discharge of old distress and much cultural change before we will reach this degree of rationality. It is certainly worth working toward, however. Just compare it to what we have now.

ON HETEROSEXUALITY AND HOMOSEXUALITY

At the present time the sexual preference of just about everyone is based on distress recordings. People associate sexual feelings with men or with women or with goats or with whips entirely as the result of what distressful experiences sexual feelings were attached to in early childhood. Thus some men develop patterns connecting sexual feelings with women, and other men develop them with men. Actually we all have accumulated distress patterns attaching sexual feelings to both men and women, but because of the particular ways in which we each have been hurt, the nature of the patterns varies from person to person.

I do not know what sexual preferences people will have in the absence of distress, or even whether everybody will exhibit the same sexual preferences. There is so much homophobia, or fear of homosexuality, rampant in our culture that it is difficult to think about what would happen if this fear were not so pervasive and encompassing.

Whatever form rational sexual behavior may ultimately take, the oppression of homosexuals in our society must cease. It is hurtful to all of us, but particularly to those human beings who happen to have sex with members of the same sex. No person deserves to be fired or treated as "different" or in any way discriminated against because s/he has a sexual preference at variance with the cultural norm.

The homophobia upon which the oppression of homosexuals is based is one aspect of the distress our whole culture puts on sex. It is one of the main things keeping men from getting close to and supporting other men, and also keeping women from each other. This attitude is harmful to relationships with members of both the same and the opposite sex, because it places undue reliance on opposite-sex relationships for the fulfillment of our needs. We thus downplay our friendships with members of the same sex and overemphasize those with members of the opposite sex. Neither set of friendships is treated with the respect and care it deserves.

Like other painful emotion, the fear of homosexuals or of being homosexual can be discharged and eliminated. The benefits of ridding ourselves of homophobia are threefold: (1) It will enable us to relate more humanly to people having a same-sex sexual preference, (2) we can be more effective in helping to eliminate the oppression of homosexuals in the world, and (3) we will have better relationships with men and women in our own lives.

I am not advocating any form of sexual behavior. What I am advocating is eliminating the distress we have accumulated in the area of sexuality so that our behavior can be based on our intelligence and not our distress patterns, and so that sex can play a constructive and beneficial role in our lives and those of our partners.

twelve
You and Children

. . . People do not have to become hurt and irrational. Children can be protected from most experiences of distress and helped to free themselves from those that do occur. It is possible for children to remain their real selves. Children can be allowed to grow up and become adults and yet remain the happy, loving, successful geniuses that they are inherently.[1]

Throughout this book we have stressed repeatedly the true nature of human beings—their natural intelligence, their capacity to love and be loved, their curiosity, their creativity, their natural zest, and above all, their ability to think freshly and creatively in every instance and to act appropriately based on the information at their disposal. What limits them is only the cumulative effect of undischarged distressful experiences.

When human beings are born, they possess all this tremendous potential. They may have suffered some prenatal

[1]Harvey Jackins, *The Human Side of Human Beings* (Seattle: Rational Island Publishers, 1965), p. 71.

or birth trauma, but basically physically healthy infants are functioning at a very high level. They sleep when tired and cry when distressed or when their needs for milk, warmth, or attention are not met. When awake and undistressed they are alert, curious, and playful, and spend their time exploring and taking in their immediate world.

There are few distress recordings inhibiting the intelligence or affecting the behavior of infants. When they are distressed they spontaneously discharge until the tension is gone and their needs are satisfied. When they are not distressed their attention is totally in the present; they have few behavior patterns interfering with their response to the immediate situation.

It follows that infants and young children are much less distressed than almost all adults. Quite simply, they have not been hurt as much as adults. Also, because they have not yet been trained sufficiently to hold in their discharge, they do not suppress their emotional release, as adults do, and they recover from their distresses much faster and more completely. The only reason adults often think young people are more distressed than adults are—they cry, "fuss a lot," and "carry on"—is that infants have more access to their discharge. Because we mistakenly equate the discharge (the healing) with the distress (the hurt), we assume that they are distressed and we adults are not—after all, we are not the ones crying.

In fact, young people are closer to the way human beings naturally behave in the absence of distress. Rather than looking down on them, we adults can look to them as models— they are zestful, curious, energetic, playful, and wanting to take charge of their activities and their lives. If you do not believe me, just observe how energetic and exuberant young people are. "I'm too old and respectable to behave like that," I hear you say. This may be part of it, but I think the main reason adults are more quiet and withdrawn than children is that we have accumulated more distress and behavior patterns that keep us from being our natural, exuberant selves.

Human infants are not necessarily born totally undistressed. If during the prenatal period the mother took drugs, smoked cigarettes, or ate the wrong kind of food, for example, the newborn infant will already have some emotional and physical distress to discharge. In addition, the birth experience itself can be very scary—which explains why most infants spontaneously cry upon being born.

Apart from the restimulation from the prenatal period and the birth process, infants feeling painful emotion are usually experiencing a new hurt rather than a restimulation of an old hurt. This distinction is important, because with new hurts it is necessary to remove the cause of the painful emotion. If an infant is crying, for example, it is usually because s/he is hungry or something in the environment is scaring him or her or s/he has an upset stomach or so on. To help the infant we must not only allow him or her to cry, but also remove the cause of the bad feelings if possible.

We thus have a unique and exciting opportunity with young people that we do not have with adults—we can prevent them from developing distress recordings and behavior patterns in the first place. We can participate in their growth and development and can help them achieve their potential without the limitations imposed by undischarged distressful experiences. They can grow to be strong and competent, loving and caring, acting to take charge of their environment, without fear, embarrassment, anger, or grief. They will not have distress recordings saying "I can't do it," "It's hopeless," "I'm no good," interfering with their thinking and their actions. This is not just an impossible dream. There are now hundreds and perhaps thousands of adults who know about the importance of the discharge process and who are applying this knowledge in their relationships with their children. This number will undoubtedly continue to grow as more people become aware of how unreleased hurts affect human behavior.

Human beings are not inherently distressed. They are not basically timid and shy, weak and irresponsible. Infants and young children want to take more and more responsibility for their lives, and if given the chance will take as much charge of their lives as they are capable of. We have all seen three- and four-year-olds literally beg their parents to let them help with the dishes and the housework. Toddlers do not have to be taught how to walk; they have a natural desire to master their bodies and their environment. Why is it that houses with one-year-olds must be "baby-proofed," that all things within the young person's reach must be unbreakable and big enough not to be eaten? Young people have an insatiable urge to explore everything in the environment— nothing is untouched.

The most constructive role that adults can play in the lives of young people is to allow them to take as much charge of their lives as they are capable of and to think constantly about what support they need to continue growing and learning. If we do both these things and provide the necessary love and attention, they will prosper and develop their potential as whole human beings. If instead we inhibit their discharge and unwittingly inflict hurts upon them, they will develop distress recordings and rigid patterns just as we did.

What children are capable of doing changes rapidly. The number of things a one-year-old can do that a six-month-old cannot is staggering. Adults do not develop nearly this fast. Thus, to think effectively about young people, we must continually reassess who they are and what they can do, based on their present behavior and not on what they did last month or last year. Let me give an example.

Angela is a good friend of mine who has two children, Chris, aged eight, and Shawn, aged six. Since they were weaned, Chris and Shawn had their meals prepared for them. For the last three years they have been living communally with several other people, and the adults were taking turns cooking for them. They would not eat what the adults were eating, so rather than trying to force them to eat food they did not like the adults cooked for them separately. Needless to say, this was quite a bother.

Last year another adult, Emily, moved into the house. She had not known Chris and Shawn before, and quickly got to know them over a month or so. While watching one of the perennial squabbles over their not wanting to eat what was cooked for them, it occurred to her that there was no reason they could not cook for themselves some or most of the time. They were smart enough, and both were physically capable of it. She started talking about the idea to the adults and then broached the subject to Shawn and Chris. They were both immediately very excited and wanted to start cooking for themselves right away. Everyone decided that it made sense to start with breakfast, with an adult around to provide support and encouragement. I was there when Shawn cooked her first egg, and I wish everyone could have seen the expression on her face. It did not matter that she used three times as much butter as necessary and that half of it ended up on the floor. She was so proud of herself! Both Shawn and Chris continued cooking their own breakfasts, and in two weeks were cooking their suppers as well, with an adult nearby to help them choose nutritional foods and assist with preparation when necessary.

This solution did not end all the problems concerning Chris and Shawn's eating habits. There remained the problem of cleaning up after dinner, and they still did not want to eat many vegetables. Nevertheless, the power struggle between them and the adults over eating diminished considerably, and more important, they took major responsibility for this sphere of their lives.

I am not suggesting that every six-and eight-year-old be forced to cook for him- or herself. In this case it was appropriate and produced positive benefits for both the children and the adults. There are no rules about what things young people can do at what age. We have to think about the individual person and what s/he is capable of, and then decide what is appropriate in the particular situation.

All too often, we relate to children in terms of rigid rules. We do not consider what their real capacities are, but instead base our behavior on what our recordings say young people should or should not do. Thus we find parents not letting their children cross the street years after they are fully capable of doing so with all due caution. We find parents not encouraging their daughters to learn how to ride bicycles years after they are ready to do so.

How effectively we think about young people has a direct correlation with how well they are able to take charge of their lives now and as adults. If we support them to take responsibility for themselves and solve their own problems with our help, they will grow up strong and confident with a sense of their own personal power. If we instead tell them what to do and what not to do, or do not give them the nessary information and support to solve their problems, then they will grow up with distress recordings saying that they are helpless. Let us look at a situation in which an adult's behavior greatly affects a young person's sense of empowerment.

Dottie, an eight-year-old girl, has been having some trouble at school lately. She has not wanted to go, and whenever the subject comes up she says that she hates her teacher. She has started refusing to get up in the morning, and recently her teacher sent home a note saying that Dottie was disrupting the class. Let us discuss some ways this situation could be handled by a parent, say her father.

1. He could tell Dottie essentially that "You just have to put up with school," that there is nothing he or she can do to change the situation. "You might as well learn right now that there are some things that you can't change," he might tell her. Maybe he agrees that her teacher is not doing a good job, but the essential message is that there is nothing they can do.

2. He can punish her for misbehaving in school and threaten her with more punishment if it continues. "If I hear from your teacher again, you'll really get a whipping!" he might say. In this scenario Dottie is essentially told that it is all her fault and that she is bad.

3. Her father can listen to Dottie talk about how bad her class is and then take the matter into his own hands. Maybe he calls the principal and complains about the teacher, insisting that Dottie be placed in another classroom. He is probably quite angry, and lets the principal and maybe the teacher also know how angry he is. Once Dottie has shared the problem with him, he has assumed it as his own. She has little input with regard to what action he takes.

4. He can listen to Dottie talk about school and encourage her to discharge. He can listen to find out what is really bothering her and can help her think about what she needs to do to improve the situation. Maybe he suggests the possibility of a meeting between Dottie and her teacher, with him present, to help them resolve the issues between them. He might call the teacher himself, to find out what she thinks is happening with Dottie in school. He also asks Dottie if she would like him to do anything, and he considers her response.

It is clear from the elucidation of these alternatives that the last is the most sensible. The others either invalidate Dottie or attempt to solve the problem for her. As a result her sense of competency and worth will diminish, and she will not develop the capacity to solve her own problems.

To think about the best interests of young people we often must set aside our own patterns and feelings and do things that feel uncomfortable to us. It may be easier for Dottie's father just to tell her to put up with her problems at school, but this is obviously not the best solution. The benefits to his thinking about Dottie and what the situation entails far outweigh his personal discomfort.

HOW TO BEST SUPPORT YOUNG PEOPLE

To help young people grow and develop without being burdened with rigid behavior patterns, we adults can do the following:

1. We can help them meet their real human needs for loving, physical closeness, touching, playing, and intimacy. We do not have to be the ones to fill all these needs, but we can think about how they can best be filled.

2. We can provide them with the necessary information so they can make intelligent decisions. We can tell them that the stove is very hot and that if they touch it they will get burned. We are not telling them what to do; we simply are giving them more information upon which to base their actions. Some important information to communicate includes knowledge about sex, how machinery operates (for example, how to flush a toilet or drive a car), how our society works, how to cook an egg, how to earn money, and so forth.

3. We can encourage them to discharge when they are tense or behaving in a distressed manner.

4. We can treat them with the full respect all human beings deserve, avoiding invalidation. We can listen to their ideas and opinions, taking them as seriously as we would an adult's. We can talk with them as peers, instead of condescending to them as inferiors.

5. We can think about them and pay attention to their successes and hurts. When they are acting irrationally, what is happening? What can be done to remove the cause of the distress?

6. We can let them know continually by our words and our actions that we love them. We do not love them for what they do, but just for being the wonderful human beings they are. Helping them maintain a sense that they are loved and okay no matter what will go a long way toward combating any sense of incompetence or powerlessness that might develop as a result of distressful experiences.

I think most people would agree that many or all of these attitudes and behaviors will help young people develop as strong, powerful human beings, capable of taking full control over their lives. Nevertheless, few adults actually relate to their children or other young people in these ways. Instead children are yelled at, physically abused, told what to do, ignored, and punished for releasing their feelings. Why?

Many things make it difficult for us to relate rationally to young people. First, we were not treated rationally when we were young ourselves. When we interact with young people today our distress recordings are restimulated, and our behavior is controlled by them. As mentioned earlier, for example, almost all child abusers were themselves victims of child abuse when they were younger.

Second, we have all received much incorrect information about how to raise children: Crying is bad, if we "spare the rod" we "spoil the child," children should be seen and not heard, girls who are physically active are "tomboys," boys who play house are "sissies," and so on. All this misinformation interferes with our thinking about the particular young person and what s/he needs to nourish her or his growth.

Third, we adults are distressed ourselves, and our feelings and patterns affect our relationships with young people. We may be too upset ourselves to think about what *they* need. (As we have discussed earlier, when we are distressed we tend to have little attention for other people.) "What about me?" the distress recording cries out, and it may not even occur to us to think about our children.

Also, adults' painful emotions are often taken out on young people. The parent has a hard day at work, comes home, and yells at the child for leaving a roller skate on the sidewalk. Or the parents just had a fight, and afterwards one of them smacks their three-year-old child for playing with the father's pipe. Because the parents have not discharged their feelings, they are directed at their children.

Fourth, to relate rationally to young people takes time, energy, and attention. It may be easier to respond to the question, "Why do I have to go to bed now?" with the answer,

"Because I say so," instead of explaining why you want the child to go to bed at this time and not an hour later. Or it might be much more time-consuming to arrange and attend a meeting between Dottie and her teacher than it would be to tell Dottie to put up with the bad situation at school. Of course, not taking the time to think about young people has a strong negative effect on their development.

Fifth, we adults are bigger and have more power than young people. It is thus relatively easy to force children to do our bidding, despite their own needs and desires. By itself this difference in power might not be significant, but in conjunction with the feelings and behavior patterns adults have, the power tends to be used in an oppressive manner. For example, it is common to find parents controlling the behavior of their children by threatening to withhold their allowances from them. This use of coercion assumes that young people are not capable of acting rationally themselves, and in fact inhibits their ability to act intelligently on their own.

Sixth, adults have distress recordings attaching their self-worth to how "good" their children are. If the children are successful in terms of the parents' values, then the parents feel as if they are "better" people; if the children fail, then the parents ask themselves the heartrending question, "Where did we go wrong?" The dependence of adults' self-images on their children's behavior interferes with their ability to see and think about their children in terms of the young people's needs instead of their own desires.

Finally, because discharge makes adults feel uncomfortable—that is, it restimulates their own feelings—they tend to try to stop the discharge of children. Typically adults threaten ("if you don't stop crying I'll give you something to cry about"), disapprove ("big boys like you don't cry"), bribe ("here, don't cry, have some ice cream"), deny the child's feelings ("what are you crying for?—that was only a dog"), and distract ("hey, look at that bird! Come on, have a look"). As we have discussed at length, by giving children the message that they should not cry, we are contributing to their distress recordings.

When we do act irrationally around young people, it usually takes the form of not giving them room to be themselves. The effect of our taking so much control and power over their lives is that they develop feelings and patterns of powerlessness. The patterns of powerlessness are deeply ingrained in each of us, and through running our children's lives, we effectively pass the patterns on to them.

The readers of this book are in a fortunate position, one unparalleled in human history. We can interrupt the cycles of powerlessness that have been going on for millennia. If we treat our children so that they are strong and confident and in charge of their lives, they will treat their children with love, respect, and attention also, and so on. The cycle can be broken.

SKILLS AND TOOLS TO HELP US THINK ABOUT AND RELATE TO YOUNG PEOPLE

The exercises that follow apply to people of all ages, and some have been presented in earlier chapters in the context of adult-adult relationships. They are presented again here because they are crucial to the humane functioning of relationships between adults and young people.

Exercise 31: Communicating love to young people. Because of our embarrassment and our other distressful feelings, we communicate affection to young people much less frequently than we would really like to. The more we hug them and touch them (with their permission) and tell them we love them, the better they will feel about themselves—and it is enjoyable for us, also.

EXERCISE 31   COMMUNICATING LOVE
TO YOUNG PEOPLE

Purpose: To encourage you openly to communicate your caring to your children and other young people.

Task: Work to communicate your love directly to young people. Two universal ways are

1. Touching—hug them, boys as well as girls, as you would hug any person you deeply loved. Establish warm, physical contact—which is different from bear hugs, pats on the back, roughhousing, or sexual caresses. Also be sure you have their permission to touch them, so that you are not forcing yourself upon them in the name of love.
2. Telling them you love them—"I love you" works quite well, as do smiles and verbal appreciation.

Try these methods. If you meet some resistance, gently continue to reach out. Underneath their resistance they are yearning to be reached by you.

Think about and try other ways you can communicate love to your children and other young people.

Evaluation:

How has your communicating more affection affected your relationship with the young person?

What will help you remember to continue to express your caring openly and directly?

Exercise 32: Encouraging young people to discharge. Control patterns are not so ingrained in children as in adults, so it is much easier to facilitate their discharge when they are distressed; often just asking them what happened is sufficient. The most important thing we can do is to maintain an attitude of relaxed attention and simply allow them to release their feelings. The benefits of allowing the discharge are enormous. The previously distressed person will be relaxed, alert, curious, and zestful, as if the painful incident had not occurred.

EXERCISE 32   ENCOURAGING YOUNG PEOPLE TO DISCHARGE

Purpose: To facilitate emotional release in young people so that they can effectively heal themselves from physical and emotional hurts.

Task: When you see your child or another young person hurting, give them your loving, respectful attention. Do what you can to make the environment feel safe; physical contact (hugging, touching, and so on) is often very helpful in this regard. If they are discharging, do not try to comfort them or make them feel better in such a way as to discourage the discharge (for example, "It doesn't hurt *that* much, does it?" or "Here, have some ice cream and you'll feel better"). If discharge stops prematurely, you might try active listening or having the person again tell what happened.

Maintain an attitude that copious discharge is absolutely natural and acceptable. You can verbally encourage them also ("It's okay to cry"). The most important thing is to be there with loving attention.

If the young person is hurting and not discharging, you can try using active listening and lovingly staying with him or her. S/he may well start dramatizing anger at you, but do not be intimidated by it. Continue to be present and to listen actively, showing your caring. If you remain and do not get angry yourself, the child will often break through the surface to the discharge that was waiting to come out.

Evaluation:

What happened?

How did it feel to you?

How did the young person feel after releasing the feelings?

What made it difficult for you?

How did your listening affect your relationship with the young person?

What will help you listen better next time?

Exercise 33: Using active listening with young people. Active listening, discussed in depth in Chapter 6, is invaluable in establishing good communication with young people. By feeding back what we hear as their real meaning, they will feel understood and validated. It will help them think through and solve their own problems enabling us to be effective allies. Through the use of active listening we can avoid the pitfalls of owning or taking over children's problems as our own. It is not our duty to make everything right for our children, and trying to do so will only make them feel less in control of their lives.

Active listening will further encourage them to share their feelings and thoughts with us—we will be safe people who communicate love and acceptance. The use of active listening has turned many parent-child relationships completely around. There is no reason your relationship should not be positively affected, also. (For a review of active listening, see pages 131–139.)

EXERCISE 33 USING ACTIVE LISTENING WITH YOUNG PEOPLE

Purpose: To help you listen more effectively to young people.

Task: The next time your child has a problem and is experiencing painful emotion, use active listening to facilitate communication. That is, tell him or her what you are hearing as the message s/he is communicating. It is important that your manner be loving and accepting. (See Chapter 6 for discussion and examples.) Continue to actively listen until the situation is resolved or the young person is no longer feeling distressed.

Evaluation:

What happened?
Was active listening effective in drawing out the young person? Why or why not?
What was difficult for you about active listening?
How could you have listened better?
How did active listening affect your relationship with the young person?

Exercise 34: Using I-messages with young people. I-messages are an excellent way to communicate our feelings and concerns when it is appropriate to do so. By taking responsibility for our own feelings, we can avoid the blame and invalidation implicit in most You-messages (as in, "You only think about yourself"; "You're so messy"; "You make me so angry!"). By using I-messages, we help young people see us as human beings, with emotions and concerns of our own. If they are not disparaged by our messages, they are much more likely to respond to us intelligently instead of from their feelings and patterns.

We must think very carefully about I-messages before we send them. It is easy to use them as a subtle form of manipulation, implying that young people should do our bidding or else we will feel bad. The most beneficial use of I-messages is to give receivers accurate information about how we feel so that they can take it into account while formulating their own course of action. We can of course tell them what we would like them to do and why, but any physical or emotional coercion on our part will only limit their ability to think and act rationally on their own.

EXERCISE 34   USING I-MESSAGES WITH
YOUNG PEOPLE

Purpose: To enable you to be understood more effectively by young people.

Task: The next time you are having a problem with a young person's behavior (that is, you are the one with the hurt, scared, or angry feelings) use an I-message to communicate your feelings. In other words, say what you are feeling directly and relate it to the child's behavior. An example of a good I-message is "When you leave your crayons on the couch I feel very angry, because I just spent two hours cleaning the living room." Try to avoid blaming the young person for your feelings by invalidating her or him ("I am angry because you are acting like a stupid baby").

If your I-message is not heard, you can repeat it. If the young person feels distressed in response, you may have to use active listening to reach a point where your message can be understood.

Evaluation:

What happened when you used I-messages?

Were they effective tools to enhance communication?

Were you able to keep from invalidating or passing judgment on your young friend in your I-messages?

If your I-messages did not help you be understood, why not?

What can you do differently next time?

Did you gain any other insights?

Exercise 35: Giving young people bedtime attention. One of the chronic problems afflicting many relationships between adults and young people is that the adults seldom give the latter their complete attention. Usually the adults are doing something else at the same time, are thinking about something else, or are simply too distressed themselves to give young people good attention. When was the last time you engaged a young person on her or his terms, when you talked about what s/he wanted to talk about for as long as s/he wanted to? Giving young people this kind of attention is tremendously helpful to both their personal growth and our relationships with them. The added benefit for adults is that such contact is as rewarding an experience as a person can have, and it can establish a degree of intimacy seldom found in adult-adult relationships.

Bedtime is an excellent occasion to give children attention. Other times can be just as good, but the relaxed period before sleep is a wonderful time to connect. Talk to them, listen to how their day has been, snuggle with them, read them stories, do whatever makes sense. Most of all, pay attention to what *they* need, and act accordingly. This kind of contact can make all the difference between close and distant relationships.

EXERCISE 35   GIVING YOUNG PEOPLE BEDTIME ATTENTION

Purpose: To provide you with the opportunity to establish warm, daily contact with your children, and to give them the chance to deal with any distress that occurred during the day.

Task: At your children's bedtime give them at least fifteen minutes of special attention each. Talk with them about how their day was, what happened, and so on. Give them the kind of attention they most need—reading them a story, hugging them, playing with them, or helping them discharge some painful feelings related to incidents that occurred during the day.

Communicate your love openly and directly, both physically and verbally. It may feel embarrassing to you, but do it anyway. The most important thing is to really be there with your full attention and your love. Make this special time a daily ritual.

Evaluation:

Did your children appreciate this bedtime attention?
Did you enjoy it?
How was it helpful to the young person and to your relationship?
Was there anything difficult about giving your children your full attention?
What will make it easier to do the next time?

These exercises are of course not meant to take the place of our thinking about the young people involved in our lives. They are essentially tools of our intelligence, to be used when appropriate. They also serve as reminders of how all people should be related to all the time—with love, thought, and attention. If we can keep this concept in mind, we will basically do a good job of parenting.

INTERRUPTING PATTERNED BEHAVIOR IN YOUNG PEOPLE

A correct attitude by a parent to a child does not include permissiveness to a pattern that is creating difficulties for the child (and the people around him or her).

A child being forced by a pattern to be messy, destructive, or thoughtless of others needs a firm interruption of the pattern by the parent (or other aware adult). The interruption will usually bring discharge and then, of course, the discharge must be permitted and assisted thoroughly.

To not interrupt such a pattern is to abandon the child to behavior which spoils his relationships with others and prevents much of his enjoyment of the world.[2]

How do we interrupt the patterns of young people? We do not want to add more distress in the process. To "interrupt" a young person's pattern of abusive language by screaming at or beating him or her will add more distress onto the recording, making it that much more entrenched. The person may no longer use abusive language in the presence of the adult, but the pattern itself will increase rather diminish as a result of the adult's behavior.

We can most effectively interrupt patterned behavior in young people in a way that does not invalidate them—by communicating love and respect while at the same time firmly interfering with the reenactment of the pattern.

I walked into the class of four year olds to observe and was greeted by most of the boys ready to kung-fu me. I took this to mean they wanted to touch me. They knew that I was a new presence and wanted to find out who I was. I asked the boy who hit me what his name was and then asked, "Do you know what I do when someone hits me?" He and the other boys looked a little trepidatious. I said: "I turn into a kissing monster." I proceeded to kiss him on the neck and he giggled. Some other boys kung-fued me. I did the same, and they giggled. Later that day, one of the boys walked over to someone else's block house and kicked it to pieces, apparently for no reason at all. The boys who had built the house went over and kissed him. He didn't want that to happen so left the block area. The children and adults in that classroom have continued to work with this particular boy in this way when he destroys things; and he is now openly asking for affection at times, and giving it himself.[3]

[2]Harvey Jackins, *The Human Situation* (Seattle: Rational Island Publishers, 1973), p. 111.

[3]Chuck Esser, "Some Incidents from the Non-Violence and Children Program (of the Friends Peace Committee in Philadelphia)," *Classroom*, No. 3 (Seattle: Rational Island Publishers, 1976), p. 38.

In this example the boys' patterns of violence were thoughtfully interrupted by kissing. The response in no way invalidated the children, and when they were kissed they discharged their embarrassment and fear by giggling. If their violent behavior were continually interrupted in this way, the patterns would soon disappear—not just because they were forced to stop acting violent, but because the way in which it was done enabled them to discharge the painful emotion behind the behavior.

We must remember that whenever a young person is acting irrationally, it is because s/he is distressed. We can be of most assistance to this person if we interrupt the patterned behavior so that s/he can discharge the painful feelings instead of acting them out. All too often adults respond to young people's patterns by getting angry and threatening or abusing them. The adults do not have any ill motives, but they lose sight of the fact that the child is distressed and indirectly asking for help.

Kitty is a ten-year-old friend of mine who has gotten a lot of support from both parents to get rid of her feelings rather than dramatize them. One incident I recall occurred when Kitty came home from school, clearly quite upset. She would not talk about it, but let everybody know she was feeling bad by slamming doors and telling everyone to "Shut up." At one point she picked a fight with her younger brother and shoved him against the wall. He started crying, and Hilary, their mother, came down to investigate. After her son recovered from the experience, Hilary thought about Kitty. She herself was quite angry; she knew, though, that something was bothering Kitty, and she was able to put her own feelings aside temporarily to assist her daughter.

She went up to Kitty's room, and knocked on the door. Kitty yelled at her to go away, but Hilary knew that this was part of Kitty's pattern. After Kitty kept refusing to open the door, Hilary let herself in the room. Kitty started screaming at the top of her lungs for Hilary to get out, but Hilary maintained a light tone and said, "I'm going to stay here to help you unload some of those bad feelings you are carrying around." Kitty came over and tried to push Hilary out, screaming and crying as she tried to do so. Hilary, maintaining a calm and loving attitude, firmly refused to leave. This behavior went on for about fifteen minutes, with Kitty sobbing heavily and directing her anger at Hilary. Meanwhile, Hilary tried to use active listening to find out what was really bothering Kitty. She had no information about the specific incident, but she knew that Kitty was having some trouble with some girls in her class. Every time she alluded to this—"You had some trouble with Lucy and Alice today"—Kitty started crying more heavily.

Eventually Kitty ceased fighting, allowing Hilary to hold her. She finally told what had happened to her, and continued crying. Hilary continued to listen and give Kitty her complete attention. After awhile Kitty seemed finished, and was soon laughing and talking in a relaxed and attentive manner. The distress responsible for her earlier behavior was gone, and the pattern was no longer operative.

If Hilary had responded to Kitty from her own anger, she would have been much less able to interrupt effectively Kitty's pattern. The typical adult would respond to Kitty's "irritating" behavior by hitting her, yelling at her, sending her to her room, or in some other way taking out the adult's feelings on her. Any of these reactions would increase Kitty's distress and would not at all deal with the cause of her irrational behavior, the incident at school about which she had hurt and angry feelings.

If Hilary had been brought up in the "liberal" school of child-rearing, she might have responded to Kitty's attack on her brother by adopting a "hands-off" policy, leaving Kitty and her brother to fight it out between themselves. Whereas frequently it is appropriate to allow young people to work out solutions among themselves, in this case it would have been tantamount to abandoning Kitty to her distress. Maybe the "liberal" approach does not add as much distress onto the recording as the "hit 'em and send 'em to their rooms" approach, but it still allows the pattern to operate and become more ingrained.

ON DISCIPLINE

What we normally call discipline usually involves trying to alter young people's behavior by threatening to use or using the power adults have over children. We threaten to hit them, take away their allowances, withhold their dinners, send them to their rooms, force them to do unpleasant labor, or otherwise impose restrictions on their mobility and activity. Discipline is sometimes used in an attempt to interrupt patterned behavior, but it is also often used to force the young person's behavior to conform to the adult's desires, no matter how irrational and capricious these wants may be. I recently observed a woman and a young boy, who appeared to be her son, standing on a subway platform waiting for a train. This three-year-old boy was naturally curious about the people and objects around him, and as soon as she released his hand he wandered a few yards away to investigate the contents of a trash can. When his mother saw this she commanded him to come back to her immediately, in a harsh and irritated tone of voice. When he returned she shook him hard with her one free hand, telling him that she would smack him if he did that again. Until the train came she insisted he remain still and quiet.

In this instance the boy's behavior was not patterned or irrational—he was displaying a natural curiosity in an environment rich with people and things and sounds and smells. He was punished merely because his behavior made his mother uncomfortable. He ceased his exploration not because he understood that he might get sick if he played with garbage, but because he would get hit if he continued.

The basis of discipline is control by fear. We instill a behavior pattern in young people attaching fear and hurt to the behavior we do not like. We succeed in controlling their behavior, but at great cost. We force them to short-circuit their intelligence and adopt rigid patterns in its place. The well-disciplined young person is a very fearful young person, and one who has lost much of her or his natural zest and creativity. Whether the behavior being interrupted is patterned or not, the price of this kind of control is too high. The use of discipline is one of the major reasons so many of us have such a hard time thinking for ourselves and taking charge of our lives. These are precisely the qualities we were punished for having as children.

Inflicting physical violence on young people is the extreme form of discipline. Hitting young people is an accepted practice in this country, so much so that many parents are incredulous at the idea of bringing up children without it. Of course, a large part of their belief is the result of distress recordings they developed when they were hit as children themselves.

Physical abuse visited on young people has all the harmful consequences that other forms of discipline have, and additionally can cause real physical damage. Human beings would simply not hurt other people were it not for the fact that they themselves were hurt in similar ways. By using physical force adults are forsaking all means of rational communication, and they send the clear message to young people that "You are powerless." Have you ever been held by several people while another person beat you? This experience is analogous to the power imbalance between the parent and the small child.

When I talk to groups of parents about the effects physical punishment has on young people, I frequently hear the concern that "If I don't hit them, I can't control them." "How can I make them stop fighting if I don't hit them?" Basically, if their behavior is irrational there is always a way to interrupt it lovingly, as in the example of the "kissing monster." If their behavior is reasonable but we just do not like it or it makes us feel uncomfortable, then we can work out an agreement with them as we could with any other human being. We may not get what we want as often as we would if we used threats of physical force, but the improvement in the quality of our relationships will more than compensate for this loss.

The most effective parenting we can do is to think well about young people, and act on our thinking. We may sometimes have to set limits on their behavior—we do not want our one-year-old child falling down the stairs, no matter how natural his or her motivation may be—but we can do so in a way that does not unnecessarily distress them—by erecting a barricade, for example.

When young people are acting irrationally, they are hurting. (The same is true of adults, of course.) If instead of responding from our own anger we ask ourselves the questions, "What is happening to that person? How is s/he hurting?" we will begin dealing with the roots of the distressed behavior. By respectfully interrupting the behavior and allowing the emotional discharge to occur, we will be helping both the young person and his or her relationships with others.

INEQUALITY IN ADULT-CHILD RELATIONSHIPS

Go to your room!
All right, no more allowance for you this month!
One more crack like that and you're grounded for the week.
Eat your vegetables!

Could you imagine a young girl saying any of these things to her mother or father? How about a young boy washing his mother's mouth out with soap for saying a dirty word? Or maybe a teenage girl taking her father over her knee and smacking him for staying out too late one night? Of course not. Young people simply do not have this kind of power over adults. In fact, these sorts of behaviors are not found among equals. Adults do not send each other to their rooms for not eating their asparagus or wash each other's mouths out with soap. The only situations I can think of where one adult has such power over another are master-slave relationships.

Adults have tremendous power over young people. In addition to near total economic control and physical control, they also have informational control. They have more knowledge at their disposal, they can use words that children do not understand, and they have more experience arguing. Young people may know that they are right, but this knowledge does not help them much in confrontations with adults.

Adults have more emotional power than young people. Young children, particularly infants and toddlers, are much more dependent on adults for meeting their emotional needs than vice versa. Parents can leave their children for days and not suffer any harmful effects, but such an event can be very painful for an infant.

Adults also have control over the mobility of young people. Adults can come and go as they please, but young people's movements are restricted from infancy. From the crib to the "Be home by nine o'clock," the behavior of children is controlled and scrutinized.

The real and assumed power adults have over young people is accompanied by assumptions about children that serve to justify the use of this power: children are incompetent and stupid, they do not know what is good for themselves, they should be seen and not heard, they are too fragile to be told about real crises in the family, they are silly, they cannot understand thoughts and ideas, and they have no rights, only privileges conferred on them by their parents. It is with these assumptions that parents try to hide their marital conflicts from their children, and then suddenly inform them they are separating. It is with these assumptions that parents tell their children they are moving, without bothering to listen to what the children think. It is with these assumptions that what young people say is virtually ignored in conversations when both adults and young people are present. They may be given a perfunctory nod or grunt, but the attention then returns to the adults.

One of the most oppressive aspects of children's absence of power is their forced attendance at school. Why should people be forced to go to school and sit still and be quiet for from four to eight hours per day, five days per week, for twelve years? At least adults get paid for their labor. As a matter of fact, much of the distress adults feel in their jobs is the result of the restimulation of painful feelings associated with school. Desire to learn is part of the nature of human beings; forcing young people to sit down and shut up and learn at the same pace as everyone else stifles real learning and takes away control of their own lives.

The best thing we can do as adults and as parents is to use our power sparingly, and never oppressively. Often as adults we do not notice or are not aware of all the power we have over children. We forget what it was like for us as children, and having so much control over young people's lives seems natural. One good way to see our own behavior is to find out how our children perceive us—how do our actions look to them?—by reverse role-playing. Reversing roles, as in Exercise 36, will give you a good idea of the dynamics of inequality in your relationship.

By giving up the oppressive use of our power, we will help our children grow and prosper and will regain their friendship. They will no longer be afraid of us or feel powerless while relating to us. Parents have such an important role in affecting every aspect of children's lives—their friendships with peers, their relations with their teachers, their ability to cope with new situations, and most of all, their sense of themselves as competent, in-charge, okay human beings.

EXERCISE 36   REVERSING ROLES WITH YOUNG PEOPLE

Purpose: To help you develop a better understanding of how your child sees you and how you act around her or him, and to remind you of what it is like to be a young person.

Task: At an appropriate occasion suggest to your child that s/he be the mother or father and you be the child, that is, that you switch roles. While playing the young person, do not use the role to convince your child of the correctness or superiority of the adult position. Play the child's role as humanly as possible, and do not exaggerate it to be very distressed and irrational. As a general rule, as the young person try to be as reasonable as possible; remember, the major purpose of this exercise is to observe how your child sees the adult role and to experience how it feels to be in the relatively powerless position of a child.

Evaluation:

How did each of you enjoy the role-playing?

How did your child play the adult role?

What does it imply about how you behave around your child?

How did it feel being in the child's position?

How did it feel to your child to be in the adult role?

How did it feel to him or her to have you in the child's role?

What did you learn about how your child perceives you?

What did you learn about how you perceive and treat your child?

Was the reverse role-playing helpful to your relationship? How?

What other insights did you gain?

CHILDREN AND SEX ROLES

Sugar and spice, and everything nice. . . .
Jack fell down . . . and Jill came tumbling after.
. . . and Cinderella and the handsome prince lived happily ever after.

Throughout our culture the conditioning of men and women into sex roles begins at an early age. Many of the more obvious means of conditioning have already been mentioned; another one is the different kinds of toys boys and girls are given and encouraged to play with: Girls are given dolls and objects with which to "play house," and boys are given toy guns and rockets and cars. Both boys and girls are disparaged for acting outside the sex role, boys being called "sissies" and girls "tomboys."

There is a wide-standing myth in our society that boys are better than girls in mathematics and science. Although studies have demonstrated that this myth has no reality in terms of the performance of boys and girls in grammar school, most elementary school teachers still believe it to be true. One of the dynamics of sexism in the education of young people is that boys are continually encouraged in these areas, whereas girls are funneled into "accommodating" and service professions, such as typing, social work, education, and so forth.

There is no concrete evidence that any inherent behavioral or psychological differences exist between men and women. We do have an enormous amount of evidence that men and women from infancy on have been forced to take on different roles through the installation of distress patterns, resulting in adult men having more economic, social, and political benefits. Both men and women, however, lose essential parts of their humanness.

No undistressed adult would ever want her or his children to have their potential limited by sex-role conditioning and related distress recordings. We only treat young people in a sexist manner because we were treated that way ourselves; and not only were we placed into these roles, but so was everyone else we knew—our friends, our teachers, our comic book heroes and heroines, and our parents.

Notwithstanding the distress patterns with which we have been laden, we all want our children to be the best, most capable human beings they can be. As adults we can greatly influence the growth of young people, countering much of the sexism in the world and helping them maintain their full humanness:

1. We can serve as role models of how men and women can be. The more we can operate outside our own sex-role conditioning, the more we will be good models for young people to emulate.

2. We can encourage all types of discharge in all young people, allowing and encouraging both boys and girls to cry, rage, tremble, and laugh when they need to.

3. We can awarely hug and touch both boys and girls. Boys need it every bit as much as girls do.

4. We can provide all young people with opportunities to learn all kinds of things, from cooking to mathematics to understanding how to change a diaper. We can also encourage them to play many different things from playing ball to playing house.

5. We can appreciate the intelligence and creativity of both boys and girls in all areas in which it is exhibited.

6. We can interrupt patterned behavior in all young people wherever it is found and help them discharge the associated distress. Because of sex-role conditioning, this step may involve interrupting violent behavior in boys and more passive, self-invalidating patterns in girls.

By treating young people in these nonsexist ways and being good models ourselves, we can help both boys and girls grow up to be strong, capable, loving people. The benefits of doing so are obvious and are certainly worth the effort. Not only will their lives be more fulfilling, but our relationships with them will be stronger and closer. What more could we ask for than to have our children be our lifelong friends?

GETTING HELP AS PARENTS

Parenting is a difficult task, particularly when we are trying to avoid hurting our children in the same ways that we were hurt. It is a monumental job for one person to try to accomplish by her- or himself; and because of the amount of attention infants need, it is unreasonable to expect one or even two people to meet the infant's needs adequately, as well as their own.

The nuclear family is a relatively recent phenomenon, having originated with the rise of capitalism and industrialization. Before this period, child-rearing was performed by many members of the extended family, including grandparents, brothers and sisters, and other young people. It is thus a recent development that one woman has nearly sole responsibility for thinking about and taking care of children. This practice can have only a limited future, because it is simply not a rational structure for helping young people grow and develop.

For all parents, I encourage you to get as much support as possible for thinking about your children. You deserve real support, not as a favor to you but as part of the responsibility all adults have for making this world a more rational place. Sharing the responsibility for nourishing young people will result in your having more time for yourself, and at the same time, will allow you to focus better attention on your children.

I urge all nonparents no longer to leave all the parenting to biological parents. Just because a young person and you have no particular genetic similarity is no reason for you to be afraid to become involved with him or her. If you see two young people fighting, there is no good reason to sit back and wait for a parent to come along to break it up. You have the same potential ability to relate well to young people as any parent does—all they have is a little more experience. Take the opportunity to get to know young people and become involved in their lives. I guarantee the experience will be a rewarding one. After all, what could be more beneficial than interacting with a bright, zestful, energetic young person, who is attentive and creative and lots of fun to be with?

Our goal is to have all human beings be intelligent, creative, caring, zestful, assertive, and in charge of their lives—which is possible for every person, without exception. Thinking about young people is one of the most important things an adult can do. We are now in a position where we can finally break the cycle of distressed people hurting their children in the same ways that they were hurt as children. As this happens, the whole course of human events will change. The amount of distress in the world will decrease, and it will be a more rational place for all of us. Every time we accord young people the love and respect they deserve, we will be contributing to this process.

Index